underbelly

The authors

John Silvester has been a crime reporter in Melbourne since 1978. He worked for *The Sunday Times* Insight team in London in 1990, and has co-authored many crime books, including the *Underbelly* series, *Leadbelly* and *The Silent War*. He is currently senior crime reporter for *The Age*.

Andrew Rule started in journalism in 1975 and has worked in newspapers, television and radio. He wrote *Cuckoo*, the inside story of the 'Mr Stinky' case, since re-issued in the collection *Sex, Death and Betrayal*, and has co-written, edited and published several other books, including the *Underbelly* series. He is a deputy editor of *The Age*.

. . . .

underbelly

A TALE OF TWO CITIES

JOHN SILVESTER AND ANDREW RULE

Published by Floradale Productions Pty Ltd and Sly Ink Pty Ltd
January 2009

Distributed wholesale by Gary Allen Pty Ltd
9 Cooper Street
Smithfield, NSW
Telephone 02-9725 2933

Underbelly: A Tale of Two Cities
ISBN   0-9775440-9-5

Cover design, typesetting and layout: R.T.J. Klinkhamer

For Paul Delianis and Carl Mengler,
who saw the door was slightly ajar
and crashed right through it.

Paul Delianis   Carl Mengler

CONTENTS

FOREWORD

It was the best of times,
it was the worst of times.

CHARLES DICKENS,
A TALE OF TWO CITIES

IN the late 1970s the underworlds of Melbourne and Sydney were changing – violently.

Melbourne was the home of old-style gunmen. Many were from generations of crooks, schooled on the waterfront in matters of theft, intimidation and violence.

In Sydney they were just as hard but they learned early that the only way to make big money was to get the police on side.

There had always been corruption – with police paid to look the other way – but in the 1970s it exploded to the point that a cell of bent detectives actually set up the 'jobs'. They franchised crime to chosen crooks, who virtually worked for them. Lennie McPherson, a handy safe breaker but no criminal mastermind, became a Mr Big because police gave him the 'green light'. Neddy Smith was a violent thug who became a big mobster because he was protected by manipulative police. The smooth George Freeman made millions under police patronage. It was so brazen that Freeman was once photographed at Randwick racecourse with the Chief Magistrate. In Sydney it was just another day at the races.

But there was a small group of honest police in Sydney – and they had to break the law to prove it. They resorted to illegally tapping the telephones of their suspects, people like Freeman and drug syndicate boss 'Aussie' Bob Trimbole. And what they discovered horrified them. Police, politicians, and legal figures were talking to crime bosses. It confirmed that in Sydney nearly everything was for sale – from knighthoods to ladies of the night.

The crims protected by bent police started to believe they were untouchable. When the Griffith mafia tired of the activities of a local businessman, Donald Mackay, who dared complain about lack of police efforts to deal with the lucrative marijuana industry, they calmly ordered his execution. They thought that by using a Melbourne hit man and ordering that the Italian weapon of choice – the shotgun – not be used, they could get away with murder and that corruption would flourish unchecked.

They were wrong. And while the politicians did little (except for the disgraceful Al Grassby, who actively worked to sabotage the case) the public was outraged.

But still the crooks believed they could do anything, including shooting an undercover policeman, Mick Drury, to stop him giving evidence in a drug case.

Meanwhile, federal police using legal phone taps in their own drug investigations, were stunned to pick up the extent of corruption – but their political masters stayed silent, preferring to do nothing rather than risk the inevitable political fall-out.

Powerful New South Wales political figures from both sides resisted federal overtures to clean up the rot. Police like Peter

Lamb – a federal expert on organised crime – could do little except try to keep his team from being infiltrated by corrupt police.

But the assassination of Mackay in 1977 and the shooting of Drury seven years later proved to be watershed moments. Politicians reluctantly ordered inquiries.

As the Sydney detectives' vice-like grip on crime (committing, not investigating it) began to loosen, the established pecking order collapsed. Ambitious new crooks were prepared to take on older, protected ones. And police were involved in setting up killings to protect their stake in organised crime.

This resulted in a series of murders culminating with that of hit man Christopher Dale Flannery, whose body was never found.

Back in Melbourne, the gunmen were at war and showed such contempt for the system that one was gunned down in the City Court on a busy sitting day. The killer was given inside information and his getaway assisted by someone with an intimate knowledge of the court complex. A small group of police remain the most likely suspects.

Gunmen were so confident of the underworld code of silence that on one occasion they did not bother to wear effective disguises even though witnesses could identify them. They had reasons to be confident. One young witness persuaded to give evidence was silenced with a bullet. Some bodies were found. Many weren't. No-one was convicted.

But while the gunmen fought over personal 'honour' and to carve up proceeds of big armed robberies, the cold winds of change were coming. They were dinosaurs and the Ice Age had arrived. Well, if not ice (that would come later), at least the Heroin Age. A new order had taken over. Drugs were king and those with access to powders manufactured from poppy seeds in

Asia made more money than the armed robbers and 'dockies' dreamed of. From then on it would be drug money, not guns, that controlled the underworld.

Terry Clark was a small-time New Zealand police informer who wanted to be a world-class crook and for a short time he got his wish. First through a massive importation of Thai 'buddha sticks' to New Zealand and then through a $100 million importation of heroin to Australia. He formed his own group, which he called The Organisation, and managed it ruthlessly.

Clark was the first man to establish an international drug empire based in Australia. He would not be the last.

While the crooks in Melbourne and Sydney continued to kill each other over the spoils of their shrinking crime rackets, Clark was quietly making a fortune in the shadows. If they had realised what he was up to, they would have surely moved in on him, removing his fortune or his toes.

Knowing what damage a police informer could do, he killed anyone he thought might give him up to law enforcement agencies. Corrupt police, officials and lawyers told him when any of his team was talking. And then he would silence them permanently.

This ruthlessness and greed would ultimately prove his downfall. When the bodies of two of his couriers, Isabel and Douglas Wilson, were found in the seaside resort of Rye, south-east of Melbourne, it became a full-on homicide investigation.

Enter Paul Delianis, then head of the Victorian homicide squad. Delianis soon realised that the Clark syndicate, known as the Mr Asia gang, had infiltrated the Federal Narcotics Bureau.

The federal government at first denied the problem but a later inquiry resulted in the whole bureau being found to be beyond redemption. It was scrapped.

Delianis' initial investigations, followed by those of the equally dedicated Carl Mengler, who headed a taskforce codenamed Trio, resulted in the syndicate's exposure and finally revealed who murdered the Wilsons and Donald Mackay.

Their investigations succeeded despite widespread corruption, police jealousies and political indifference. It was a long road but the Mr Asia syndicate was finally smashed and Clark died in an English jail.

As Charles Dickens once wrote: 'There are dark shadows on the earth, but its lights are stronger in the contrast.'

There are many old men who retired as respected police, judges, lawyers, journalists and politicians who would count themselves fortunate that their telephones were never tapped back in the bad old days.

Or were they?

SLEEPING DOGS LIE

CONTRACT KILLING FOR THE MAFIA

> He told them why they were to
> die and shot Wilson first, then
> his wife. But he did not shoot
> their dog.

THE bitch was a stray – part cattle dog, part fox terrier, mostly lucky. When she wandered into the Altona street where a meat inspector called Dennis Brown and his wife lived in the mid-1970s, instead of calling the dog catcher the couple adopted the little black and white mongrel. They called her Mitzy.

When the Browns bought an unfinished fibro holiday shack in the ti-tree behind Rye on the Mornington Peninsula, Mitzy was in her element. There were kangaroos and rabbits to chase, smells to investigate on walks along the tracks winding through the scrub-choked vacant blocks. The only danger was snakes in the grass.

Almost thirty years on, Danny Street is filled with houses, some of them expensive. But in 1978 it was an unmade road with a handful of shacks in it. The Browns were at Lot 55, and the two blocks to the south were covered in scrub. Dennis kept a few bee hives in the ti-tree and sometimes went shooting rabbits, Mitzy at his side. Man and dog didn't miss much.

Early that year, Brown was checking his hives when he noticed that a long, narrow hole had been dug in the sandy soil under the ti-tree on Lot 59. Intriguingly, it had been covered with scrub. On visits after that, he would glance at the hole. For more than a year, nothing changed. But in April, 1979, he saw that the unknown digger had cleaned out and deepened the hole and covered it again with some fresh scrub.

About five weeks later, on 18 May, a Friday, Mitzy and her master came down early for the weekend. They were going for their usual walk when she stopped where the hole was and started to scratch furiously. Brown realised that the hole had been filled in – and saw signs that foxes and other dogs had already been scrabbling in the freshly turned sand. Whatever was in the hole attracted carnivores.

A less observant man might have missed it. A less curious one might have shrugged it off. Dennis Brown had worked at abattoirs all over Australia, among rough men in a tough business, and his instincts were high. Since he'd first seen it, he had fancied that the long, narrow hole looked a little too much like an empty grave. Now it was filled in, his fancy hardened into suspicion: if it were a grave, maybe it was no longer empty.

He whistled his excited dog away, got into his maroon 1976 Holden Kingswood and drove the four kilometres into Rye to talk to the police about the sandy grave in Danny Street.

At first, local cops thought it might be a cache of stolen property. Then they stuck a probe into the sandy soil and caught a whiff of something that made them feel sick.

The homicide crew came late that afternoon and forensic experts soon after. Portable generators throbbed all night to power the crime-scene lights. Dennis Brown didn't hang around to see what he had found; he had a pretty good idea it wouldn't be pretty and he was right.

There were two bodies. The first out was a young woman, fully dressed except for one boot – the other was later found on the road nearby. It didn't take ballistic experts to see that she had been shot through the breast and the head. Underneath her was a man of about the same age. He had been shot twice in the chest and once in the neck.

Some distinctive clothing and jewellery – wedding ring, brooch and hair comb – gave the police a lead, but they must have suspected who they were looking for. It took less than 48 hours to identify the dead pair as Douglas and Isabel Wilson. It was, as police were learning to say in the 1970s, clearly drug-related.

The Wilsons were from New Zealand and they had form. The Victorian homicide squad, then headed by the renowned Paul Delianis, were keen to talk to their associates. Especially a Martin Johnstone and one Terry Sinclair, who had recently changed his surname by deed poll from his birth name. Johnstone and Sinclair were also New Zealanders, who had joined thousands of their countrymen to flock to the bright lights of Sydney.

So why had the Wilsons turned up dead outside Melbourne, a full day's drive and almost 1000 kilometres south of where they had been living in Sin City? Delianis and his detectives were determined to find out. Not everyone in other Australian law enforcement bodies seemed to have the same enthusiasm for the task.

THE path that led the Wilsons to a shallow grave in a sleepy Victorian holiday town started on the other side of the Tasman where, a decade earlier, the teenage Douglas Wilson started dabbling in drugs while an above-average student at Auckland Grammar. But when his family treated him to a year in America in his final year, he developed a taste for drugs, spurning his private-school education and a comfortable middle-class start in life by dealing to support his own growing habit – and his scorn for the workaday world. His slide across the social divide to the dark side continued until he dropped out of a university accounting course and was arrested for trafficking marijuana and LSD in early 1972 when he sold an undercover cop some drugs. This slip earned him a short jail sentence.

Jail hardened Wilson's habits into vices, pulling him further from the life he might have led into the one that would destroy him. By this time, he already knew Isabel, who was a year younger and had been mixing in a group which used drugs after she'd left home at sixteen.

Not long after getting out of prison in mid-1973, Wilson had returned to working as a tiler with his father's business when a small-time crook recruited him to sell Thai 'buddha sticks' to the university crowd that the middle-class Wilson could mix with more comfortably than working-class criminals could. The man who recruited him was Terrence John Clark, who would use a string of aliases and later change his surname to Sinclair.

Wilson met Clark through a small-time criminal called James McBean, sometimes referred to as 'Jim the Grammar School man', who had helped Clark sell buddha sticks.

Wilson was good at selling dope: he sold 40,000 of a payload of 200,000 sticks that the edgy Clark and his smooth-talking associate Martin Johnstone had smuggled into New Zealand on a yacht called *Brigadoon*, netting each a million dollars at a time when that was enough to buy a street full of houses. But Clark and Johnstone weren't interested in real estate just yet. They were bankrolling a bigger foray into international drug trafficking.

For all three, this early success was the bait that would lure each to his destruction. As for Isabel, she was fated to hook up with the drug-dealing, freewheeling Wilson as well as to drugs, and went along for the ride. She married him in 1977, and rarely left his side, but devotion didn't help. It was a fatal attraction. They both ended up with raging heroin habits and clouded judgment. And that would eventually put them in the wrong place at the wrong time, with a ticket to a sandy grave.

THE wrong place and time was the Gazebo Hotel in Brisbane in June, 1978. By then the Wilsons had been in Australia a few months. They were just two of several 'kiwis' Clark had recruited to distribute heroin in his expanding empire. Douglas Wilson was being paid a retainer of $400 a week by Clark, who had skipped bail and left New Zealand two years earlier, in 1976, after being charged with importing two cigarette cartons full of heroin fetched from Fiji by a woman friend. He had been living in Brisbane and Sydney under a string of aliases, moving from place to place. All the while building the drug running syndicate he liked to call 'The Organisation', but which would later become tagged by the media as the 'Mr Asia' syndicate.

Clark had developed a theory of avoiding detection through caution and planning. If he had stuck to the rules he laid down for the rest of the gang, he might have made and laundered millions of dollars and eventually lived the dream of 'going legitimate' and getting out in time.

Recruiting the Wilsons was an early example of the flawed reasoning and carelessness that would bring him undone. According to his contemporaries, Clark despised drug addicts, almost as if he wanted to ignore the effect of his obscenely profitable trade. But despite this contempt for 'junkies', he had chosen the Wilsons to work for him as drug and money couriers – and even part paid them in heroin for their own use, as well as the hefty retainer.

In Australia, he favoured using fellow New Zealanders and perhaps saw the Wilsons as more malleable – more reliant on him – because they were slaves to the drug he could supply along with the easy money they needed to support their indolence. Clark came to realise that slaves might obey cruel masters because they have to – but are not loyal to them. He could rule by fear, but fear is a form of hatred.

At first, Clark had encouraged the Wilsons to seek medical help to get 'clean', by entering a private hospital. When this failed, he turned against them, as he had done before – and would do again – with people that he lured with fast money then ruled by intimidation. So when Clark invited the Wilsons to Brisbane in June 1978 for a boat cruise to help get over their addiction, they accepted the offer at face value, as far as their contemporaries could tell. But – as they would subsequently confide – Clark had started saying things that played on their minds. He had a black sense of humour and made cryptic comments that fed junkie paranoia.

Before the Brisbane trip, talking about the proposed boat cruise, he asked if the couple's dog, a pampered Belgian keeshond called Taj, would get seasick. When Wilson said he didn't think so, because keeshonds were 'barge dogs', Clark deadpanned: 'Does he freak out on guns going off?'

As the late Richard Hall observed in his book *Greed: The 'Mr Asia' Connection*, 'Whether the plan was to kill the Wilsons or just give them a convalescent cruise will never be clear, for ... Clark was about to pay the price for that sense of humour.'

Clark fancied himself as a cool and cautious criminal 'executive' who made a show of running his drug syndicate on pseudo-corporate lines, but behind the cool mask was a boastful smart-arse who couldn't help wanting to show how much cleverer he was than the herd. So when he checked into the Gazebo Hotel he signed the register not with one of his many aliases, some of them backed with false passports, but with the words 'J. Petersen, MP'.

He might have got away with 'Petersen' but adding 'MP' was stupid for a man with so many reasons to avoid attracting attention. The Hon. Joh Bjelke-Petersen was at the time the long-serving Premier of Queensland and a nationally-famous public figure, respectively loved and lampooned by his many admirers and detractors. Using the Petersen name in vain was asking for trouble, and he got plenty.

The worried hotel manager spotted the false name and concluded the hard-partying guests were not only subversives mocking the Premier but running up a huge champagne bill, and so probably were fraudsters who would not pay their bill. He called the police.

Queensland consorting squad detectives of that time were what are now sometimes referred to as 'old-fashioned' and 'robust'. When the squad came knocking, they found the sort of evidence that quickened an old-fashioned detective's pulse: $5276 in cash, for a start. After what Clark would later describe as some tough questioning, they searched his Jaguar and found an unregistered pistol which, it would turn out, was probably a murder weapon. Meaning Clark was in big trouble. As were his Brisbane 'representatives' and his right-hand man, Jimmy Shepherd, also pulled in by the police. More significantly, so were the Wilsons, taken in for questioning after arranging to meet Clark at the Gazebo.

The Queensland police and the Narcotics Bureau soon ran checks establishing that Clark was wanted in New Zealand on heroin charges laid two years before. Clark, a dab hand at corrupting officials, tried and apparently failed to buy his way out, although word might have spread about his almost bottomless financial resources.

A detective sergeant, Ron Pickering, later dutifully reported that Clark had offered $50,000 to obtain bail. The obvious conclusion was that had Clark got bail, he would have disappeared again, using one of his many false identities.

In other circumstances – such as, say, if Clark had been picked up for drink-driving and fingerprinted – the old heroin charge hanging over him in New Zealand might have seemed disastrous. But, given the gravity of the charges he risked in Australia, being extradited to New Zealand might well have been a better bet than facing the music here – a fact that later stuck in the craw of Victorian police investigators who began to question how and why Clark had been released to New Zealand when he was a suspect for so many serious crimes in Australia, including murder.

These accusations came to light within days of the Gazebo Hotel arrests, when the Queensland police interrogated the nervous Wilsons.

'Still suffering from the long, drawn-out process of withdrawal, frightened of Clark's growing coolness, and finally apprehensive of his growing talk about the sound of guns, they talked. A lot.' writes Hall.

By the end of the week, when the Wilsons (and their pampered pet dog) were turned loose with strict instructions not to bolt, the police – and, by extension, the Narcotics Bureau – had heard a long, rambling story painting Clark as a huge heroin dealer, a callous killer and, significantly, a high-level corrupter. In the 112-page transcript of the tapes the police secretly made over six days, they made some startlingly specific allegations.

One was that Clark had a senior Customs official in his pocket in Sydney – 'an embittered, cynical old copper' on a $25,000 annual stipend plus bonuses for extra valuable information. They told how Clark and his helpers stashed heroin in Thermos flasks buried in Frenchs Forest in Sydney and that Clark had recently bought blocks of land in Fiji. But, most tellingly, they said that the purple Jaguar and the pistol Clark had brought to Brisbane were the same car and weapon he used to murder a drug courier known as 'Pommy Harry'.

It would not have taken much checking, even in the pre-computer age, to reveal that 'Pommy Harry' was the nickname of one Harry Lewis, who had disappeared in late May 1978, soon after being apprehended at Sydney Airport with some Thai buddha sticks. As would be revealed later, Lewis had been nabbed at the airport on 13 May and released on bail posted by one of Clark's lieutenants, Wayne Shrimpton. On 19 May, just six days later, the Narcotics Bureau opened an individual file on Clark. Clark knew this because his 'inside man' leaked it to him in return for cash. The fatal conclusion was that Lewis had said too much under interrogation.

Clark, in Singapore enjoying a secret liaison with Wayne Shrimpton's girlfriend, Allison Dine, at the time of Lewis's arrest, had flown back to take charge of the situation like the trouble-shooting executive he fancied himself to be. He arranged to drive Lewis to Brisbane, promising him he had arranged for him to escape on a boat. Lewis agreed. He had little choice: to run from Clark, without any money to survive, would prove conclusively that he had ratted, something he did not think Clark could know for sure. He had to keep up the pretence of normality, hoping Clark meant what he said about an escape by sea.

But Lewis was doomed. He was given a 24-hour reprieve because Clark saw the chance to hook up with the opportunistic Allison Dine, a former trainee kindergarten teacher with an eye for the main chance. After sending Dine's boyfriend Wayne Shrimpton to Singapore to buy gems, Clark calmly postponed the Brisbane trip to take Dine to the Hilton Hotel, as his wife Maria was in hospital having some plastic surgery. The lovers got drunk, booked the king size suite and stayed the night.

When Lewis came around to the Sydney Hilton next morning for the trip north, he struck Dine as 'pensive'. She thought at the time (or so she would claim later) that he was sad about leaving his girlfriend. Perhaps Lewis's instincts were stronger than hers, and he feared driving 1000 kilometres with the man he'd informed on the week before.

Clark was driving a new purple Jaguar. Somewhere in northern New South Wales, they damaged the exhaust system and Clark decided to head back to Sydney – his intention all along. At dusk he pulled over, claiming the transmission was slipping, and asked Lewis to have a look under the bonnet. Obediently, he obliged and Clark shot him in the head.

It would later be revealed that Clark, the supposed cool master criminal, lost his nerve and bolted after rolling the body into a ditch. After driving for more than an hour, he turned back, found the body and loaded it into the boot and took it down a bush track. Then he lugged it into the bush and dumped it, after cutting off the hands and smashing the teeth to hinder identification. Having made the mistake of killing Lewis instead of sending him far away, he compounded it by not burying the body so it would never be found. Then he drove back to Sydney, wearing blood-spattered clothes, and promptly told Dine his version of the killing – that Lewis had attacked him.

The story of Pommy Harry's murder was soon known to everyone in The Organisation ... including Douglas and Isabel Wilson. Clark no doubt meant Lewis's death to inspire fear, but it was never going to guarantee silence. The Wilsons were so frightened they would be next that it would become a self-fulfilling prophecy. By talking to the police, they signed their own death warrant.

The question still is: did anyone in authority believe the Wilsons' tale when they told it? Or was it, in the beginning, more convenient to dismiss it all as the paranoid delusions of heroin addicts?

This decision to allow Clark to leave the country – and to shelve the charges against him in Queensland – would later be prodded in court. In committal proceedings against two Narcotics Bureau officers and a bent law clerk in Sydney in April 1980, a senior Victorian policeman, Assistant Commissioner Rod Hall, made withering answers under cross examination that made it clear the Victoria Police suspected Clark had been given a 'green light' by inept, or corrupt, investigators.

Hall knew his stuff. He had run a joint Victoria, New South Wales, Queensland and Federal investigation into the Mr Asia drug syndicate but without the powers to check bank records and demand answers.

He said the experience showed him there was a need for a standing Royal Commission or National Crime Authority.

Many senior police were concerned that Hall had broken the coppers' code of silence and was prepared to publicly speak of corruption.

Three decades later, he remains unrepentant. 'There is no doubt that Clark was paying off investigators inside the Narcotics Bureau,' he told the authors.

He also found that some states involved in the taskforce were more enthusiastic in uncovering corruption than others.

Later in his investigation when Clark was jailed in Lancashire, Hall went to England and asked a local policeman to interview the inmate. 'What questions do you want asked and what answers do you want written down?' the local responded.

It was, after all, a different era.

The evidence against the Narcs was damning. So much so that Justice Sir Edward (Ned) Williams in yet another Royal Commission into Drugs eventually called for the Narcotics Bureau to be disbanded and its role to be absorbed into the newly formed Australian Federal Police.

One of the criticisms of the Bureau was that it took credit for the jobs conducted by state police. Some things never change.

Meanwhile, back in Brisbane, Terry Clark was in an uncomfortable spot ...

TWO Queensland undercover police put in the cells with Clark and Jimmy Shepherd overheard conversations between the pair that supported what the Wilsons were telling their colleagues in an interview room not far away. Clark and Shepherd whispered to each other about running The Organisation. Why such streetwise operators would be so careless is hard to say – unless Clark was already confident he could pull strings in Sydney or Canberra to get extradited. And that he was equally confident he could bribe enough witnesses to beat the old New Zealand heroin charge. (Which, in fact, he later boasted of doing.)

Whether it was apathy or something more, Sydney police did not do anything to protect the Wilsons from Clark's revenge. On 30 March 1979, Douglas Wilson called the New South Wales homicide squad. He said he was frightened because Clark had come to his house the previous day and threatened him. A detective called Dawson gave Wilson his home telephone number and reported the call to Sergeant John McGregor, telling him Clark was in New Zealand and under surveillance. But ten days later the homicide squad got a fax from New Zealand police informing them that Clark was in Australia. Notwithstanding this, the police did not put the Wilsons in protective custody, or even contact them.

It was odd. Somehow, the Wilsons' story was not considered strong enough to hold Clark and investigate him for murder and serious trafficking. And yet someone, somewhere – perhaps in the Narcotics Bureau – thought the Wilsons' story *was* strong enough to sell. And Clark certainly thought it strong enough to buy. He complained later that he'd had to pay $250,000 for the Wilson tapes. And another $250,000 to have them killed.

To do that he needed local talent – a trusted middleman who could arrange a hit.

Enter 'Aussie Bob' Trimbole.

FOR a Calabrian peasant's son raised in the secretive ways of the sinister mafia organisation known as N'Dranghita, Robert Trimbole was different from most of his contemporaries. His parents and many of his relatives had come to Griffith in boatloads, migrating en masse from the poverty and crime-ridden town of Plati in Calabria before and after World War II. They left the grinding poverty behind but brought the crime with them: relatively humble members of the so-called 'Honoured Society' established themselves high in a new pecking order in the new country. And because they came in such numbers, and stuck together so strongly, in some ways they still lived in the village their parents had left behind in southern Italy.

But Trimbole, born in Griffith in 1931, showed the ability from an early age to get along with people outside the tight circle of what the Griffith Calabrians called, among themselves, La Famiglia – The Family – the local cell of N'Dranghita. While the clannish Calabrians didn't all share Trimbole's gregarious nature and easygoing engagement with the wider world, the senior figures in the secret society recognised his potential usefulness and would exploit it. Unusually, Trimbole married outside the Calabrian community – where cousins often married each other – when he wed Joan Quested, an Anglo-Australian secretary he met while working in Sydney in 1952. They would have several children, all with 'Australian' Anglo names – one son was called Craig – and Trimbole did not follow his parents onto the irrigation block. A talented mechanic, he did his apprenticeship in

Sydney with Pioneer Tours and later ran a garage in Griffith. But he was always a punter and, inevitably, he lost more than he won in the 1950s and 1960s, although he was well-known for shouting the bar at the local club when he'd had a good win. And although he was good 'on the tools', the garage barely supported his growing family and his punting. In 1968, he was declared bankrupt.

'His trouble was he wanted to be a mate to everybody and never charged enough for the work he did,' a former garage employee said of his former boss to journalist Keith Moor in the late 1980s.

'Customers took advantage of his good nature and he was always a soft touch for a hard luck story. He accepted all sorts of things in payment for work done, even down to race tips. He was always a gambler – bet on anything, he would. He was forever nipping away from the garage to put a bet on and racing broadcasts were a constant background noise at work.'

To the outside world, the young Trimbole was a battling small businessman, a mug punter, a loving father and a good mate. The description 'good bloke' was often used about him, even after he was disgraced. But no matter how well Trimbole got on with outsiders, he was still connected by birth, geography and instinct to the shadowy organisation that flourished in the irrigation districts of Griffith, Mildura and Shepparton, and whose tentacles reached the fruit and vegetable markets in Sydney, Melbourne and Adelaide.

For decades, the Family hierarchy extorted money from fellow Italians by standing over growers and stall holders. But by the early 1970s, there was a new cash crop in town: marijuana.

As proved in the Prohibition era in America in the 1920s, the banning of a substance that was impossible to stamp out and easy to supply created a multi-million dollar black market, created and enriched a criminal class, and corrupted police, politicians, public servants and the judicial system. Not to mention jockeys, horse trainers and racing officials because, one way or another, black money tends to find its way to the racetrack as well as to casinos. Crooks, with rare exceptions, are gamblers by both nature and nurture. More importantly, gambling is a swift and relatively simple way to launder the proceeds of crime.

Marijuana produced mountains of black money that had to be filtered some way before it could be spent on visible assets. Trimbole was never the 'Godfather' of the Griffith Family, but he was its most active operator – a fixer whose main task was to handle the marketing of marijuana and the laundering of cash. Punting was in his blood. Now he could attempt to rig races himself or to buy information from race-fixing gangs who bribed or intimidated jockeys and trainers and had horses doped.

As Moor outlines in his book *Crims in Grass Castles*, the first known turning point in Trimbole's fortunes came in 1971 when the manager of a local club, Archie Molinaro, suggested he might be interested in taking over a business selling, leasing and repairing pinball machines throughout the Riverina. Trimbole had the necessary mechanical skill to repair the machines, and so he took it on in partnership with Molinaro – and with a Melbourne man called Gianfranco Tizzoni, a onetime debt collector with interesting contacts.

Tizzoni, three years younger than Trimbole, was also Italian but not a Calabrian and, although he was an associate of the Griffith crew, he lived in suburban Melbourne and was never an insider like Trimbole. It was an association that would make them both rich, eventually, and then infamous. But it wasn't the pinball machines that made the big money. It was the new crop being grown under cover in the middle of the irrigation blocks. Local wags called it 'Calabrese corn' and there were stares and whispers around the Riverina as battling 'blockies' suddenly accrued the trappings of wealth on irrigation blocks that had been hard pressed to support a family for decades.

Tizzoni would later tell police that it began in 1971, when Trimbole said to him that he had to raise some money for an operation on the eyes of a friend's son – and that he proposed to sell marijuana to get the money. Whether the story of the eye operation was true is debatable, but Tizzoni agreed to arrange marijuana distribution in Melbourne.

'He told me there was an endless supply from the Griffith area, and that Tony Sergi was organising the growing part of it and the supply part of it,' Tizzoni told police.

'Different farmers were growing it for him (Tony Sergi) and Tony Barbaro was supervising the farmers. Bob Trimbole was organising the distribution and my job was to distribute in Victoria under Bob's instructions.'

That was the beginning of a decade of greed. By the time Trimbole became one of Australia's best-known 'racing identities' a few years later, he had laundered tens of millions of dollars for himself and the Griffith godfathers, including the aforementioned Sergi and Barbaro. Along the way, the professional 'good bloke' had compromised scores of useful people from jockeys and strappers to some of the highest in the land: politicians, senior police and public servants, lawyers and judges.

By the time Terry Clark asked for Trimbole's help to get rid of Douglas and Isabel Wilson in 1978, he had already arranged murders. One, in particular, would go down as one of the most shameful episodes in Australian history. That was the murder of another 'good bloke' from Griffith – this one a decent man called Donald Mackay.

IT happened on a Friday evening in winter. At 5.30pm on 17 July 1977, Don Mackay closed the furniture store his family had run in Griffith since the 1920s and drove his mini-van to the nearby Griffith Hotel. He had earlier told his wife, Barbara, he would be home by 7pm to look after the youngest of their four children while she went to a meeting.

The Mackays were that sort of family – public spirited, generous, industrious and honest. And also fearless. If there was one thing Don Mackay had, it was moral courage. But in Griffith, in 1977, moral courage was a dangerous quality. Perhaps it still is.

The known facts are bleak, and haven't changed in half a lifetime.

At the pub, Mackay had a round of drinks and chatted with friends – largely about his efforts to draw attention to the open scandal of large-scale marijuana crops being grown in the area – before buying a cask of white wine in the bottle shop and heading to the car park to go home. He was never seen again.

It was dark, the street almost deserted. Two people were working late in the office building on the other side of the car park. One was Mackay's solicitor and friend, Ian Salmon. The other was an accountant called Roy Binks.

Salmon heard nothing, although he was later called from home to look for his missing client. Binks, however, later told police he'd heard a noise 'like someone being sick' and that he thought he'd heard a sound like 'whip cracks'.

Years later, understandably, Binks' recollections were even vaguer. In 1997, on the twentieth anniversary of Mackay's murder, he obligingly pointed out his old office to the authors – and where Mackay's van was parked. But he didn't want to rake over the embers of fading anger and sorrow.

In fact, he seemed faintly embarrassed and nervous, an attitude shared with many other honest Griffith citizens, who still tend to start sentences warily with 'It's all such a long time ago'. The unspoken suggestion is that it's easier to let sleeping dogs lie.

Binks was anxious about being quoted. He didn't want to stir up trouble, he explained apologetically.

Ian Salmon was not quite so shy. After 33 years in Griffith, he moved interstate to retire and often thought about what happened that Friday evening after a worried Barbara Mackay called to say Don hadn't come home.

Salmon agreed to drive around looking for him, as Mrs Mackay was reluctant to call the police immediately.

At first he didn't feel it was sinister, only that it was out of character for Mackay not to go home. But, by midnight, he was getting worried and contacted police. He kept looking and found the mini-van in the Griffith Hotel car park.

First, he noticed the imprint of an adult hand on the driver's window. Then he swung his car around so the headlights lit the scene. That's when he saw pools of blood and three spent .22 bullet shells glinting on the ground.

DON Mackay's body has never been found. No one has been convicted of his murder. No one is likely to be.

An old and dangerous man called James Bazley, criminal and gunman, was convicted in 1986 for conspiring to kill Mackay and for another drug-related double murder, but he's not the talking type. Finally released in 2001, aged 75, he has never broken his silence to say anything useful, except that he'd been 'told' that Mackay's body was buried on a large Griffith rice farm owned by Gianfranco Tizzoni, the man whose evidence helped put him away on murder conspiracy charges. Where, he couldn't say.

Neither is George Joseph saying much. The one-time gun dealer sold Bazley a French .22 calibre pistol believed to be the murder weapon and recommended Bazley to do the 'hit' when approached on behalf of a Griffith marijuana syndicate keen to hire a killer.

With the exception of Robert 'Aussie Bob' Trimbole (who would eventually die on the run in Spain in May 1987) those who ordered Mackay's death – many of them publicly named by a royal commission – are still going about the business of turning illicit millions into legitimate assets. They do this with the best legal and financial help money can buy. The way, some say, they bought police and politicians.

Mackay's family, friends and supporters see this but they are powerless where governments and police have pointedly failed. Some avoid certain shops in Griffith, or cross the street rather than share the footpath with certain people. None have ever been willing to be quoted.

It's hard to credit this nightmarish undercurrent in the bustling main street of an outwardly peaceful country town. But the Riverina, for all its Banjo Paterson red gums and sunlit plains, is in secret ways a little Calabria, still a stronghold of the so-called 'Honoured Society'.

Sydney had a dark side, too, like Al Capone's Chicago, where for decades corruption seeped upwards like rising damp, regardless of which premier or police commissioner was in power. Some people in Griffith still wonder why investigations went nowhere, about who tipped off Trimbole to flee Australia in 1981 and why he was not arrested after Victorian police passed on his address to other authorities.

They recall the times that visiting political figures would go straight to the shop of a Calabrian identity, now dead, known locally as 'The Godfather'. It was suggested that this man – once charged with having unlicensed pistols – could deliver blocks of votes. It was speculated he could also deliver campaign funds. What isn't certain is what favours he scored in return.

'Don't let anybody fool you,' one long-time Griffith businessman told the authors in disgust. 'In this town, crime pays. Crime is probably the biggest industry here.' By this he means drug money used to establish legitimate businesses.

It costs millions to buy and set up modern, irrigated vineyards and orchards but some families have no trouble finding the money, although neighbours on identical farms remember the same people battling to get by before the 1960s – before the marijuana boom.

The businessman points at a house nearby, owned by a family whose common Italian surname, Sergi, figured prominently in the Woodward Royal Commission's report in 1979. He remembers former local member (and Whitlam Government Immigration Minister) Al Grassby's Commonwealth car, Australian flag fluttering on the bonnet, arriving as guest of honour at a family gathering.

The Riverina, like Melbourne's northern fringe, has many 'grass castles' – eruptions of brick, tile and concrete so huge and ugly that they're worth less the day they're finished than the total cost of construction. These are not built as an investment but as a self-aggrandising way to soak up black money. There are always tradesmen who will work for cash.

Marijuana growing has ensured some words have entered the local language. When Riverina people talk of a 'crop', they don't mean wheat or rice but marijuana. They talk of 'crop sitters', pawns who specialise in the greedy business of being gardener and guard to million-dollar dope plantations.

The accepted wisdom is that the Griffith irrigation area soon became 'too close to home', too closely observed by agricultural pilots and local police keen to clean up the tarnished reputation of their predecessors, of whom three went to jail for corruption in the early 1980s.

Later, the crops were grown much further afield – as far as outback Queensland and the Northern Territory. But, even so, if there was a police raid interstate it was odd how often a Griffith connection was made so far from home: trickle irrigation equipment from a Griffith supplier; bags stamped with Griffith producers' names; crop sitters from Griffith families.

The younger members of such families disappeared from town for a few days or weeks then returned flush with cash. 'They've got a crop off somewhere,' locals muttered to each other. But not too loudly, and never on the record.

Meanwhile, money keeps pouring into an already prosperous district. The town where tax investigators in the 1970s estimated half the banks' cash flow was from marijuana has remained remarkably recession-proof. Some suggest the same of Shepparton and Mildura.

DONALD Bruce Mackay was, according to Ian Salmon, more than a decent man. He was a good bloke, too. Like Mackay's widow Barbara (until her death in 2001) and adult children, Salmon resented the headline writer's shorthand that labelled Mackay an 'anti-drug crusader'.

It's a tag that ignores the warmth, intelligence, humour and strong physical presence of a husband and father, businessman and sportsman. It leaves a lingering and offensive suggestion that he was a naive, wowserish zealot who blundered into trouble. As if, somehow, it was his fault. Blaming the victim has been popular in some circles ever since the murdering Mafia peasants used their tame politician, Grassby, and bent police and others to try to poison public opinion. There were those, prominent in politics, the mob had compromised long before.

The truth, says Salmon, is that Mackay was big – in size, intellect and heart – and brave enough to stand by his principles when lesser people shuffled their feet and looked the other way. Two days after he disappeared, Barbara Mackay told reporters her husband believed if good people 'didn't do anything, then evil won'.

The weasel tendency to blame the victim has crept into references to Mackay by some who didn't know him, which suits those who plotted his death. It has also suited them to suggest that support for Mackay and demands for a full investigation are somehow harmful to the harmonious relations of an area that is more than half Italian, mainly Calabrian.

For thirty years it has been repeatedly asserted that '98 per cent' of Griffith people are law-abiding citizens, which is undoubtedly true. What some find galling is that the other two per cent – representing organised crime – have much to gain by repeating that assertion.

The feeling is that the corrupt few can hide among the law-abiding majority, at the same time leading a refrain that it's unfair to brand all Calabrians as crooks. It would, of course, be unfair – but that is a convenient loophole for the people who plotted murder.

Ten days after Don Mackay disappeared, 5000 people crowded the lawns of the local hospital for an ecumenical memorial service. Shops closed. People wept.

Two weeks later, 2000 people jammed a local club to take part in a television special hosted by famed British interviewer David Frost, who flew in for the event. Al Grassby was jeered off stage at the same event when he claimed he'd had only one complaint of marijuana growing. The snake in the grass was posturing for the benefit of his long time sponsors – the crims in grass castles.

Meanwhile, a reward of $25,000 soon leapt to $100,000 with pledges from local business people – and there were predictions it would reach the then staggering sum of a million dollars.

Members of Concerned Citizens of Griffith were widely quoted about the need to investigate and clean up drug trafficking and corruption.

But as the years came and went without any sign of Mackay's body, the group ran out of energy and its members rarely met and would not be quoted. Time dulled the outrage and the determination but not quite all the fear.

EVEN Barbara Mackay, the most articulate and fearless of women, grew to feel that there was little to be gained by repeating herself. When the authors visited her in 1997, she would talk off the record but saw no point in spoiling the harmony of her family's life by appearing publicly bitter.

At 61, and a grandmother, she lived then in a tasteful unit overlooking a park in a quiet street. She was gracious, almost serene, given what she had suffered. She had faith in both God and in Griffith but not so much in the system that had let her down so cruelly.

She said she had written a book that had been shelved by her publishers because of fears of defamation writs but she planned to revive the project. That idea would die with her in 2001.

Meanwhile, her eldest son, Paul, was still running the family furniture store his grandfather had started just after World War I. But the youth who was outspoken and angry in the first years after his father's death was, nearing 40, gruff and suspicious when the subject was brought up. Like everyone else in town, he did not want to be quoted. After all, all the talk in the world couldn't undo the great wrong done to his family.

But the facts speak in favour of the Mackays. They have been accused by the stupid and the self-serving of being 'anti-Italian' and 'anti-Griffith' yet Barbara never considered moving and Paul married a woman called Maria Minato, whose mother's family is from Plati, a stronghold of N'Dranghita and birthplace of many Griffith Calabrians.

Barbara Mackay went to her grave still tortured by speculation about what happened to her Don's body. The reality couldn't be worse than all the rumours, she sometimes told friends.

One story is that the body was put through a pet food grinder, another that it was burned in a hospital incinerator or an old brick kiln, another that it was weighed down and dumped in a river, or set in concrete underneath a building.

She never did get the truth about his death. What she had, though, was the truth about his life.

Three days before he died, there was an attempt to lure him to Jerilderie, 160 kilometres away, to meet a mysterious 'Mr Adams', who claimed he was a lottery winner who wanted to furnish an entire house. It was later to become clear that it was the hired hit man, James Bazley.

Mackay missed the appointment, instead sending an employee, Bruce Pursehouse. The reason? Mackay was arranging the funeral of a poor man called Harold Craig, one of many people he had helped in Griffith. 'If the truth's known,' Pursehouse would recall, 'Don probably paid for the funeral as well as doing everything else.'

He was like that. Three days later, he paid for his social conscience with his life. The question remains: was it in vain?

Two years later, in 1979, a Queen's Counsel assisting the Woodward Royal Commission into Drug Trafficking put it this way: 'One school of thought is that people behind the (drug) trade have been incredibly stupid in acting against someone as prominent as Don Mackay. The other school says it was a masterstroke which has created enough fear to keep people's mouths shut for the next ten years.'

More than thirty years later, mouths are still shut. After thousands of hours and millions of dollars being spent on investigation, the truth behind a crime that shamed Australia is as elusive as it was the night Don Mackay was killed.

AROUND the race tracks and clubs and restaurants favoured by the big spenders they called Trimbole 'Australian Bob', later contracted to 'Aussie Bob'. It was part of the casual criminal slang favoured by people who liked the quasi-anonymity of using nicknames and aliases rather than the surnames on their birth certificates. Not that they had any trouble, in the 1970s, getting fake birth certificates, driver's licences and passports. Trimbole had a book of 100 birth certificate blanks filched from a public building in Griffith. Nothing was a problem to Aussie Bob. He was everybody's mate, because he never knew when they might come in useful.

One of the people Trimbole knew from the racetrack – and from eating in Tati's restaurant in Oxford Street, Darlinghurst – was Jimmy Shepherd. They had much in common: both were huge punters who laundered – or sometimes just lost – drug money at the races. Clark met Trimbole through Shepherd in the Sydney scene. As the Griffith marijuana business got a little 'tropical' after Donald Mackay's murder in 1977, the two grew closer. Outwardly dissimilar, they had interests and abilities in common.

Trimbole, the bridge builder, started playing an active part in Clark's organisation and would eventually pay, on behalf of his Griffith principals, some $30 million to take over the Australian end of what the media would later call the 'Mr Asia' syndicate – Clark's Organisation – while Clark stayed overseas. He, too, by mid-1978 was getting 'tropical'.

On appearances and background, the scruffy, big-bellied Italian racing identity and the flinty, physically fit and impeccably-dressed Clark, who despised punting as a mug's game, had little in common except an aversion to honest work and access to ob-scene amounts of black money. The first real test of their fledgling business relationship was when Clark asked Trimbole to solve a problem for him. He wanted Douglas and Isabel Wilson killed.

His instructions were chillingly specific: he wanted the pair to disappear, as if they might have done a runner and changed their identities. Knowing how devoted they were to their dog, he wanted it killed, too; presumably because anyone who knew the Wilsons knew they wouldn't leave the dog. And, just before they were killed, they were to be told why: 'You get this for talking to the police in Queensland.'

Trimbole was keen to please. He said he had just the man: one who had done another 'job' for him. He meant the middleaged painter and docker James 'Iceman' Bazley.

According to 'Frank' Tizzoni, who would later testify against Bazley, Trimbole called him on 27 March 1979, and asked him to pick him up at Melbourne Airport. When Tizzoni did, they went to a hotel car park, where Trimbole told him Clark wanted to get rid of two people who had talked to police in Queensland. Tizzoni said he would find out if the hit man who had killed Mackay was available. Trimbole relayed the instructions about killing the dog, and about leaving the Wilsons' car in the long-term car park at the airport to make it look as if they had fled using false identities.

Tizzoni, himself a middle man, called the shifty Melbourne gun dealer, George Joseph, who by virtue of his occupation had friends on both sides of the law – criminals, police and security guards. Joseph had set up a meeting between Bazley and Tizzoni two years earlier at Trimbole's request.

The meeting took place at the same spot: in a car parked in the leafy residential street running behind Kew Cemetery. Tizzoni relayed the orders but Bazley resented the order to kill the Wilsons' dog, Taj. 'Why do the dog? Dogs don't talk,' he said, in a bizarre display of compassion.

Tizzoni shrugged it off, and told Bazley the Wilsons would drive down from Sydney, expecting to meet a person at a Seymour motel (north of Melbourne) that they had been told they were 'taking over from' in Melbourne. Bazley would pose as that person. He suggested the following Sunday, 8 April, and asked for $10,000 for each victim. Tizzoni readily agreed, as Trimbole had made it clear there was much more money available than that. He agreed to drop the Wilsons' car at the airport and to ensure the bodies would never be found.

'There's no worry about that; I'll put them through the mincer,' Bazley promised. These barbaric details were music to Clark's ears when later relayed to him by Trimbole.

When Trimbole heard Bazley was reluctant to kill the Wilsons' dog, he remonstrated and Tizzoni spoke to Bazley, who reluctantly agreed.

The Wilsons left Sydney that Sunday and drove south down the Hume Highway to Seymour, an hour north of Melbourne's suburbs. But Bazley had to cancel at the last minute because he had hurt his arm, which was in a sling. It was too late to head off the Wilsons. Trimbole flew to Melbourne and Tizzoni drove him to the Seymour motel the Wilsons had booked into, to make sure they were there, and had not suspected anything was amiss.

The Wilsons returned to Sydney, their lives spared for five more days. Two days later, Bazley told Tizzoni his arm was better and suggested the 'job' go ahead that Friday. This was proof, if nothing else, that Bazley was neither religious nor superstitious.

It was Friday the 13th, and also Good Friday.

This time Bazley was waiting for the unsuspecting couple. No one knows exactly where he asked them to follow him, but it was most likely to a suburban house with a garage somewhere close to the airport. He told them why they were to die and shot Wilson first, then his wife. But he did not shoot the dog.

Taj the keeshond was found wandering the streets in the northern suburbs on Easter Monday, and was taken in and cared for by a man who later handed him in to police. Like Bazley, the Wilsons and Dennis Brown, the man who found their bodies a month later, he was a dog lover – which was more than could be said of Terry Clark. He loved only himself and money – or, rather, the power it bought him over others.

Clark couldn't resist boasting about the murder to his third wife Maria Muhaury, mother of his son, Jarrod. During an argument, he threatened to get the same hit man to kill her if she caused any trouble. This might explain why she had no qualms about testifying against him later. But it doesn't explain why so many women threw themselves at Clark. His own theory was that it was the money.

LADY KILLER

THE RISE OF TERRENCE CLARK, DRUG DEALER

When a hit man was sent after
him, Clark sat the gunman down,
opened a bottle of wine, lit
him a cigar and cleared up
the misunderstanding. He was
carrying a vintage Luger pistol
and his associates had no doubt
he would use it.

LATER, when his world had crashed around him, Terry Clark
would sit in court reading Norman Mailer's *The Executioner's
Song*, the true story of a death row prisoner who chose to be executed. A decade earlier, as a small-time crook with big ideas,
Clark would have seen *The Godfather*, a film classic that inspired
a generation of would-be gangsters. More literate than the usual
run of thieves – he fancied himself as an artist – Clark most likely
also read the Mario Puzo novel that inspired the Godfather films.
And if he ever read Puzo's pithy line about what drives men to
compete, he would have understood it, because it fitted him.

Men compete to succeed, Puzo said, so that beautiful women
will love them. When detectives asked Clark about photographs

of his beautiful lawyer girlfriend Karen Soich rolling naked in money he replied: 'Women like money, don't they?' Money was a means to an end, and for Clark a potent attraction was the power it gave him over women. It meant he could buy them, use them and discard them, often brutally.

After the author Richard Hall investigated Clark's background in New Zealand, he painted a picture of a small town loner – a skinny kid with a chip on his shoulder, without the physical or mental gifts to put him above his peers. There was nothing about him that marked him as special, except for the most important thing of all: an ego that drove him to do whatever it took to feel superior to the common herd. He wanted to be number one. To do that, he turned to crime the way some turn to sport and others to study or music. Unlike most people raised in relatively normal family circumstances, he showed no inhibitions about breaking the legal and moral rules.

Terrence John Clark was born in Gisborne on the east coast of New Zealand's north island – the first city in the world to see the rising sun each day. When Clark was born on 13 November 1944, the biggest business in town was the abattoirs and freezing works, where his father, Leo, worked when Terry was young. 'Good old Leo', as locals called him, was from a farming family and was a sportsman, a surfer and a founder of a local surf lifesaving club.

But while the father was a public-spirited sportsman in a sports-mad community, Terry wasn't. Not big or strong, he soon developed into a loner at school. He affected being a rebel without a cause. In that time and place, that meant being a 'bodgie', with a Cornell Wilde haircut and a roll-your-own cigarette hanging from his lip. Whereas his younger brother Paddy was good at school and at sport, Terry went the other way: he played tough guy.

But there was ambition and a shrewd streak of business sense in the family. In the early 1950s, while Terry was in primary school, Leo bought the local pie-cart – a caravan that sold pies, sausages and bacon at night. Soon after, he bought a better house. And by 1957 he set up the first driving-school in the town. Leo the farmer's son was not content to be an abattoir worker all his life. But while his family was bettering itself, Terry Clark was going the other way: he was unusually aggressive in schoolyard fights and so determined to be seen as tough he talked about carrying a knife and being prepared to use it.

Like a lot of kids from provincial towns, Terry Clark got out as soon as he could. By 1962, he was in Auckland working as a welder's assistant. He fancied something that paid better than handing welding rods to a tradesman but he wasn't going to follow his father into a life of hard work. He wanted short cuts.

It didn't take him long to collide with the law. The police picked him up for interfering with a car. He was given probation. Other youngsters in the same boat might have 'pulled up' but Clark wasn't other youngsters. He was drawn to the dark and dirty side. In Auckland in the 1960s, that meant thieving. Illicit drugs were still almost unknown, armed robberies were rare. Burglary, theft and receiving were what Kiwi crooks did. Top of the pecking order were the safecrackers.

In 1963, Clark had begun what would become a habit: acquiring women. That year, while still on probation, he married a girl called Sally R. They moved into a flat. Meanwhile, Clark combined panel beating with minor rackets: stolen cars and shop breaking. But, already, he was receiving stolen goods from other thieves, which meant they did the dirty work and took the bigger risk. This set a pattern.

After a farcical foray into safe blowing – he left the gelignite on top of the safe, instead of drilling it, and blew up half the service station it was in – he started to combine receiving with informing. The sneaky, calculating loner convinced of his own superiority soon became a regular police 'fizz'. Ordinary in so many ways, he was not quite normal, even for a 'delinquent': unlike most young criminals, he wasn't a tearaway who hung around with his mates, drinking in pubs, fighting and thrashing and crashing cars. He lived quietly with his wife – first in a flat, then in a state-owned rented house.

Writes Hall: 'His informer role helped to make him deeply suspicious and cautious. He insisted on meeting his police contacts well away from the suburbs where he lived. The detectives who used Clark remember him with a special dislike ... One detective recalls that Clark became so hostile that he had to be passed on to another, the detective deciding that he was too shifty to deal with even as a grass.

'From time to time Clark undertook regular work, but he always made sure the experience paid an extra dividend. One land sale company that employed him for a short time was burgled five times in the next year.'

While still living with Sally, Clark had several women friends, several of them prostitutes. One, Norah Fleet, was an early heroin addict in Auckland's fledgling drug culture. The cold-blooded Clark smelt an opportunity for fast money. In 1969, he bought 24 capsules of 'heroin' to re-sell – not suspecting it was a police sting. But fate had another trick in store – when the capsules were sent for testing, they turned out to be codeine and milk powder. Clark, who in the next decade would become one of the biggest dealers on Earth, had been conned. In the process, he had beaten the rap. But, for all his precautions, his luck was running out.

'As a grass, Clark was getting out of control,' Hall would write. 'Some say that when Clark was picked up attempting a safe in the country town of Napier in March 1971, he had been deliberately set up by police to get rid of him.' Maybe it was because he had aimed too high: 'lagging' respected crooks with their own ways of getting back at him. Whatever the reason, they threw the book at him. In March 1971 he was sentenced to five years prison. Proof, perhaps, that no-one likes a rat. Except, it would turn out, several women who should have known better. But that was later, when he had far more money than they had sense.

WI TAKO prison, at Trentham, north of Wellington, was a mini-mum-security jail for first offenders. As such, Clark would prob-ably have been sent there automatically. Typically, though, he claimed he had got there through inside influence – a contact at the Justice Department. Although he won a reputation as a jail 'heavy', and was twice charged with fighting, he made sure he didn't do anything serious enough to get him sent to a tougher jail full of hardened offenders. Working in the joinery workshop, he invented a yachting self-steering device. He was keen on boats and read voraciously about them. Mainly, though, other inmates would remember him as a wheeler-dealer with a talent for cor-rupting people. And for deceiving them. One of his contempo-raries recalled him selling dried dock leaves to six other prisoners who thought it was marijuana.

A fellow prisoner who later wrote a book about prison life describes Clark as having 'that cold, implacable look that dulled his face when he spoke of dealing it to people.' He also describes a tense prison visit from Clark's parents where Clark's broken-hearted father said bitterly he was prepared to set his son up in any legitimate business when he got out – 'but no, he doesn't want my money. He just has to make it himself by being a big-time crook.'

Clark used to boast that if 'you have enough bread, you can buy anyone'. About the only person he showed respect was the jail chaplain, for whom he drew the head of Christ in black ink, a picture the chaplain would hang in his office for the rest of his career.

By the time he was released in 1974 he had divorced Sally R and married his heroin addict prostitute, Norma Fleet. It is hard not to conclude he saw her as a way into the heroin dealing world. If so, he was on the money. In just a few years, drugs had taken over from the traditional forms of crime. The old underworld hierarchy of thieves was irrelevant. Norma was to die the following year from an overdose of Mandrax. Clark went to work dealing Thai 'buddha' sticks. Where other dealers flashed their money by buying big American cars, Clark stuck to a battered old English car, which blended in. He behaved himself – and he was no longer an informer.

Careful as he was, Clark bumped into some high-living drug dealers. One of them was Martin Johnstone.

Johnstone, younger than Clark, had been born in 1951 in a farming district near Auckland. He had a brother and a sister and their parents were a successful, hard-working business couple. After dropping out of a private school, he'd soon got into trouble for theft and burglary. Then he worked in an Auckland menswear shop – Collar'n'Cuffs – where he met an Englishman called Andrew Maher. By 1973 Johnstone was dealing in marijuana, but very small time. He was arrested that June in possession of two plants and told police he had developed an interest in horticulture because he was too poor to buy his own grass. The arresting detective described him as 'a friendly, easy-to-approach person who would readily admit to offences.'

But Marty Johnstone had no intention of remaining small time. While he and Clark were almost opposites in character they shared one personality trait – ambition. First it was local leaf then he moved up to imported Thai sticks. He bought the sticks from a connection on the Royal Dutch Orient Line, which sailed from Asian ports and whose Chinese crewmen easily outwitted New Zealand's crude customs regime, mainly by tossing contraband overboard at pre-arranged spots to be picked up by small craft. The middle man on the Dutch boats was Choo Cheng Kui, known as 'Chinese Jack'.

Johnstone and Clark did shady 'business' together but there was always an underlying tension. Clark had done time and was street smart, but the younger Johnstone was tall, dark and handsome and had the insouciance of the well-dressed, private-school dandy he was. Charming and gregarious, he was also prone to melancholy – and not as ruthless and resilient as Clark. One thing they had in common, besides a taste for easy money, was a love for boats. Johnstone owned a speedboat he used to pick up contraband. Clark bought a 51-foot sloop, a symbol of success.

Johnstone loved playing the prosperous businessman. A confidential New Zealand police report said, 'He was becoming noted for his flamboyant lifestyle and jetset image.' While Clark worked in the shadows, Johnstone sought the spotlight. It was another reason the two men were not destined to be long-term partners.

Johnstone set up a group of companies and used one of them to buy a 36-foot boat, the *Brigadoon*, captained by one Peter Miller, who had been a member of the Exclusive Brethren religious sect. Johnstone put together a syndicate of backers to finance a voyage to buy half a million buddha sticks from Thailand – a plan police and customs soon got to hear about on the grapevine. Clark didn't invest but became 'wholesaler' for the operation, agreeing to pay $3.50 per stick.

The voyage of the *Brigadoon* was more Marx Brothers than mastermind. After a series of minor disasters, an Australian trawler skipper called John Chatterton agreed to tow the *Brigadoon* from Indonesia to near New Zealand, where police and customs had heard long before that a shipment of marijuana was on the way. But the *Brigadoon* was running so late that the surveillance had been eased. Even then, the syndicate speedboat had broken down and the cargo of 36 bags of Thai sticks had to be ferried ashore by rowing boat.

Clark took delivery of 458,000 sticks. Johnstone cleared about $1 million plus the yacht. Eventually, Clark cleared about $1 million, too, retailing the sticks at $7 each over the following year. Two other partners – a local solicitor and a Greek businessman – made a handsome profit. At a time when people worked for $10,000 a year, it was enough money to set up a legitimate business and go straight. Clark, however, was already moving into heroin. In late 1975 he persuaded a woman called Valerie Kairua to smuggle some back from a Fiji holiday. But the two fell out, police raided Clark and he was charged with trafficking offences that carried ten years jail. Clark had no intention of going back inside. Instead, in the new year of 1976, he jumped bail and headed to the bright lights of the big city most New Zealanders go first ... Sydney.

IN Auckland, Clark had befriended several fellow inmates of Wi Tako prison, which was probably the single worst decision any of them ever made. One was Greg Ollard, by this time also in Sydney. Another was Wayne Shrimpton. Another was Errol Hincksman. Then there was Douglas Wilson, who had 'moved' $200,000 worth of buddha sticks for Clark. And, of course, the urbane Martin Johnstone. Ollard was already in Sydney when Clark got there, and the rest would follow.

The attraction towards Clark and 'Sin City' was a dangerous one. No-one, even Clark in his darkest moments, could have guessed then that soon he would have arranged the murder of three of his old Auckland 'mates' (plus two women associated with them), stolen the girlfriend of another, and caused Errol Hincksman to be charged with one of the murders.

Ollard was Clark's first contact in Sydney. He stayed with him in King's Cross when he got there. Unlike Clark, who despised addicts, Ollard used heroin as well as dealing in it. He had worked for the EMI record company and hung around with rock groups, including Rose Tattoo and the New Zealand band Dragon, which by 1977 would be Australian *Rolling Stone* magazine's 'Band of The Year'. Ollard was a groupie; he loaned the band members money and picked up bills in return for reflected glory. Dragon's drummer, Neil Storey, died of a heroin overdose in June 1976, most likely because of the free 'smack' Ollard handed out at parties.

Meanwhile, Johnstone was living high on the $1 million he'd made selling the buddha sticks wholesale to Clark, whose 'representatives' in New Zealand were steadily 'retailing' them for him. Johnstone settled in Singapore and made his name as a profligate party-giver and ladies' man. He once boasted of spending US$11,000 on one long weekend party.

New Zealand police were still tracking him. 'Johnstone lives in Singapore, again leading a lavish lifestyle, allegedly living in an expensive apartment, driving an XJ6 Jaguar car and creating the impression that he is a successful businessman. It is known he has spent vast amounts of money on purchasing ocean-going vessels in Singapore and has also spent a great deal of money in Auckland,' they wrote.

While the New Zealand police could see that Johnstone was moving onto the world drug stage, international authorities did not seem to grasp the size of the operation. They did not understand that the former shop assistant was positioning himself to wholesale the deadly white powder. On 23 December 1977 Johnstone was seen walking through Sydney airport with an Australian woman. Both were stopped and searched. The woman was found to have heroin valued at $1.5 million strapped to her body. She was arrested. He was released.

Meanwhile, Clark was busy. He now had a third wife, Maria Muahary. On a visit to Malaysia and Singapore later in 1976 he renewed acquaintance with 'Chinese Jack' and did some business: sending two couriers back to Australia with heroin strapped to their bodies. While Johnstone dreamed of setting up a big-time legitimate business, Clark was setting up a big-time illegitimate one, which they called The Organisation. While Johnstone postured outrageously in Singapore's expatriate social scene, Clark moved around quietly under a string of aliases: John Templar, Phil Scott and Phil Perkins were three of many he would use over the next three years. Not standing out from the crowd was now useful for the former nondescript kid from Gisborne: for the time being, Clark was a shadowy figure on the fringe, under the radar while others attracted attention. But he showed some nerve. There was a claim he had cheated someone, and a hit man was sent after him. Clark sat the gunman down, opened a bottle of wine, lit him a cigar and cleared up the misunderstanding. At the time, he was carrying a vintage Luger pistol and his associates had no doubt he would use it.

By the end of 1976 the man who had made his first million wholesaling buddha sticks in New Zealand had switched to being a heroin importer. The potent and fabulously expensive powder could be smuggled in relatively small amounts and sold on for instant profit, leaving the 'dirty work' of selling it on the streets to others down the food chain. As usual, he separated himself from unnecessary risk – and from being close to the addicts that were the end result of his immoral trade. He prided himself on selling 'Number One Chinese White', which was around 90 per cent pure. Much later he was to tell police: 'I know it sounds funny, but people in the game think I'm honourable.' In a twisted way, the heroin dealer had a little of his father 'good Old Leo' in him: he valued his reputation for square dealing because it was good for business. This would explain, later, why he was so angry when Johnstone hurt The Organisation's reputation by 'cutting' a batch of heroin.

There was no single 'Mr Big' running drugs into Australia, but by 1977 Clark's organisation was certainly one of the bigger syndicates operating. He had five main competitors, the most significant of which was run by a bent businessman, William Garfield Sinclair, who used drunken footballers on sex tours of Thailand to act as 'mules'. Sinclair would be arrested in Bangkok along with Warren Fellows and rugby player Paul Hayward. But there were always others. And, in Australia and New Zealand, there were wholesalers who stood to make millions. Not all of these shadowy figures belonged to the traditional underworld, although they were as amoral as any bank robber. Clark's biggest wholesaler, for instance, was a supposed property dealer from Brighton, Melbourne's premier bayside suburb, and he dominated the Victorian market. He sent his sister to Sydney to sell heroin into the expanding market of addicts in the western suburbs, and regularly flew north to keep an eye on things. In Sydney, he stayed at the Crest Hotel in King's Cross, and Clark would meet him there to share fine wine and cigars. The slaughterman's son from Gisborne had come a long way in a short time.

It was inevitable that Clark's drug running brought him into contact with the vice empire run by Abe Saffron, Sydney's 'Mr Sin'.

Saffron, nephew of a judge, had expanded from sly grog in pubs and clubs to pornography, extortion, prostitution and drugs. Many of the prostitutes who worked from his premises were addicts, and there was no way the greedy Saffron and his parasites were going to let anyone else profit from supplying them. It was an evil vertical monopoly – paying prostitutes at inflated street prices in heroin bought wholesale from Clark and others. The supremely corrupt Saffron kept clear of handling drugs himself. Not that it mattered – he had a network of corrupted or compromised senior police, judges, politicians and public servants who would protect him all his life. Those he didn't bribe he could blackmail with photographs of them indulging their favourite sexual vices in Saffron's premises, which were fitted with one-way mirrors and a camera.

In the 1970s, most of Saffron's dirty work in Sydney was done by James McCartney Anderson, who would later turn against him. According to Saffron's son Alan, Anderson had arranged the murder of wealthy Sydney heiress Juanita Nielsen, who had opposed Saffron-backed development of King's Cross. It was Anderson – who later gave evidence against Saffron – that handled the heroin for Saffron's organisation, allowing the hookers to stash their personal supplies in his nightclub safe.

But the canny and clannish Clark decided to hedge his bets. In 1977 he asked another New Zealander, 'Diamond' Jim Shepherd, to come from Auckland to act as a heroin wholesaler exclusively for The Organisation. Shepherd, a gregarious man who loved the racetrack, bought heroin wholesale and sold it down the line to middlemen and street-level dealers.

The authorities could not keep up with this runaway drug culture. An early and ultimately unsuccessful attempt was the formation of the Federal Narcotics Bureau in 1969. Because it was difficult to prove drug-trafficking conspiracies, the bureau (like its state police equivalents) tended to gather much intelligence. This created a de facto market for information. The danger, of course, was that markets attract buyers as well as sellers. Clark became an early buyer. The onetime informer had reversed roles completely – and he had deep pockets.

Starting in 1976, the bureau had been gathering intelligence about New Zealanders under the code name Operation Tuna. Exchanges with the New Zealand authorities led to clandestine raids on Sydney addresses, and agents started to put together a list of names. One was Martin Johnstone. Another was Greg Ollard, the man who supplied rock bands with heroin. And the agents found out that another Kiwi had arrived: he used the name Wayne Shrimpton, and his girlfriend was Allison Dine.

Clark, meanwhile, was still known only by aliases that meant nothing to the bureau. And he knew it, because his sources were impeccable.

What vaulted Clark to become Australia's biggest heroin importer was one massive shipment brought in by trawler, the *Konpira*. With nearly 100 kilos of heroin in more than twenty old square kerosene tins on board, the trawler skipper John Chatterton made his way down the east coast in June 1977.

Chatterton was quick to spot the surveillance plane that appeared on the horizon every day so at night he would speed up, giving him time to stop if he needed.

During a storm he took the trawler to the safe side of an island off the coast where the heroin was unloaded. But during the cargo drop in rough seas two of the drums were lost.

Eventually a motor launch was despatched to the island and the heroin taken to the mainland. By the time suspicious customs officers searched the trawler at Eden, the heroin was buried in thermos flasks in the bush at Frenchs Forest in outer suburban Sydney. When customs officers checked the remaining cargo, one accidentally smashed a large terracotta pot, slicing his arm and requiring him to be taken by ambulance to hospital. The remaining officers soon lost interest in continuing the search. Blood on the decks will do that.

It is believed some of the syndicate returned to the island and recovered at least one of the lost drums.

While the syndicate continued to import heroin, using couriers, it was the Frenchs Forest stash that made Clark Australia's biggest heroin distributor long before police grasped the fact he was a major player. And it was when that stash ran out and police started to close in that Clark sold his Australian interests to

Bob Trimbole. 'Aussie Bob' didn't realise he was being taken for a ride.

Within weeks of the trawler heroin shipment, Clark insisted that Ollard and his girlfriend Julie Theilman – both addicts – should 'dry out' by going to a motel on the northern New South Wales coast. But when the pair returned to Sydney that August and got back on 'the gear', Clark decided they had to die. He knew the Narcotics Bureau was closing in on Ollard. Agents had secretly broken into two premises used by Ollard and cracked his telephone codes and the false names in which he held bank accounts. As soon as the agents brought Ollard and Theilman in for questioning, Clark knew they would not stay silent for long. There was another, deep-seated reason why he wanted Ollard out of the way: Ollard had refused an offer from Clark to buy him out of his heroin dealing business. Clark knew that Ollard was capable of competing with him – and competitors can be dangerous in criminal circles. They have a motive to inform on each other. Ollard knew far too much about Clark's operation. This was fatal for his girlfriend, Julie Theilman, because she would have to go, too.

Julie Diane Theilman, born in 1956 in New Zealand, had developed bad habits early. Arrested for 'keeping a brothel' at the age of eighteen, she had to give up being a nurse because of the hepatitis she had contracted from intravenous drug use. She and Ollard often travelled back to New Zealand from Sydney. Once, they left a small suitcase in Theilman's room at her parents' house. Her mother later opened it and found it was full of money, wrapped in brown paper. She shut the case, put it back and never talked about it. Perhaps she should have.

The odd thing is that before they disappeared in September 1977, Ollard and Theilman told friends they intended to go overseas on a long trip and not to worry about their whereabouts.

They told other friends they were returning to Auckland to announce their engagement.

They never arrived.

When one insider, who took over Ollard's role on The Organisation, asked where they had gone, Clark replied: 'I have retired Greg and Jules', a clear hint that they had been killed. Others were told they had 'gone east' – overseas – but Clark started dropping hints to insiders that they were buried under concrete construction work at Sydney airport.

Typically, it was only a half-truth, calculated both to instil maximum fear and to lay a false trail. The truth was revealed when the bodies were located five years later, in late 1982, as a result of information received: Ollard's remains were found in Ku-ring-gai Chase National Park near Sydney, three days after Theilman's were dug up at Mt Victoria in the Blue Mountains.

A secret witness told the Stewart Royal Commission that Clark had called him in mid-September 1977 and asked for his help. The witness drove Clark to a dirt track in Ku-ring-gai National Park. On the way Clark told him he had killed Ollard earlier that day, then he led the way to Ollard's body, lying off the track. It had been too heavy for Clark to lift into a hole he had dug earlier. They buried the body and put a branch over it. Clark said he'd lured Ollard there on the pretext of hiding a stash of heroin. Later the same day Clark and the witness picked up Julie Theilman from the house she shared with Ollard at Avalon. They gave her two 'snorts' of heroin and said they were going to Parramatta to meet Ollard. They drove to the Blue Mountains and down a dirt road between Blackheath and Mt Victoria, to a place where they had hidden heroin in the past. Clark shot the drug-affected woman in the head, then twice in the chest. They dragged her body behind a tree and covered it with rocks.

Less than two years before, Clark had stayed with Ollard

when he first arrived from New Zealand. But he could buy inside information and he was prepared to kill to ensure silence, to punish leaks or to remove those he saw as weak links or likely competition: a deadly combination for those close to him.

CLARK already had two children in New Zealand. On Boxing Day, 1977, Maria Muahary gave birth to his son, Jarrod. But Clark, always the opportunist, was already eyeing another conquest: he wanted Allison Dine, girlfriend of his old jailmate (and employee) Wayne Shrimpton. It was partly to cut his reliance on Shrimpton that he recruited yet another Kiwi to run errands for him – the ill-fated Douglas Wilson, who had sold 40,000 buddha sticks for him in Auckland a couple of years before.

Meanwhile, Clark was making passes at Allison Dine who, at 23, was bored enough with Shrimpton to be up for a fling with the boss. Born in Rotorua, Dine had trained as a kindergarten teacher but had dropped out to work as a waitress in Auckland. She'd met Shrimpton in 1976. He offered excitement – or, at least, life in Sydney, where they arrived on New Year's Eve. Later she would claim she didn't know Shrimpton was involved in anything illegal but if that were true, she was a fast learner. By the following August, she broke the law for Clark, carrying $10,000 to Singapore for Johnstone. It was the start of a year or two of living dangerously for the girl from Rotorua. Clark showed her a good time whenever Shrimpton wasn't around, which was whenever Clark could arrange it. If she were unavailable, it didn't worry Clark much. While his woman, Maria, looked after the baby, he would go into the city on business, and pick up women. He said that if you kept yourself fit – which he did, working out at a gym in Crows Nest each morning – then handling a couple of women a day was no problem. Despite this narcissistic streak, he was careful not to make a splash: he had no favourite restaurant, and was careful not to tip too lavishly. Unlike Jimmy Shepherd, who ate most days at Tati's in Oxford Street with other racing identities, and threw money around like a flash gangster. Shepherd was a huge punter, which Clark then thought was 'a mug's game'. But it was how Shepherd came to be friendly with another big gambler, Bob Trimbole, a fixture at city race meetings in the late 1970s.

Clark drew Allison Dine closer into The Organisation by asking her to recruit another courier. She came up with Kay Reynolds, a strapping redhead who had learned to live hard and fast since leaving her home district of Barcaldine in Queensland. Reynolds, who worked in Sydney massage parlours, was keen on what looked like 'easy money' to be made from being a drug mule.

Clark went to the west coast of the United States to sound out his grand scheme for a global drug network: running heroin to the west coast and cocaine back to Australia and New Zealand. But he had not dropped lusting after Allison Dine. He stopped over in Singapore to meet her secretly, having previously arranged for her to courier $25,000 there from Australia. But after just four days, he got news of trouble back in Sydney: 'Pommy Harry' Lewis had been sprung at Sydney Airport with a load of Thai sticks. Clark had to interrupt his romantic interlude to fly back and kill him.

It was May 1978. Clark's growing reputation for ruthlessness was becoming self-fulfilling. But reputations are dangerous things, as many a tough guy has found too late: the fear he struck in the people around him did not breed loyalty. Like Macbeth, he had so much blood on his hands he had to keep going because, as he saw it, retreat was becoming impossible. He had created a vortex of violence that could end only with his own destruction. But not soon enough to save several others.

ON Sunday 28 May, another New Zealander who thought Sydney was New York arrived at Kingsford-Smith Airport with a false passport and an unregistered pistol in his luggage. It was a .38 replica modified by some backyard gunsmith to fire .22 rounds: crude but effective and highly illegal. The surname in the passport was Andrews, but when the customs officers seized the pistol and started asking lots of personal questions, they were interested to find that the name on the supposed Mr Andrews' driver's licence was Duncan Robb. This was his real name but it did not satisfy their curiosity. They took him on a tour of the addresses he claimed to be using in Sydney. One flat would not open because his key did not fit the door, but the next one Robb took them to, in Mosman, did open. In it they found five grams of heroin. The customs men grew more interested. Robb's nerves frayed fast, as he was a heroin user hanging out for a fix, and he wasn't going to get it any time soon.

Robb was an old friend of the 'vanished' Greg Ollard and another Organisation runner called Mark Fitt, who had been killed – in a genuine traffic accident, amazingly enough – not long before. Douglas Wilson had been using him to run money and drugs interstate and across the Tasman and Robb knew all the names – including Terry Clark's. So when a shrewd narcotics officer called Graham Brindle took him along to his superior, the calculating Richard Spencer, Robb rattled off a dozen names – and details of phone codes and numbers used by The Organisation. The trafficking charge against him could be reduced to 'possession' if he helped set up Clark. Which might have seemed like a good deal for a desperate man, except that was playing against a stacked deck: Clark's contacts high in customs, the Narcotics Bureau or police immediately told him that Robb had rolled over. In fact, they sold the tip-off to Clark for $10,000, as would later be revealed.

The Stewart Royal Commission would later find that corrupt narcotics officers provided Clark with confidential information, using crooked law clerk Brian Alexander as a go between. Alexander worked for Sydney solicitor John Aston, whose trust account was used to launder the syndicate's turnover.

Alexander was laundered in a different way. He was thrown from a boat with a gas stove attached to him. His body was never found. Nor was the cooker.

What happened next was described a couple of weeks later by Douglas Wilson in Brisbane after the Gazebo Hotel debacle. Wilson told police and, interestingly, a Narcotics Bureau member that a 'guy at the top of the customs in Sydney ... actually met Terry and played him the tape of the conversation (with Robb).'

On Friday 1 June, Robb was 'taken for a ride' by Clark, Andrew Maher and another of their gaggle of itinerant Kiwi crooks, Patrick Bennett. They took him north to Frenchs Forest, where Clark raved at Robb in what must have seemed like the last words he might ever hear. Two things Clark said would stick in his mind: that he had 'a little bird in the office' who leaked information; and that he already knew Robb had given the gang's phone code to the interrogators.

At some point Robb must have decided he wasn't going to be killed, as he asked to urinate so he would not wet himself during the bashing. Clark agreed then methodically belted him with a baseball bat, breaking his fingers and one arm. When they left, Clark told him to lie still for ten minutes or he would be shot. Robb was lucky Clark wanted him to be a walking, talking example of what happened when you crossed The Organisation. As opposed to being the other sort of example: corpses like Greg Ollard, Julie Theilman and 'Pommy Harry' Lewis. Robb repaid this 'mercy' by going straight to the Narcotics Bureau investigators and telling them about the beating, but he did nothing about setting up Clark. The latter, meanwhile, underlined the 'lesson' by taking his baseball bat and a knife to Robb's Mini Cooper – slashing the upholstery, denting every panel and smashing the windows. Days later, a public-spirited neighbour reported the state of the car to the police, who traced the registration to Robb, who said he wanted no action taken.

Meanwhile, Allison Dine was becoming Clark's favourite both in and out of bed. Apart from her assignations with him in luxury hotel suites, he used her flat to break up and bag the imported rock heroin, and she did a couple of cash runs overseas and would soon take twenty five bags of heroin to New Zealand strapped to her waist. She had also recruited her friend Kay, the massage parlour girl, to run drugs and money. But Clark had more on his mind than sex and money: he was already making plans for his old 'mate' Douglas Wilson, whose heroin addiction Clark saw as a fatal flaw. Douglas and Isabel had gone to hospital that May 'to dry out' but Clark doubted the effectiveness of the cure. He suggested they might like a boat trip, and invited them to the fateful meeting at the Gazebo in Brisbane. Which, of course, would end up destroying them all, as the betrayers themselves became the betrayed. But whereas the Wilsons were already teetering towards a shallow grave, Clark was still flying high. Too high.

WHEN Clark's fingerprints were taken in Brisbane in June 1978, they were automatically cross-checked on the national register, which flagged that he had jumped bail in Auckland in 1976. That much was routine. But the fact he was let out of Australia, given Douglas Wilson's statement linking him to serious crimes, did not appear routine to everyone, although a later review by Justice Donald Stewart absolved police of any deliberate wrongdoing. Clark would later claim that he had not offered Detective Sergeant Ron Pickering $50,000 to get him bail, and accused Pickering of soliciting a bribe, but the Stewart investigation found nothing to support Clark's contention. As Pickering said, and other police agreed, the allegation about Harry Lewis's murder was unsupported – there was no body and no evidence. And they had been assured by New Zealand police that Clark was certain to get twelve years jail on the old heroin charge. 'We knew where to find him,' one policeman said.

In any event, after a rough few days in custody that left him battered and bruised, Clark was sent to New Zealand to lick his wounds and face the heroin import charges.

Despite the New Zealand police's confidence that they had Clark stitched up, it was like letting Brer Rabbit into the briar patch. On his home turf, Clark bought the best legal talent that massive drug money could buy, something that would later tarnish the reputation of at least two legal professionals seen to have 'crossed the line' of ethical behaviour. One of these was Karen Soich, who would cross the line several ways, mostly with her clothes off.

At 23, Soich was a confident only child of doting and prosperous parents. From the best-equipped rider at the Kamo pony club near Whangarei to the law student whose fond father handed her the keys of her own MG sports car, she had always been able to get what she wanted, particularly from men. By the time Terry Clark turned up, wallet in hand, Karen Soich was an assistant in the office of New Zealand's then top criminal advocate, Peter Williams. Although male prisoners are famously fond of female lawyers who visit them in jail, not everyone loved Karen Soich. But she hit it off with Terry Clark almost from the moment she was first sent to see him on remand after his extradition.

Clark was still showing signs of a 'robust' interview when Soich was ushered into a prison room to see him. But, despite his own woes, she would say later, he charmed her by jumping up and clearing a spot for her to sit. He had learned a few tricks and was moving up from the fringe-dwelling women of his earlier days – those who, if not hookers and drug addicts, were at home in such circles.

Clark had always been attracted to women with a hard edge, but to him the attractive young woman with the law degree, educated voice and string of show ponies was 'classy'. She stirred something in him. Likewise, he apparently stirred something in her: as a young female lawyer with ability and ambition in New Zealand at the end of the 1970s, she had nowhere to go without someone to bankroll the trip. A generation, or even a decade before, she might have resigned herself to the dull certainties of a 'good' marriage. But it was 1979, and Soich was up for skating across the thin ice of the permissive age. To her, the cool villain with the icy blue eyes and bottomless pockets must have looked like excitement. The combination of adrenalin and money could be addictive, especially if spiced with cocaine. The torrid affair would last only eleven weeks but it would forever link her with the drug syndicate. She would later say Clark would never swear in front of her and had impeccable manners. He may have been a drug dealer but at least he didn't burp at the table.

Soich was soon using her professional visits to take letters from Clark out of prison and handing them to a female who took them to Australia to the rest of the gang. While Clark was away, Dine had become head of couriers and Jimmy Shepherd handled most of the Sydney wholesaling, although Clark was suspicious of Shepherd's freewheeling ways.

Clark drew up a drug-smuggling blueprint: rules to reduce the risk of arrest. Couriers were never scruffy or 'hippy' looking, should pay all hotel bills in cash (leaving no record of their real identity), should do no more than two trips, and should take a Valium tranquiliser an hour before landing to keep calm while clearing customs.

Later, when giving evidence, Allison Dine would outline some of this elaborate courier code. For instance, in Singapore, the courier would be met by 'Chinese Jack' or another trusted contact at a hotel. Jack would take the courier's suitcases away and arrange to meet the courier a few hours later. In that time, he would transfer the courier's clothes into new (but similar-looking) suitcases – false-bottomed ones with up to 7.5 kilograms (but usually less) of compressed and sealed heroin hidden in disguised panels. He would then drop the courier and the bags to a new hotel for the rest of the courier's 'holiday'. Before the courier (usually an attractive young woman) flew out, Dine would visit and check that dirty underclothing was packed at the back near the false bottom. This was to discourage zealous searching by customs officers. Finally, she would wipe down the entire bag with a damp cloth to remove any stray fingerprints.

'As the courier was checking her bags in at the Singapore airport Jack would hover in the background, to see that everything went all right,' Dine described in her statement. 'They usually had to pay excess baggage ... due to the weight of the suitcase and the heaps of clothes that had to fill such large bags. Bags had to be full to look good. Jack would go out and buy some easily breakable toys to put amongst the clothes and they would normally break or he would break one before he put it into the bag, the reason for this being ... the broken toys would take the attention of customs officials and make the courier feel more relaxed having something to talk about ... The customs officer would always feel sorry and would let the courier through without further ado.'

Clark was behind bars for four months. In that time the *Auckland Star* ran an expose stating that a two-year police investigation to smash New Zealand's biggest drug syndicate had been derailed because two witnesses refused to testify against the gang's leader – an Aucklander living in Asia that the paper dubbed 'Mr Asia'. That was, of course, Martin Johnstone. The story proved to

Clark that his own rank in The Organisation was still little-known – he was still one name among many – but that the careless playboy Johnstone was dangerously exposed.

The first thing Clark's big-time barrister Peter Williams did to earn his fee (reportedly $56,000) was to get his trial switched to Wellington on the grounds of possible prejudice. When the trial began, Williams used all his court room tactics to sway the jury. Meanwhile, if Clark's boasting were to be believed, Clark was doing all he could to sway certain witnesses, some of whom were not as positive as they had been during the committal. Whether this is true is hard to say, but Clark often claimed later that the acquittal cost him $250,000. When the jury returned the 'not guilty' verdict Karen Soich raised eyebrows by embracing Clark in court, a gesture more courtesan than counsel. French champagne flowed in a hotel room that night; next day Clark bought a new Jaguar to celebrate. He drove it to visit a friend in his old 'boarding school', Wi Tako Prison. The message, to warders and prisoners alike, was clear. While they were stuck inside, Terry Clark was conquering the world. It was a long way from the shifty thief and informer he'd been only a few years before.

Clark was juggling women as well as risks. Allison Dine flew from Australia to 'celebrate' with him. They celebrated their brains out in a luxury hotel suite in the daytime before Clark would return to Maria for the night. When Dine returned to Sydney, Clark followed, heavily disguised. He told everyone he was going by ship, and then flew, to buy himself three secret days in Sydney with Dine. For the moment, his budding relationship with the glamorous Soich was on hold. But each had baited a hook. For her, it was Hollywood meets Chicago. She was going to play a part in a real-life drama – a bigger role than she would get in the law.

Meanwhile, Martin 'Mr Asia' Johnstone was sinking into a marijuana-induced haze that pushed him steadily lower in

Clark's bleak estimation. 'Chinese Jack' reported that Johnstone was too stoned to do business properly, that he was taking short-cuts, doing deals on the side to cut out The Organisation, and short changing people who were owed money. These included the crew of a trawler called *Konpira* and a couple of other boats, which were supposed to be 'legitimate' fronts but which Johnstone neglected: the boats deteriorating and the crews idle and unpaid. Clark saw all this as risky.

By the new year of 1979, Johnstone had joined the Wilsons on Clark's list of things to do. He had enlisted the aid of the English knockabout Andy Maher, who had worked with Johnstone at an Auckland menswear shop in the early 1970s but had returned to Northern England, where he was a useful member of The Organisation as it spread into the UK. By the time the Wilsons were killed in April 1979, Clark was quietly planning Johnstone's demise – and Maher was part of the plan. It would be a classic set up: to use someone close to Johnstone to destroy him.

A week before the Wilsons' decomposed bodies were found at Rye, Clark flew to London with Maria and their baby son, Jarrod. He booked into a suite at the London Hilton and bought a Mercedes, but left the hotel on 20 May – straight after the Wilsons' bodies were found – and moved into an expensive Mayfair flat, rented by Jim Shepherd in a false name. They hired a woman called Argentino Colaco as a nurse to look after the baby Jarrod, and a chauffeur, Sylvester Pidgeon, who had in fact lost his driving licence for drunk driving. The man driving a big international drug smuggler around London had no licence – a huge risk if the car were stopped by an inquisitive policeman.

BACK in Australia, the syndicate was starting to fray. The same week that the police pulled the Wilsons' bodies out of the sandy soil at Rye, one of the syndicate's new couriers, a woman called Joyce Allez, codenamed 'Buckteeth', was arrested at Sydney airport bringing in heroin from Singapore. It was a random arrest: an alert customs officer had noticed that the tartan suitcases were unusually thick at the bottom. Allison Dine and her friend Kay Reynolds had been waiting for Allez and panicked when they saw her arrested. They were even more alarmed when police spoke to Allez's workmates at the Chinatown massage parlour where they had recruited Allez. The courier had not revealed where she got the heroin, insisting it had come from an unknown stranger in Singapore. The police soon caught up with Dine and Reynolds but they, too, said nothing. Dine got in touch with Clark in London and he called on Trimbole to help, proof that the friendly Godfather from Griffith had effectively taken over the Australian end of The Organisation.

Trimbole shifted the two women to a flat he owned in Sydney's western suburbs. They moved on swiftly, with investigators tailing them. After seven days of pressure Dine 'cracked' and persuaded a friendly doctor to commit her to a psychiatric hospital. It was not a mad idea. When Trimbole contacted her with an escape plan the over-stretched Bureau of Narcotics wasn't watching. Trimbole told her to slip out of the hospital and get a passport photograph taken, wearing a wig and glasses. He handed her a blank passport application form and told her to fill it out in the name 'Royda Lee Blackburn'. Two days later, she met him at the gates of Centennial Park in Sydney – a spot from where it would be easy to see if she were being followed. She wasn't being tailed; the 'narcs' were too busy. Dine flew to London to join the entourage, chaperoned by an Argentinian called Roberto Fionna, a punting mate of Trimbole's and Shepherd's and the nominal owner of their favourite Sydney restaurant, Tati's.

In London, The Organisation was in trouble, but no one realised yet. The crew lived hard – partying like those with much to forget. Which, especially in Clark's case, was true.

Within weeks the inveterate gambler Shepherd had persuaded Clark (under the name 'Sinclair') to join Ladbroke's private casino. And Trimbole soon flew in and joined them at the West End gaming tables, setting the scene and making the contacts – although he might not have known it then – for the fugitive life he would be leading within a couple of years. The group lived high and fast, their days revolving around manic spending sprees with the endless supply of cash Clark kept in bundles around the apartment. The others had always been punters – like most criminals – but heavy gambling was a new vice for Clark, who had always seen betting as a mug's game.

Now, instead of playing his cards close to his chest, he played them recklessly – dropping tens of thousands of pounds on the gaming tables. He had boasted he had so much money he 'couldn't spend the interest' and his housekeeper would later paint a bizarre picture of a man who had money to throw away – literally.

She would see him scrunch up new banknotes, put some in his pocket, drop some on the floor and throw others in the waste paper bin. He was also drinking heavily and early in the day and no longer worried about physical fitness the way he had in Sydney.

Interestingly, given his father's stern opposition to his early criminal tendencies, his own family seemed to have turned a blind eye to the possible source of his astonishing wealth. Clark led an outing to the countryside outside London for the wedding of his sister, who lived on a farm. The entourage was growing. Some found the lure of the high life hard to resist, and were willing to make compromises.

But the danger of being close to Clark was that eventually he would turn on you. And they all knew – or feared – what that could mean. After another courier, Carolyn Calder, was picked up in Sydney, Allison Dine felt a chill from her sometime lover, who blamed her for recruiting Calder through Kay Reynolds. Clark still had the contacts to know that Calder had told the police too much. Calder and Reynolds were so nervous they flew out from Sydney to London – without telling Clark – on the theory that it might be safer there than Sydney. Dine knew this but would not tell the suspicious Clark when he questioned her about her friends' whereabouts. Eventually, he told her to go back to Australia – promising her he would send $25,000 so she could set up a beauty salon. But she didn't like the way he said goodbye.

'I did not like the look he had in his eyes ... his look was very final,' she would later state. 'I did not know whether he meant his goodbye just like that or whether he intended to have me shot.'

It got worse. Back at Dine's Neutral Bay flat, six Narcotics Bureau officers arrested her. After getting $5000 bail, she fled on a false passport – to the USA, via London. But she did not tell the increasingly-erratic Clark where she was. She sensed murder in him. She knew his form.

IF Martin Johnstone was not already a dead man walking by mid-1979, he sealed his death warrant with an abortive heroin-buying trip to Thailand in August, around the same time Dine was arrested in Sydney.

He went to Bangkok with a woman called Monique and his sometime friend Andy Maher, the Englishman he'd met in Auckland years before. Ostensibly keen to salvage his standing with Clark by pulling off one big deal by himself, Johnstone negotiated to buy several kilograms of heroin direct from Thai gangsters – three armed men who insisted that they be paid in full as they handed over the drugs.

Johnstone was armed with a .45 revolver but it seemed the playboy dealer was no match for tough Thais on their home territory. He was driven along a lonely jungle road with the cash to meet the gangsters and do the switch. When the gangsters appeared they opened the door of their van and showed him the package of heroin. Then they took the money from him to count it – but slammed the doors of the van as Johnstone went to take the heroin, and drove off. He wasn't up to shooting at them, he said later. With odds of three to one, he might have lost his life as well as the money.

Johnstone was desperate. He took a 700-gram sample of the heroin he had been given and cut it with castor sugar and sent it to the UK with a courier. It was suicidal stupidity. Clark knew of the debacle within days; apart from anyone else, Johnstone's alarmed friend Andy Maher had told him. Maher knew it would be better to tell Clark first rather than to let him discover it when the complaints started to flow from angry wholesalers duped into buying castor sugar.

Clark was furious. One of the cornerstones of The Organisation was its reputation for delivering near-pure heroin. Maher was convinced that he himself was lucky not to be partially blamed for Johnstone's debacle. It meant that when Clark asked him to kill Johnstone, he agreed. The combination of fear and greed was potent.

Johnstone deluded himself he could recoup the loss – of about $250,000 – by selling 15,000 Thai sticks in the UK. He was trying to ignore other problems: he owed Clark about $2 million; various 'front' businesses had gone bad, wages bills were outstanding for the crews of the syndicate's three unused boats.

Maher was now a double agent. When he told Johnstone he had buyers for his Thai sticks in Scotland, Johnstone fell for it. Clark sealed the set-up with a long telephone call to Johnstone in which he acted friendly and forgiving. Maher, meanwhile, was recruiting help: his father's cousin James Smith, an ex-soldier who had seen action in Northern Ireland. Smith, in turn, recruited two more Scots, another ex-Guardsman called Kingsley Fagan, and a neighbour called Gerard Keegan. Clark reinforced Maher's willingness to do the deed by telling him he had ordered the death of a woman and her child for crossing the syndicate. Maher took this as proof that if he didn't do what Clark wanted, his own wife and baby daughter could be killed.

As well as the implied threat, Clark duchessed Maher: inviting him and his wife Barbara to a two-day cocaine party at the London flat on the last weekend of that September. Johnstone flew into London a week later. He had $200 in his pocket and owed $2 million. When Maher told him he had buyers in Glasgow with plenty to spend on his Thai sticks – but that the Scots insisted on talking to Johnstone personally – it wasn't hard to persuade him to drive north.

Earlier that week one of Maher's mates in the Lancashire town of Preston went around buying a motley collection of hardware – an axe, a rope, a lorry jack and several weights. Maher got a sheet of polythene and some sawdust. They had everything but a gun. Clark took care of that, getting a London underworld contact to buy a .38 pistol, parcelling it up and paying his chauffeur's teenage daughter to take the parcel on the train north.

Johnstone and his latest girlfriend, a former local beauty contestant called Julie Hue, visited Maher and his wife in their house at Leyland, near Preston. Hue noticed 'a bad atmosphere' and Johnstone told her later it was because Maher had told him he wanted to settle down and no longer wanted to work for him. Martin Johnstone even 'cried a little' about losing his friend of seven years. This was Maher and Barbara's Judas moment. The couple had been so close to Martin Johnstone they had called their baby 'Marti' after him. Now they were plotting his murder.

Johnstone took Julie Hue back to London to go shopping, then returned to Lancashire ready to do the supposed big Scottish deal. He had a drink with Maher and his 'mates', the ex-Guardsmen Smith and Fagan.

They set off in the evening, laughing and joking as they carried luggage out to the old Jaguar bought for the job. Fagan stayed behind, and they dropped off Julie Hue at her mother's and drove north. But not for long. Maher turned onto an old highway, then through several towns until the village of Carnforth, where he pulled over into a lay-by on a quiet section of road and asked his friend if he wanted to drive. As Johnstone got out, Maher shot him in the back of the head. Then, over the next few hours, it got unspeakably worse as they butchered the body to make it unrecognisable before disposing of it.

It was 9 October 1979.

CLARK got the call from Maher next morning. It was at least the sixth murder he'd organised or done. 'Good one,' he grunted.

Four days later, on Sunday morning, two novice scuba divers went diving in the Eccleston Delph, a flooded quarry known for the number of stolen and wrecked cars dumped in it. The pair swam around underwater until they noticed what one thought was a shop dummy on a rock shelf about 25 feet down. Then he saw 'the squiggly tubes and mess coming from the vicinity of the stomach' and 'the severed wrists'.

It was one of the biggest cases the Lancashire police had seen in years, and 60 detectives would be assigned to it. Their difficulty was to identify a body with no hands and whose face and teeth had been smashed beyond recognition.

In the end, it would not be the power of forensic investigation but the weight of guilt that would bring the killers undone. And, by extension, bring down Clark's evil empire.

For almost two weeks Maher's de facto, Barbara Pilkington, had distracted Johnstone's girlfriend, Julie Hue, by telling her Johnstone had been called away on business. Barbara took Julie to Spain, where Maher's father had a bar on the Costa Brava. Julie wasn't a big reader but on 21 October, nearly two weeks after the murder, she saw a newspaper story about the body in the quarry near her home town in Lancashire. Barbara broke down and told her the truth, explaining how Maher had been forced into killing his friend. The two distraught women attempted to commit suicide with sleeping tablets, but it didn't work. After a long sleep and big talks, they flew to London. Barbara called Maher (who was by then in Singapore) and blurted out that she didn't love him any more. He suggested the two upset women go to Lancashire. For him, it wasn't good advice. As soon as they got there, Julie Hue told her devout Seventh Day Adventist mother the truth. The shocked and pious woman called the police.

CLARK fiddled as his empire burnt. With Allison Dine hiding in America, Karen Soich had arrived from Auckland to join the party in London. Clark's long-suffering wife Maria had also left, so Soich had Clark to herself, accompanying him to casinos and parties. Most days, she rode a hired grey hack along Rotten Row, a pampered pet in a fool's paradise.

Maher was arrested as he stepped off a plane at Heathrow. Early next morning Scotland Yard police avoided the fortified entrance door to Clark's apartment, instead forcing the back door. They found Clark and Soich in bed together. Soich yelled at the police: 'Get out of the room and let me get dressed. What is going on? I am a lawyer!' She told Clark not to tell them anything except his name and address and she demanded to see a warrant. Police were to accuse her of trying to kick a diary under the bed.

Soich claimed she did only the washing and cooking. This did not tally with the evidence: police found photographs Clark had taken of her rolling naked in hundreds of banknotes on the double bed. The pictures were 'art', Clark told detectives. Asked about it later, he said: 'Well, women like money, don't they?'

After that it all unravelled. Police made arrest after arrest, each leading to the next. Eventually, most of them 'rolled over', telling various versions of the truth: that they'd been pawns in Clark's murderous game. Oddly enough, it was the seasoned Clark who talked a lot – boasting about his feats as a drug dealer in Australia and New Zealand but insisting unconvincingly that he had come to England to retire. Inevitably, he made a mistake, telling the police he had supplied the pistol to Maher, which he claimed was for Maher's protection. For a man who had spent millions on lawyers over the years, it was a foolish slip. He was charged with Johnstone's murder and several other serious charges, as were Maher and Smith and two other men who had helped them. Karen Soich and six others were charged with conspiracy. By 5 November they had all been remanded without bail.

They buried Johnstone's desecrated remains a couple of weeks later in Lancashire. Only his mother, Julie Hue and Barbara Pilkington mourned the foppish rogue who had once thrown the biggest parties in Singapore. The only other person at the gravesite was Detective Superintendent Phil Cafferky of the Lancashire police.

The police soon traced Allison Dine in the US. She was travelling under a false identity and might never have been found except that she had picked up an American boyfriend in Sydney and someone knew that he came from Orlando, Florida. When he visited his mother in Orlando, the local police identified Dine's Celica car. She was soon traced to the west coast, and offered a deal to give evidence against her former lover and his organisation. Her old boyfriend Wayne Shrimpton would do the same.

Dine would be a star witness in four proceedings – including the Clark committal, the Wilsons' inquest in Melbourne and a conspiracy case against three suspect Narcotics Bureau officers accused of selling information to Clark. In return, she went free – returning to the anonymity she'd had just three years before.

The trial took 115 days, fourteen of them summing up the evidence of 175 witnesses. It took the jury another week to deliver a verdict. Clark was guilty on three counts of murder and two drug conspiracies. All the co-accused were found guilty except a minor player called Jack Barclay ... and Karen Soich, who walked away.

Clark was sentenced to life with a minimum of twenty years, and ordered to pay a million pounds towards the cost of the trial, the highest ever in England. It was barely seven years since he'd come out of a New Zealand prison with nothing but the ruthlessness to succeed in an evil trade. Now he was going back. It is said that after the sentence was passed, the sardonic Clark said to Soich's mother that she had got both things she wanted: her daughter's acquittal and Clark locked up for twenty years.

Meanwhile, two big players in The Organisation were absent. Jimmy Shepherd slipped away to America and disappeared into the huddled masses of the great republic, not heard of again for a long time. That left 'Aussie Bob' Trimbole in charge of the tattered remains of The Organisation. He had returned to Australia. But he, too, would soon be on the run.

TERRY Clark died in Parkhurst Prison in August 1983. Officially, he died of a heart attack, an unusual fate for a 39-year-old prisoner. But in his Royal Commission into drug trafficking tabled in Australia that year, Mr Justice Stewart suggested that Clark was smothered by several other prisoners. A likely explanation is that Clark the onetime 'grass' merely fell foul of the violent code of behaviour inside – making the fatal mistake of offering to inform on fellow prisoners. Unless, of course, there was an even more sinister explanation ... a long-range conspiracy to silence him to prevent any chance of his revealing which police, public servants and lawyers had been on his payroll in Australia.

3

FRIENDS IN HIGH PLACES

HOW BOB TRIMBOLE BEAT THE ODDS

'The Commonwealth, New South
Wales, Victorian and Queensland
Governments have established
a judicial inquiry into the
possible drug trafficking and
related activities of Terrence
John Clark and other persons
associated with him. It will be
headed by His Honour Mr Justice
Donald Gerard Stewart of the New
South Wales Supreme Court ...'

WHEN the Stewart Royal Commission was born on 30
June 1981, the words were formal but the meaning was as plain
as the plot in any western: a new sheriff had been handed a badge
and a posse to round up the bad guys.

The Stewart inquiry had many fathers – its birth was announced by the acting Prime Minister, Doug Anthony, and the
premiers of Queensland, New South Wales and Victoria. It was
rigorous, vigorous and blessed with many investigators – detectives, lawyers and accountants. But a Royal Commission is not

born overnight. There had been a long gestation. Since the arrest of Clark and his lackeys for Martin Johnstone's murder, and the inquest into Douglas and Isabel Wilson's murder in 1979, it had been inevitable the authorities would be forced to shine light in dark places, to ask questions dodged too long, to break what a family friend of the murdered Donald Mackay called 'the appalling silence' about the drug lords who corrupted police, politicians and the judiciary.

Long before Judge Stewart's posse started knocking on doors, dragging in witnesses and asking them tough questions under their draconian powers, the dogs had been barking about the new inquiry. And no one knew more dogs than 'Aussie Bob' Trimbole, a man whose adult life had been spent cultivating contacts as skilfully as his Calabrian cousins cultivated cannabis among the rows of irrigated grape and tomato vines and citrus trees around Griffith, Mildura, Shepparton and South Australia's Riverland.

The racecourse members' bar and betting ring is where the social and professional barriers of the outside world can be broken down by a powerful lubricant – the desire to back a winner. In Sydney, especially, it was routine that judges, lawyers, politicians, captains of industry and senior police rubbed shoulders with 'colourful racing identities' whose sources of income were a mystery or an open secret, depending on who was asking.

In this group, a powerful currency is The Tip – inside information that this horse will win or that favourite won't. That such 'certainties' can hardly be predicted without some form of conspiracy has never stopped otherwise honest people from falling under the spell of those who regularly tip winners – and losers.

The organised crime figure who uses punting to launder black money can buy influence beyond the crude buying power of the tainted cash he uses to bribe jockeys, stablehands and trainers, to pay doping gangs or to pay criminal race-fixers, perhaps even to 'sweeten' racing officials. Not only does bribery improve the odds of achieving his main aim of laundering black money by landing winning bets – but in the case of the gregarious Trimbole, fixing races gave the opportunity to claim acquaintance with and influence powerful or useful people otherwise beyond his reach. How? Because people that would not dream of accepting a bribe will scramble for a tip like children for lollies. They will blithely – and blindly – bet on 'sure things' that common sense suggests are probably the fruit of organised race rigging. This gives the tipper, if he uses his corrupt inside information carefully, a hidden power, just as effective but far less risky than the blackmail racket of setting up targets with illicit sex and threatening or implying exposure, as the sinister Abe Saffron did for decades to compromise those in power. Whereas many people secretly disliked or feared Saffron, most people who knew Bob Trimbole liked him. He loved racing and a lot of racing people returned the compliment. The most common phrase used about him was that he was 'a good bloke', a view some people stuck to even after he was exposed as a mobster with a murderous streak.

What was the secret to Trimbole's appeal? That question teased Carl Mengler, a senior officer in the Victoria Police in the early 1980s who would head a task force on the recommendation of the Stewart Royal Commission when it made its report in early 1983. Mengler would spend years dissecting Trimbole's public and private life, reading documents and interviewing scores of his associates, and probably knows as much about him as anyone alive.

It was Mengler who told crime reporter Keith Moor a story that captured the deft way Trimbole got to people who were useful to him and, by extension, to the Calabrian crime family he belonged to and to other crime outfits he knew.

'There was this quite prominent chap interviewed about his association with Trimbole,' said Mengler. 'He said he hadn't wanted anything to do with Trimbole at first, but they had become friends over time. Now this bloke was a racing man, frequently at the track, as of course was Trimbole, and that's how they met. This man was of high social standing and in a position of being able to influence a lot of prominent people; he was from a very respected family.

'He recalled this untidy little man often being near him. Now, Trimbole was an expensive dresser, but never quite looked the part. His belly was hanging over his trousers and the trouser bottoms were just that bit long that they hung over his dirty shoes, not the sort of man our influential friend would normally associate with, him being a real toff and mixing in all the right circles.

'The toff started to take notice of this man being around him wherever he went. He would look along the bar and this bloke would nod at him. After a while Trimbole got to saying hello to the toff. The toff said he hadn't wanted to talk to this "little scrag" and had more or less told him to "piss off". A week or so goes by and the toff sees Trimbole, again at the races, and the toff has a guilty conscience about having been rude to Trimbole, so this time when Trimbole says hello the toff has a brief chat with him.

'A week later the toff was at the bar and the waiter brought a drink over and said it was from the bloke at the other end of the bar, and of course the bloke was Trimbole.'

And so the story unfolds to its inevitable conclusion, as the patient Trimbole, the onetime mechanic who shouted the bar when he won on the punt, played the 'mark' like a fish. As the casual race-day conversations moved naturally from small talk to the real business of the day – punting – Trimbole wormed his way into the other man's estimation with the one thing that's at a premium at the track: inside information.

The toff fancies himself as a racing man, on first-name terms with owners and trainers, and one day he suggests Trimbole back a particular horse. It so happens that Trimbole knows something about that particular race and suggests that a different horse, at longer odds, will win. The toff shrugs – but can't help being puzzled and impressed when Trimbole's tip romps in and his own doesn't. This is the bait. He takes the hook the following week, when Trimbole tips him a winner, which he backs. Trimbole doesn't have to tip many – but when he does, they mostly win. And the toff puts plenty on them. So he starts seeking Trimbole out, inviting him to lunch and dinner regularly. It is a complete role reversal, so that in the end Trimbole calls the shots because he is owed the favours and still supplies the 'mail'.

Call it the power of ten to one.

TRIMBOLE might never have needed to call in a favour from that particular man but the toff was only one of many he had cultivated and compromised. And many of them knew people in high places: state and federal police, politicians, lawyers and public servants. Some were actually paid for favours done – to have charges dropped or sentences made lighter. Others were befriended, just in case. For Trimbole and the shadowy people behind him, this was like an insurance policy. In early 1981, it was time for Trimbole to make a claim.

The international publicity surrounding the Mr Asia trial had exposed the network of corruption that Terry Clark had exploited, and posed questions that Trimbole and others would find difficult to answer. Despite Trimbole's ability to foil the law, it was becoming obvious to some of his well-placed contacts that the looming Stewart Royal Commission would make him too 'hot' to be around. After years of his acting with relative impunity, there would be nowhere to hide ... at least, not in Australia.

Even if Trimbole had been brash enough to think he could tough it out in the witness box, his publicity-shy backers in the La Famiglia, the Griffith cell of the Honoured Society, were anxious to get him out of the way to avoid a repeat of the scrutiny they'd endured during the earlier Woodward Royal Commission prompted by the Donald Mackay murder.

After years of being the secret society's front man, Trimbole had become something of a liability. The public backlash over the Mackay scandal had been followed by the debacle of Isabel and Douglas Wilson's murder, and now there was the link to the murderous 'Mr Asia' heroin syndicate to scandalise the public.

So, by the new year of 1981, Trimbole was getting the message loud and clear. He had done a deal to 'buy out' the Australian arm of the Mr Asia business for $30 million, and had visited Clark and his crew in London for long periods in 1979, where he combined gambling in West End clubs with making shady new European contacts involved in arms smuggling as well as drugs. Perhaps he was thinking ahead, making contingency plans, because when the warning signals started filtering through more than a year later, he seemed ready to step into a new world.

Secret telephone taps that New South Wales Criminal Intelligence Unit detectives illegally put on Trimbole's telephone in April 1981 show that four prominent people – a Sydney lawyer and a doctor and two senior New South Wales police officers – each warned Trimbole that the Stewart inquiry was going to open and that he would be called before it. The doctor had links with illegal SP bookmakers in Melbourne and organised crime figures. Police telephone taps also picked up Trimbole talking to leading trainers and jockeys. During one taped conversation, much quoted later, a jockey famously told Trimbole that another rider 'doesn't care if he gets six months. He'll almost strangle a horse to pull it up.'

Transcripts of telephone tapes later leaked to the legendary investigative reporter Bob Bottom showed that Trimbole telephoned a former Labor Party power broker on 4 April 1981 and asked him if he had yet spoken to a State judge 'so we can see where we're up to'.

The Labor man: *I've talked to a lot of people.*

Trimbole: *Yeah, but have you spoken to him or ...*

Labor man: *No, I couldn't. They couldn't get to the judge* (then adds) *I spoke to someone very close to him.*

Trimbole: *I see, fair enough, all right mate. Well, I just wanted to know because if not I've got a bloke who knows him pretty well, too.*

Labor man: *It never hurts to have more (than) one talking to...*

Trimbole: *I just didn't want to double up.*

Labor man: *Yeah, you don't want to overplay.*

Although each is too wily to mention specific names on a telephone, the meaning is clear. Later in the conversation the Labor man says: 'I spoke to somebody a bit down the line that's probably got more influence and I think they're all worried about the situation.' He then says that he will be having lunch with the judge the following week ('I've been a mate of his for thirty years') and warns Trimbole not to overplay his hand through other approaches because 'sometimes judges get a bit touchy.'

Less than four weeks later, on 1 May, Trimbole spoke to a senior Sydney policeman who asked to meet him to avoid talking on the telephone. There was a clear inference he had 'hot' information to give Trimbole. Next day, a Sydney doctor told Trimbole on the telephone, 'the heat's on'.

Asked who was putting the heat on, the doctor says: 'You might be washed up, do you get me? Re down south; they're pretty wet, you know.'

Another senior policeman warned Trimbole on 2 May there was definitely a 'set-up' and referred obliquely to a new investigation. Trimbole lapsed into racing slang. '... it looks as though I better get me ... on and keep fit. We'll just see what happens. One thing, if I break down I've got plenty of assistants.'

A Sydney lawyer arranged to meet Trimbole on 6 May in offices in the city. During a telephone conversation the previous day, he told Trimbole: 'Well, I would be thinking I would be having a holiday if I was you.'

The letters patent for the Stewart Royal Commission were issued by the Governor-General in the last week of June 1981. But the reluctant star witness, forewarned from so many quarters, had already flown.

On 7 May, under an overcast sky, Trimbole walked through Customs at Sydney Airport with the confidence of a man who knew something others didn't. He was flying to Europe via the United States on his own passport but he had filled in his flight departure card with a false birth date, a detail he knew would be enough to throw off the Customs computer programmed to detect his exit.

As usual, Aussie Bob the race fixer had inside knowledge and had set up a 'boat race' for himself. Luckily, too, the police taps on his telephone had been suspended two days earlier. That's what friends are for.

THE Australian public would not glimpse Trimbole again for more than three years. But those who knew where to look could find him if they wanted. This did not seem to include the relevant Australian authorities.

Trimbole's old partner-in-crime Gianfranco 'Frank' Tizzoni knew where to look. The Melbourne-based Tizzoni had first linked up with Trimbole in 1971 to sell and service pinball machines before moving into marijuana distribution with him. In July 1982, Tizzoni visited France and met with Trimbole, who was using the name Robert White and living in luxurious circumstances in Nice with his long time de facto wife and her daughter. He was not the only Australian villain to see the wanted man in France: the disgraced doctor Nick Paltos visited Trimbole after getting through Customs by mysterious means despite being under investigation for massive medi-fraud. But that's another story. By this time, unknown to Trimbole and the rest of the Honoured Society, Tizzoni was already talking to the Victoria Police, a choice he had made after being picked up by what he was told was 'pure chance' while driving back to Melbourne from New South Wales on 31 March 1982.

But that was later. To understand what a can of worms the Mackay case posed to various law enforcement bodies, it is necessary to go back to where the mess began – to the appointment of a New South Wales policeman to handle the case. He was Joe Parrington, who in the 1970s was a poster boy for the New South Wales Police Force. Big and handsome in a lantern-jawed way, he was a double for laconic American tough-guy actor Lee Marvin.

The disappearance of Donald Mackay was a big case but Parrington believed he was up to the challenge. In 1977 the Detective Sergeant (second class) considered himself 'the most senior and most experienced operational homicide investigator' in the state.

Despite the crime scene including bullets and blood that matched Mackay's type, rumours began early that he had engineered his own disappearance. The rumours were peddled by the corrupt local politician, Al Grassby, bent police and senior members of the New South Wales government, as outlined in a separate chapter. The media was briefed behind the scenes not to 'jump to conclusions' that Mackay had been killed. This was despite the fact that Mackay was a devout Christian and a committed family man who ran a successful business and had not moved any money as part of some mad plan to set up another life. There was not a skerrick of evidence to justify the claims but the hurtful rumours would persist for years.

The irony was that the group of faceless men who had ordered the murder had first considered compromising Mackay by setting him up with a woman but concluded he was too moral to fall for the trap.

Despite national outrage and public memorials in Griffith, the New South Wales government's response was as cynical as it was pathetic. It offered a paltry $25,000 reward for the 'missing' man. Soon the reward reached $100,000 – through public donations.

Enter Parrington – a man supremely confident in his own ability. History would show his confidence was misplaced.

The previous year he was given information on the murder of Maria Hisshion that with a little luck and a lot of digging could have linked the killing back to the Mr Asia drug syndicate. Parrington chose to ignore it – a decision Justice Stewart would later describe as 'astonishing.'

A year after Mackay was killed, Parrington presented a sixteen-page summary of the case to the Woodward Royal Commission, still claiming a 'lack of direct evidence to clearly indicate the reason for Mackay's disappearance'.

Despite the size of the investigation, when Parrington was promoted to the breaking squad in 1978 the Mackay file went with him. Any calls to the homicide squad on the murder were simply transferred to Big Joe.

As Parrington climbed the New South Wales police managerial ladder he remained in charge of the controversial case. By the end of 1981 it had stalled and would have remained unsolved if not for a split-second decision made by a policeman far away from the grass castles of Griffith and the political intrigue of Sydney. Which is where Trimbole's old pal Frank Tizzoni was forced into a starring role.

IN 1981 the New South Wales police and their federal counterparts agreed to run a risky stratagem that would effectively allow the Griffith Mafia to grow massive crops of marijuana in the hope that police would be able to gather enough evidence to arrest the principals.

The operation, code-named Seville, discovered the group would produce up to ten crops at a time because it worked on the theory that some would be discovered.

In March 1982 police watched as their targets met some unidentified men in Canberra and transferred nearly 100 kilos of marijuana into a vehicle.

But instead of heading to Sydney as expected, the men headed towards Melbourne in two vehicles. One was a gold-coloured Mercedes sedan; the other a van. Once they crossed the border into Victoria, the New South Wales police would have no jurisdiction.

Dismayed surveillance police made frantic calls to the Victorian Bureau of Criminal Intelligence with a request to follow but not intercept the vehicles.

An experienced Melbourne detective, John Weel, was instructed to tail the two vehicles as they reached Melbourne's northern outskirts. But because it was close to evening peak hour the policeman feared he could lose the targets, so he took a punt. He took it upon himself to pull them over – and found a bale of marijuana in the boot of Tizzoni's Mercedes, as well as more of the illicit crop in the van, driven by one Robert Enterkin. (A third man, Tony Barbaro, one of a notorious Griffith family, was a passenger in Tizzoni's car. Tizzoni said later it was Barbaro who had asked him to pick up the marijuana from near Canberra.)

Some cynics would later wonder why the careful Tizzoni would use his own car to carry part of the haul. But it was a different era: things were done differently then.

After his arrest, Tizzoni used a private investigator to discreetly inquire if Weel could be bribed. When he realised Weel was an honest cop, he knew he was in trouble. Tizzoni, Barbaro and Enterkin were charged and bailed but Tizzoni – neither Calabrian nor a sworn member of the Honoured Society – started looking for ways to trade his way out of trouble. A former debt collector and private detective, he saw himself as a businessman, if a shady one. He had been in partnership with Bob Trimbole in the pinball machine business since 1971, and had become increasingly involved in wholesaling marijuana in Melbourne for Trimbole's Griffith connections. The easy money had appealed to Tizzoni but the outwardly respectable middle-aged family man from Balwyn, who had invested his drug earnings into several properties, had never been the sort of criminal who sees prison as an inconvenient occupational hazard. Somehow, he wanted to covertly negotiate his way out of a prison sentence without the risk of actually telling all he knew about the Honoured Society.

Two respected Bureau of Criminal Intelligence members, Bob Clark, an expert on Italian organised crime, and John McCaskill, an intelligence specialist, turned Tizzoni into Australia's most important informer.

He eventually told them the story of how Trimbole had used him to recruit a hit man to kill Mackay and, later, Isabel and Douglas Wilson.

To provide a cover story for the fact that police dropped drug charges against Tizzoni, Weel pretended to be corrupt and to have been bought off.

The story was so realistic that a Mafia figure paid Tizzoni $30,000 as part of the bribe money. Naturally, Tizzoni kept the cash. He may have reformed but thirty grand is thirty grand.

Tizzoni volunteered to travel overseas and find Trimbole, and did. Because his wife and children were in Melbourne, and he owned a farm at Koo-Wee-Rup south-east of Melbourne, and at least one property at Griffith, he was not considered a bail risk. He went to Europe three months after his arrest and came back with Trimbole's address (and alias and car registration number) in Nice.

The Victorian police were keen to use the tip-off to nail Australia's supposedly most wanted man, who at that stage had been 'on the run' for fourteen months, but there was nothing they could do but hand the address to 'relevant authorities'.

Victoria police formed a taskforce, code-named Trio, under the command of Carl Mengler, to verify Tizzoni's claims.

Discussing it later, Mengler was tactful but critical: 'I certainly believe that if such an address is given to police, and known to be accurate, as was the case with the address supplied by Tizzone, then every conceivable effort should be made to act on the information immediately and bring the person to justice. That didn't happen in Trimbole's case.'

Mengler said the information should have gone 'straight to the Prime Minister', who should have authorised a small task force to go to France with special warrants to request the French to arrest Trimbole and extradite him. He said if it were true that the Stewart Royal Commission had been unable to do anything more than send a letter to the French authorities nominating Trimbole's address in Nice, it was pathetic – and that a golden opportunity had been wasted.

'You don't write letters giving the address of somebody who is supposed to be Australia's most wanted man,' Mengler said. 'You knock on his door.'

The truth was that the Stewart Royal Commission, for all its powers to ask questions, could only recommend that certain action be taken by the authorities. It was not Judge Stewart's fault no-one was sent after Trimbole. If it were anyone's fault, it lay elsewhere, somewhere among the silent alliance of politicians, public servants and police who had their reasons for looking out for their mate Bob.

'He was protected in high places,' was Tizzoni's pithy postscript to the affair. It seems the only explanation for the lack of action.

If the Victorian police had been allowed to build on the confession they might have cracked the Mackay case. But the Trio taskforce was not looking to charge Tizzoni, Bazley and Joseph with Mackay's murder because it had happened over the border.

Instead, they settled on 'conspiracy' because the murder plot had been hatched in Melbourne.

Detectives in Victoria were optimistic but their New South Wales counterparts were not happy. Parrington, especially felt it was a New South Wales case and believed the Victorian prosecution was doomed to fail.

Not for the first time, he was wrong. He had not endeared himself to Trio detectives: once refusing to discuss the case with expert investigators and demanding to be briefed by a commissioned officer. He made the comment that in New South Wales 'we talk to the organ grinder and not the monkey.' Clearly he thought he was the big banana.

If it had just been trivial interstate rivalry it wouldn't have mattered but Parrington appeared to be concealing evidence that could have been used in the Melbourne prosecution in the hope he would use it later in New South Wales.

Bazley was sentenced to life in 1986 for the murders of the Wilsons, nine years for the conspiracy to murder Mackay and a further nine years for a $270,000 armed robbery

A subsequent judicial inquiry into the New South Wales handling of the case by retired judge John Nagle, QC, left Parrington's professional reputation in tatters.

'Parrington anticipated that the Victorian conspiracy prosecution of Bazley would fail and wanted to hoard Pursehouse's evidence (a key Mackay witness) for a New South Wales prosecution ... It was his all-consuming, but unthinking determination to bring the killers of the Donald Bruce Mackay to New South Wales that has proved his undoing,' Nagle wrote.

Nagle found that Parrington, 'Presented as a stubborn man with little imagination or breadth of vision and no mental resilience ... it involved impeding Victorian police officers and Crown law authorities in the prosecution of murder.

'It is the commission's view that his motive was to gain cred-it for himself as an investigating officer and for the New South Wales police by a successful prosecution of Bazley in this state.

'There is evidence warranting the prosecution of Frederick Joseph Parrington for the offence of attempting to pervert the course of justice.'

On 13 March 1987, Parrington was charged departmentally with two counts of neglect of duty and fined $500 on each charge, and removed for twelve months from his post as manager of criminal investigations.

Parrington was an honest man who wanted Mackay killers brought to justice in New South Wales. But his refusal to co-op-erate with Victorian authorities could have resulted in the case remaining unsolved.

Meanwhile, Tizzoni was the star witness ... but did he tell the truth? According to one key investigator, 'Frank told his version of the truth and made sure his role was minimised.'

Some wonder if Bazley, a small middle-aged man, could have shot a big man like Mackay in the Griffith Hotel carpark and bundled the body into a car then disposed of it on his own.

Mackay was a fit squash player, ruckman size at 192 centime-tres and 95 kilos. Bazley was about 168 centimetres and lightly built. Almost certainly he would have needed help and many be-lieve Tizzoni was his assistant. But if Frank had confessed that he would have opened himself up to murder charges.

In October 1984 he pleaded guilty to conspiracy to murder Mackay and the Wilsons and was sentenced to five years' jail. He was released into witness protection after just a year. In February 1986 he was released on parole and moved to Italy. He died there in 1988.

He had previously bought a grave in a Melbourne cemetery and pre-paid his tombstone. Both remain unused – he was buried in Italy.

His co-conspirator, the gun dealer George Joseph, became a prosecution witness and was sentenced to a maximum of seven years jail but released early in October 1984. He went on to be an occasional judge in various Miss Nude contests.

There is no justice.

IN March 1984, when the long-awaited inquest into the death of Donald Mackay began in Sydney, a barrister called Brian Morris made an odd submission to the coroner, Bruce Brown. 'Business interests' overseas made it inconvenient for 'Mr Trimbole' to attend just then, the lawyer said. Trimbole, in telephoned instructions, had not said he was unwilling to attend – merely unable to do so for some time. Morris then applied for leave to represent Trimbole – a request he would later withdraw on grounds he could not be properly instructed by his client.

Pressed by the Crown advocate to explain how he came to be appearing for a fugitive, Morris said he had originally been briefed by Trimbole before he had left Australia two years earlier – and that the instructions had been confirmed by telephone.

When the advocate inquired if Morris happened to know Trimbole's current address, the barrister said he did not have the exact address. Asked to produce a document giving Craig Trimbole power of attorney for his father, Morris produced one ostensibly signed by Trimbole senior and witnessed by a solicitor on 15 May 1981 – a week after Trimbole had fled Australia.

The inquest underlined the scandalous official silence about Trimbole's whereabouts. When it moved from Sydney to Griffith later that month, the sham was further exposed when a friend of Trimbole's wife, Joan, and daughters, Glenda and Gayelle, surprised the court with a frank picture of how easily the family stayed in touch with the man who had set them up in relative luxury.

Vicky Greedy, described to the inquest as a regular visitor to the Trimbole's Griffith home in the 1970s, told the coroner she knew that his married daughter Gayelle Bignold had kept in close contact with her father in the three years since he had fled overseas. Gayelle had told her she intended to send her father a videotape of her small son's birthday party. Most damaging, perhaps, to those authorities supposedly looking for Trimbole, was the revelation that she knew of a photograph taken of Trimbole and his small grandson – who had been born after Trimbole's departure from Australia in May 1981. And Gayelle Bignold had shown friends clothing for the child which she said her father had sent 'from France'.

The coroner and his counsel could not ignore Greedy's evidence. When the inquest resumed in Sydney, Glenda Trimbole appeared and admitted that she, her sister Gayelle and Gayelle's husband, John Bignold, had visited Trimbole several times in his apartment on the French Riviera. They were a little more forthcoming than their brother Craig Trimbole, who told the inquest he had been to Nice with his wife, but he claimed he had not seen his father there. He even claimed he had not known whether his father had been in Nice at the time.

Although he held his father's power of attorney, Craig claimed not to know what type of business Trimbole senior was involved in and said he was not curious enough to ask. Under cross examination he denied telling his father to call him on Saturday evenings at his mother-in-law's house, where he always had dinner, rather than use his (Craig's) home number in Cabramatta. He denied that he had set up the Saturday night hotline arrangement because he thought his home telephone might be tapped by police. This was not widely believed.

Earlier, at the Griffith hearing, Vicky Greedy said she had been a regular visitor to Joan Trimbole's house until Donald Mackay's disappearance in 1977. Sometimes Robert Trimbole had been at the house, and she would see him speaking 'in a confidential way' in Italian with his 'great friend' Joe Calabria. This was unusual for the Australian-born Trimbole, who normally spoke English to anyone who could speak English, which Calabria could.

Another local woman, Olive Middleton, gave evidence that Trimbole and Joe Calabria had, while visiting her property at Coleambally, asked her for some empty cans to use for targets because they wanted to 'try out some new guns'.

Middleton said she and her husband had sold the property to Calabria in June 1975. She had assumed Trimbole was Calabria's business partner from Sydney.

The Coleambally connection soon came up again, when a detective sergeant, Ronald Jenkins, of the New South Wales drug squad, told the inquest he had met Donald Mackay at a Griffith motel in November 1975. Mackay had given him information and handed him a sketch map which showed marijuana crops in the area. As a result the police had arrested and charged several Calabrian men who had more than 30 acres of marijuana growing – a massive crop that would have produced $25 million in 1975 values, a staggering amount when the entire farm on which it was grown had cost $45,000.

During the marijuana conspirators' subsequent trial, the in-built flaws of the legal system had exposed Mackay as the secret police source because Jenkins' police diary was freely available to defence lawyers. One way or the other, the Calabrian crime syndicate got to know Mackay's name, and started to plan his death. And Trimbole had been at the centre of it, as the Mr Fixit for La Famiglia – the Griffith cell of N'Dranghita.

Now he was long gone. And although friends and family and potential enemies like Tizzoni could reach him at will, it looked as if no-one else wanted to find him – bar those who didn't have the authority to do so.

IN July 1984, Trimbole was reportedly spied at the Los Angeles Olympics, but it barely raised a ripple. Sleeping dogs were allowed to lie until October that year, when committal hearings were held against the two men Tizzoni had named as co-conspirators in Donald Mackay's murder: the hit man James Frederick Bazley and a North Melbourne gun dealer, George Joseph, who had recommended Bazley for the 'job' at Tizzoni's request.

Much to Tizzoni's anger, he was also charged over Mackay's death, despite his calculating efforts to earn immunity from prosecution by informing on Trimbole, Bazley and Joseph – although he was too canny to directly implicate any of the Griffith syndicate by name. Because Mackay had been killed in New South Wales, the three accused could not be tried for murder in Victoria and instead were charged with conspiracy to murder, because they had arranged the murder in Melbourne.

The committal forced the story back onto the front page – and heightened public interest in the 'mystery' of Trimbole's whereabouts and the scandal that he was not hunted down. Coincidentally, given the three-year hiatus, Australian Embassy officials in France announced on 8 October 1984, that a man matching Trimbole's description had been arrested by French police. The story went nowhere – although clearly Trimbole did – but it might have stirred public unrest about Trimbole's dream run as a fugitive.

Just two weeks later, Victoria's Director of Public Prosecutions, John Phillips QC, called for a 'massive effort' by Australian and international police to track down Trimbole.

'Grave public disquiet' about the Trimbole affair would 'not be dispelled' until he was brought before an Australian court, Phillips said. There was enough evidence to charge Trimbole with complicity in the murders of Donald Mackay and Douglas and Isabel Wilson. He even proposed an unprecedented step: to appoint one magistrate to conduct all proceedings against Trimbole, whether in New South Wales or Victoria.

'When this has been done it will be incumbent on the Australian and international police services to mount a massive effort to secure Trimbole's arrest,' he said. He was backed by the Victorian Attorney-General, Jim Kennan, who said he was 'anxious to see all steps should be taken' to bring Trimbole back to face justice. Fine words. Noble sentiment. But not much use.

Even if it were Trimbole that had been arrested in France in early October, the French authorities had not bothered to identify or to hold him. The inference was that he had bribed his way out and then fled France because it was getting a little too 'hot'. Either way, the next time Trimbole was heard of, he was in Ireland. Where, as it turned out, he had already established a hiding spot.

Meanwhile, back in Australia, a story broke that he had once tried to lobby three Queensland knights in an attempt to nobble a Queensland Turf Club inquiry. Telephone taps showed that before he fled Australia, Trimbole had called former Labor Party stalwart Sir 'Jack' Egerton and asked him to speak to former Federal Defence Minister, Sir James Killen and a former Supreme Court judge and QTC chairman, Sir Edward Williams. All because he wanted a favour for a mate, a horse trainer who had been 'rubbed out' and wanted to be granted a Queensland trainer's licence. It didn't work this time, but it showed how comfortable Trimbole was about approaching friends in high places. And how good he was at making new ones.

THE real Michael Pius Hanley was as much of a mystery as the man who took his name. No one managed to track Hanley down later, supposing he was even alive, to find out just how a fugitive Italian-Australian drug baron came to buy, borrow or steal his identity. Or, to be precise, to ask how the Australian came by the real Hanbury's driver's licence and social insurance cards.

The address on the cards led to a run-down tenement block behind Dublin's law courts. But if the real Michael Hanbury had been there, no one was telling nosy Australian reporters who came calling on the last weekend of October 1978. A man describing himself as Michael Hanbury's brother, Jimmy, was there with his wife but neither was inclined to clarify where or who Michael might be. Neighbours guessed he might have gone to London – or perhaps even to Australia. Or, and this was pause for thought, that he might be dead.

Trimbole, like Terry Clark and his associates in the 'Mr Asia' organisation, was a master at obtaining false passports. A favourite scam they had used in Australia was to take details from an infant's gravestone inscription or death notice then use them to apply for a passport, which could then be parlayed into a string of other identification documents used to open bank and credit accounts. But finding someone down and out who found they could use extra money more than they could use a passport also solved the problem in those unsophisticated days.

When 'Michael Hanbury' and his wife, Anne, and their daughter, Melanie, first turned up in the little tourist and fishing town of Westport on Ireland's west coast in March 1984, the locals noticed that he had an Australian accent but took his claims of Irish heritage and citizenship at face value.

Given that Ireland's main export for two centuries had been people, the Irish were used to thousands of distant 'cousins' visiting the old country to dig over their family roots. It was true that Michael Hanbury didn't quite look or sound like a transplanted son of Ireland but why would anyone question it? He was gregarious, generous, loved horse racing and, whether in a pub bar or the best restaurant, had a knack of making friends. He always had great 'craic' about him – and plenty of money. It helped, of course, that he talked about spending big – making plans to buy land and build a house.

The Hanburys enrolled Melanie at a remote convent boarding school called Kylemore Abbey, in April. By that time they had already become friendly with a local builder and deep sea fisherman called Padraic Conlon, a trusting soul who, with his wife Mai, grew fond of the cheerful Australian and his wife. The helpful Conlon helped his new friend select land and plan his new house in a quiet spot a little out of Westport. Ireland's sleepy west coast was the ideal place to stay out of sight yet be close enough to the main hubs of Europe that a businessman with diverse interests could stay in touch.

Later, when most of his movements were unravelled, it became clear that 'Michael Pius Hanbury' came and went from Ireland several times in 1984, which might have accounted for the report of him being 'arrested' in France early in October.

Given the lack of a co-ordinated international push to trace him, Trimbole's cover was good enough that he could move with relative impunity. If he hadn't been diagnosed with prostate cancer that October, perhaps he would never have been caught at all.

For three years he had stayed in touch with family and friends in ways that had evaded whatever rudimentary steps the Australian authorities were taking to monitor communications. But when he took ill and was told it was potentially terminal, it seems that the usual evasive tactics were abandoned. The calls made to the Trimbole family were intercepted, and it was so clear that worried family members would go overseas to see him that it was impossible to miss – or ignore, given the pressure building over Trimbole's absence during the highly-publicised Mackay inquest. So when Glenda Trimbole left the family home at Griffith and flew overseas, probably early that October, all the investigators had to do was follow. Like tracking an elephant through snow.

Martin 'Mr Asia' Johnstone: playboy dealer whose murder destroyed Clark's empire.

Douglas Wilson:
from Auckland
Grammar to a
shallow grave.
Isabel Wilson:
hitched to Douglas,
hooked on heroin,
hit by Bazley. Inset:
Taj, the Wilsons'
pet, which Bazley
refused to kill.

'Aussie Bob' Trimbole: from Griffith grease monkey to globetrotting Godfather.

John Spooner's
'Irish' Bob
Trimbole, 1984.

Life in a country town ... Joan Trimbole's house in Griffith, 1983.

Trimbole arrested in Ireland as 'Michael Hanbury' in 1984. He beat the courts but not the cancer.

Below: his loyal de facto Anne Marie Presland.

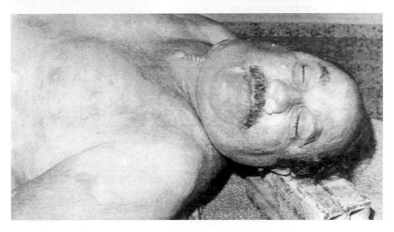

The end of the road: Trimbole's body in a rural Spanish morgue, 1987.

Donald Mackay: capable, honourable man murdered for Calabrian
Honoured Society.

Terry Clark: smalltime crook who built an international drug empire while no-one was looking.

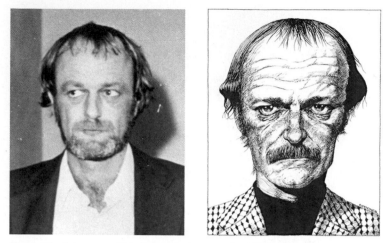

Terry Clark in one of his many guises and as *The Age*'s John Spooner saw him.

The million-dollar house Clark built in New Zealand's Bay of Islands, but never got to live in.

The high life ... Clark loved boats and fishing. Here pictured in the Bay of Islands with son Jarrod and 'Chinese Jack'.

X-rated: Allison Dine, former Clark lover and drug courier. Subsequently gave evidence against him as Miss X.

The many faces of Terrence Clark, alias Alexander Sinclair, alias ...

Gianfranco Tizzoni: informed on Trimbole, Bazley and Joseph – but did he tell all? Died peacefully in Italy.

Police picture of James Frederick Bazley.

Hard man, soft life: Brian Kane relaxing on the Gold Coast shortly before he was killed in Melbourne.

Les and Judi Kane: bash artist and bashful beauty. Pictured (top left) with a friend called Vinnie and top, with baby son Justin, 1974.

Les Kane was hard on humans but kind to pups. Pictured at
Beechworth Prison, where he helped train seeing-eye dogs.

Brian Kane and brave friend Sandra Walsh. She tried to save him after he was shot by two masked men.

Doomed love: the glamorous Fran Kear on holidays with Brian Kane in Queensland. She loved the man but not the way he made money.

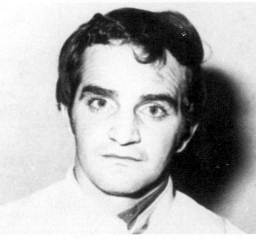

Leslie Herbert Kane: street-fighting man whose body was never found.

Brian Raymond Kane as a young standover man: quick to the punch but too slow on the draw.

Death of a gangster, Melbourne-style: Brian Kane had given
Pentridge Prison chaplain Father John Brosnan a car and air tickets
to Ireland. Fr Brosnan gave his former pupil a eulogy.

THEY arrested him just after he left the Gresham Hotel in Dublin on 25 October, a Thursday evening. He was with Anne-Marie Presland and his daughter, Glenda, who had unwittingly led investigators to him almost three weeks earlier. The arrest, the authorities claimed, was the result of joint undercover work by investigators from Australia, Ireland and Britain.

After tracing the origins of calls following telephone intercepts in Griffith and Sydney, police had watched Trimbole from when he and Presland and her daughter Melanie had arrived back in Ireland from Switzerland on 7 October. The trio had then flown in a light plane from Dublin to the west coast to avoid a four-hour journey by road, and stayed at the Hotel Westport, where they were well-known from previous visits.

The hotel receptionist would later tell reporters that the Australian she knew as Mr Hanbury 'did not look at all well.' She was right. Trimbole was suffering severe abdominal pains that had driven him to seek treatment in Zurich. He was in so much pain that his friend Padraic Conlon told him that he should join him in going to a hospital in Dublin, where Conlon was already booked in for a check up. They all drove to Dublin next day, where they met Glenda Trimbole. The women booked into the luxurious Gresham Hotel while Conlon and Trimbole went to the Mater Hospital.

Conlon left the hospital after his check-up but 'Michael Hanbury' stayed for two weeks, while Ann Marie Presland, her daughter and Glenda lived at the hotel. In that time he had an exploratory operation that confirmed the cancer had spread and would kill him, probably in a matter of months.

When the party checked out of the Gresham Hotel next day, set to leave Ireland, the police swooped. Within hours, Australia's most wanted man was in Mountjoy Prison and Australian reporters were on their way to Ireland.

While the Melbourne *Herald's* Steve Price filed his exclusive about sleeping in Trimbole's bed at the hotel in Westport, *The Age's* veteran correspondent John Stevens covered the strange chain of events that would unfold over the next few days.

It seemed clear that the Irish police had bent the rules a little to accommodate their Australian counterparts, a decision that would throw the whole case against Trimbole off course. 'At best it can be described as unorthodox, even questionable,' wrote Stevens. 'Perhaps it would be unkind to describe the whole strange affair as very Irish.'

The reason for the raised eyebrows was that Trimbole was arrested not in his own name but as Michael Hanbury and held under Section 30 of the Offences Against the State Act on suspicion of possessing a firearm, a catch-all measure sometimes used to hold IRA terrorists. But although 'Hanbury' was suspected of dealing in arms as well as drugs – probably with IRA contacts – no firearm was ever found, leading a High Court judge to conclude that the gun charge was a sham concocted to hold Trimbole for the Australian police while bureaucrats and lawyers scrambled to arrange a one-off extradition deal with Ireland, which had no formal extradition treaty with Australia at the time.

'A man from Foreign Affairs reached Dublin white-faced and exhausted after a non-stop flight from Canberra, bearing information to support the warrant – allegations of eleven offences including the murder of Donald Mackay and Douglas and Isabel Wilson,' wrote Stevens.

None of this impressed the High Court judge at a special sitting on the Friday evening, the day after Trimbole's arrest. This underlined the apparently strange decision by the Irish police, the Garda, to run the bogus gun charge when they already had firm information from telephone taps that the Australian, regardless of his real identity, was a known associate of IRA terrorists and had been supplying them with weapons. If they had offered the real information to justify the Australian's arrest, the court would probably have been obliged to rule that the arrest was lawful. So what was the problem?

The most likely reason, it emerged later, was sensitive local politics. The embarrassed Irish police probably did not want to reveal the truth about their sources: the gun-running intelligence had been passed to them by British police, a fact they would rather hide. The British-Irish relationship during 'The Troubles' was strained. And the relationship between different police forces is strange at any time, even among the different state and federal police back in Australia.

It was just the loophole that Trimbole needed. He might have looked like 'your average suburban greengrocer', as one reporter described him, but he had the spending power of a mafia don. Ireland's most eminent criminal barrister, Patrick MacEntee, appeared for him with two other counsel and a solicitor, Con O'Leary. This elite legal team demolished the faintly farcical police case, which rested on alleged possession of a non-existent gun, but 'Hanbury's' freedom was as short-lived as it was expensive: after 15 minutes he was re-arrested outside the High Court and whisked to the District Court to face an extradition warrant – as Robert Trimbole – that had been hastily patched up by the Federal Attorney General's department in Canberra.

Anne-Marie Presland, meanwhile, kept up the charade. She would answer only to 'Mrs Hanbury' and told reporters outside the Dublin police station that police had the wrong man. 'I don't know what the hell is going on here. I don't know what the hell the police are talking about. My husband's name is Hanbury. He was born in Ireland,' she insisted. Not even the Irish police believed her. But, for a few days, his lawyers stuck to the Hanbury story.

The silver-haired and theatrical Patrick MacEntee, veteran of defending IRA terrorists, predicted it would not be easy to get his client back to Australia. For a start, he said, the authorities would have to prove beyond doubt that the man in Mountjoy Prison *was* Trimbole. 'Then there are the legal issues involved in extradition,' he said, which could take 'months rather than weeks' to sort out. His client had refused to give his fingerprints, which hindered formal identification.

Others well qualified to know Trimbole had no doubt he was the prisoner. Apart from his daughter Glenda being present, her brother, Craig Trimbole, flew in with a *60 Minutes* television crew to film the circus. Two days later, lawyers appearing for the absent Trimbole at extradition proceedings in Australia officially admitted what the whole world knew, that the man in jail in Dublin was their client.

But the circus wasn't over by a long way. When *60 Minutes* went to air on the Nine network in Australia the following Sunday, Trimbole's estranged but loyal born-again Christian wife, Joan, admitted only that the man being held in Ireland had 'an incredible resemblance' to her runaway husband, and that he was certainly in the company of their daughter Glenda. Not to mention their son, Craig, of course.

In the interview with Jana Wendt, Joan Trimbole revealed that her pet name for the man she hadn't seen in three years was 'The Godfather'. This was because, she explained, 'he was always helping other people and always looking after his friends.' To her eternal credit Wendt, the consummate professional, kept a straight face.

THE hasty decision by an Irish policeman to hold Trimbole on the bogus gun charge hung over the drawn-out proceedings that followed. By Christmas week, two months after his arrest, Trimbole had appeared in court nine times to play a mute part in a show that he was paying for. And there was more to come in the new year of 1985.

While Trimbole's son, Craig, and another in-law, Tony Addabo, flew to Italy twice, obviously to get cash from some secret source, the most expensive battery of defence lawyers ever seen in Ireland worked on a case to prevent Trimbole being extradited to Australia.

Putting Trimbole's case were not only two of Ireland's most senior barristers but an English QC regarded as the best extradition lawyer in the business and a junior counsel and two instructing solicitors, one from London. It was the first time an English barrister had appeared with an Irish barrister in a Dublin court since 'The Troubles'. The Irish barrister MacEntee was said to be paid a retainer of 1000 pounds a day. But that was nothing compared with the latest addition to the team, an 80-year-old Nobel Peace Prize winner called Sean MacBride – Irish nationalist hero, world-renowned civil rights lawyer and co-founder of Amnesty International. This venerable figure was turning out for the short, fat crook from Griffith – at a price estimated to be several thousand pounds a day. But he was worth it. Reporters noted that the judge, Justice Egan, paid close attention to the great MacBride's arguments against extraditing Trimbole.

If Justice Egan mulled over the case during the legal vacation during Christmas and New Year, he thought of nothing to undermine MacBride and MacEntee's case for Trimbole. On 5 February, the judge directed that Trimbole be released and ruled that because the first arrest had been unlawful, everything that flowed from it was tainted with that illegality. The Australian Government officials assigned to the case were disappointed – but their chances of holding Trimbole until a legal way could be found to re-arrest him were scuttled when the Irish Supreme Court ruled that, once released, he could not be placed under surveillance, as that would technically be like remaining in custody. The law, at great expense, had been turned inside out to give the cancer-stricken drug baron and murderer a loophole. In essence, the

Irish police had to let him escape in order to re-arrest him with clean hands. And he was never going to let that happen.

Trimbole walked out of Mountjoy Prison at 2pm on 6 February 1985 and stepped into a car driven by his solicitor Con O'Leary. Local and Australian television crews gave chase and a helicopter hovered overhead as the car sped away. It was last seen heading towards Dublin airport. He most likely left the country in a chartered aircraft later that night. He was gone. Nothing was left behind but rich lawyers and a smell that would not go away.

THE rumour was that Trimbole was in Spain, where so many wanted men went because the attitude about extradition was so relaxed that jokes about the 'Costa del Crime' were standard. Anyone with enough pesetas could hide from their past. But if there were any information about Trimbole's whereabouts, no Australian authorities acted on it. Cynics speculated that Trimbole knew too much to be too hotly pursued. They suspected that the faceless men in the Honoured Society had contacts at every level and could reach out and touch key people when needed. The theory went that Trimbole's years of compromising people were an insurance policy: if bribery weren't enough, blackmail could be.

Another view, of course, was that the failure to pursue Trimbole after the long, expensive Dublin debacle was not a conspiracy but a stuff-up, a bureaucratic and legal tangle that could not be pinned on one person or department. Unspoken, but not forgotten, was the fact that he was dying anyway. That 'Aussie Bob' lived so long must have been an embarrassment to all except Trimbole's family and shrinking band of friends.

The news broke on a Melbourne autumn morning in 1987, when an astute reporter called Geoff Easdown got a tip from a police contact that Australia's most wanted man had died in Spain. The leak was that Craig Trimbole had telephoned the Australian Embassy in Madrid asking how he could get his father's body home. (It would turn out that Craig had flown straight to Spain in secrecy – so secret that his passport showed no record of his leaving Australia, an offence for which he was later fined.)

Easdown stood the story up well enough to get it on page one of *The Herald* and then agitated to fly to Spain to follow up his exclusive. But the newshound was blocked by the bean counters, who ruled it would be cheaper and faster for the group's London correspondent Bruce Wilson to cover it.

The wily Wilson was in a Fleet Street pub when he got the call. He hastened slowly, stopping off in Madrid to recruit the services of a newspaper 'stringer' called Ed Owen, who spoke excellent Spanish, before flying to Alicante, already widely tipped as the area where Trimbole had been hiding.

It was Saturday morning when they landed near Alicante. Their first stop was the local hospital, where they found that Craig Trimbole had signed the death certificate of one 'Senor Witte', who had died of a heart attack three days earlier. They were told the body had been moved to the mortuary at a nearby cemetery at Villajoyosa. While Wilson distracted two National Guard members guarding the mortuary, a helpful gravedigger showed Owen the body on the slab.

It was a grotesque sight: the naked body was bloated and discoloured, the head resting on a brick. It turned out later that Craig Trimbole, who had reached Alicante just four hours before his father died, had paid an undertaker to dress the body in a smart suit and tie but that somewhere between the hospital and mortuary the clothes had disappeared. 'Somebody stole the God-father's clothes,' Wilson later deadpanned.

He obtained a picture of the body. Trimbole, born a peasant, looked like one again with his body slumped on the slab in the crude outbuilding in the Spanish backwater. It was only after the body was flown back to Sydney in a lead-lined casket that the ostentatious trappings of his gangster lifestyle were restored. He was embalmed, placed in a silk-lined coffin and dressed in a white suit: Liberace meets The Godfather. But the photographs of the naked body in the morgue, published nationwide, became the enduring image of Trimbole's death, to the anger of his family and friends.

Anne-Marie Presland, Trimbole's de facto wife for fourteen years, later told a women's magazine that she had almost vomited when she saw the photographs.

'I never ever thought that they could stoop so low as to do that to someone. He was a man of pride ... he was very proud ... and they took all that away from him. They stripped him of something he had always had,' she said. But that was later. In Spain on that Saturday in May 1987, Bruce Wilson was still chasing the story.

AFTER leaving the mortuary, Wilson spread the word among English-speaking ex-patriates that he was looking for a woman and teenage girl connected to a man who had just died. The same night, two teachers from the local international school said a girl called Melanie at the school had left it the previous Thursday because her father had just died. Wilson headed to a pub where ex-pats drank and found a youth who said he went to school with Melanie – and that he knew where the family had been living.

The boy took them to Villa Conchita, a white bungalow set among fruit trees, vegetables and palms

'There was nobody home,' Wilson later told Keith Moor. 'I went through the garbage and found a couple of hypodermic syringes and some phials of painkiller. I was looking for anything that would confirm it was Trimbole's house.'

He saw some people next door picking fruit and showed them the picture of Trimbole's corpse. They said it was their neighbour 'Senor Wittig'. This was the proof that Villa Conchita had been the trio's home almost from the time they had fled from Dublin more than two years earlier. They had lived under the name Wittig – Anne-Marie Presland's maiden name.

By the time two National Crime Authority officers arrived from Australia next evening, Wilson had the story nailed down. The officers could not or would not confirm that the man in the morgue was Robert Trimbole, although their continued presence was silent proof they believed it was him. Further proof was that they tried to prevent media access to the morgue, but a Spanish magistrate overruled the Australian lawmen and allowed the gathering media pack to film the body, to the anger and distress of the dead man's family.

Wilson filed a story suggesting that if Trimbole had been Australia's most wanted man, then the second-most wanted man could sleep very soundly indeed.

TRIMBOLE'S body arrived in Australia in the cargo hold of a British Airways jumbo jet on 21 May, a week after his death. It was almost another week before the funeral at St Benedict's Church in the Sydney suburb of Smithfield on 27 May.

The time and place of the funeral Mass was the worst-kept secret in Sydney, although the police supposedly did not know about it. Trimbole's body arrived in an expensive hearse, followed by two black Ford Fairlanes. His son Craig, wearing a black suit, dark sunglasses and with a black scarf hiding his face, entered the church through a rear entrance with his wife Josephine, flanked by other men. Anne-Marie Presland and her daughter, Melanie, and Trimbole's daughters, Gayelle and Glenda, also attended, though there were no reports of Joan Trimbole and her oldest son, Robert junior, who had reportedly become a born-again Christian under the strain of having such a notorious namesake as his father. The 150 mourners contained many who were obliged to be there because of the Calabrian Honoured Society's code of showing respect. But they resented publicly exposing their link with the notorious organised crime figure responsible for Donald Mackay's murder. Some of them attacked and abused gathering reporters, photographers and cameramen.

One man leapt from a car, wielding a long baton and scuffled with television crews, screaming abuse. Someone tried to rip a camera from a Channel Seven cameraman. Famously, an ABC reporter, Max Uechtritz, suffered a bloody nose and suspected broken hand after he went to help a photographer, Nick Andrean, who was being bashed and kicked by six men. Uechtritz held his own against three would-be assailants, an effort that won him plenty of admirers.

As the service began, police started to arrive in response to emergency calls and by the time it ended an hour later were organised enough to prevent any more ugly scenes. A cortege of more than 60 cars drove to the Pine Grove Memorial Park near Blacktown in Sydney's west, escorted by police cars and with media helicopters overhead. The coffin was placed in a large family crypt near his parents, Dominco and Saveria, where there was room for another ten bodies. A Blacktown councillor later attacked the Trimbole family for tarnishing the area's image by burying the murdering mafia fixer in his municipality, calling on them to exhume the body and move it to Griffith.

'He should have been buried in Griffith where he came from. It's their shame, not our fame,' he said.

The Prime Minister, Bob Hawke, telephoned Max Uechtritz to congratulate him on defending the photographer in the brawl at the funeral. When this became public, Craig Trimbole was incensed and called talkback king John Laws on radio to attack Hawke over it. Maybe he thought that because La Famiglia, the 'family' of murderous drug traffickers, owned Hawke's cabinet minister Al Grassby, that they had bought the entire Government.

He was wrong, of course. But it wasn't hard to see how he had got the idea.

4

SNAKE IN THE GRASS

A POLITICIAN'S DOUBLE LIFE EXPOSED

One sentence buried Grassby:
'no decent man could have
regarded the general attacks on
the Calabrians as justifying him
in propagating the scurrilous
lies contained in the
anonymous document'.

BARBARA Mackay loved her husband fiercely but she was a realist: she did not entertain unrealistic hopes after his disappearance. With the blood, the bullet shells, the silence, the situation ... she knew he was dead. She gathered her strength to get herself and her children through shock, grief and loss. Paul, 19, happened to have travelled down from Sydney for the weekend and James was only 3. Ruth, 16, and Mary, 13, came home from boarding school.

Barbara's mother, the elderly Mrs Dearman, moved into her daughter's house and when Barbara said she was worried about the way her daughters were thinking and talking, and felt she should have 'a big talk' with them, Mrs Dearman seized the opportunity to make it happen.

She said, 'Look, I'll go to the bathroom and you can talk, just the three of you.' In the bathroom she slipped, fell and could not get up, waves of pain coming from her injured leg. But the old lady was staunch. Not a whimper escaped her while Barbara was speaking to the girls. She just gritted her teeth. When it was over, she was found and taken to hospital. Like mother, like daughter: when the weekly pre-natal class was held after the murder, physiotherapist Barbara Mackay was there to take it as usual.

She was in the media spotlight, every face muscle analysed for its emotional content. Some found the Methodist Ladies College Old Girl's calm assurance a passionless way for a newly-widowed woman to behave. Rumours flew: one had it that Don Mackay had a secret lover and that his van was seen parked outside a motel the night before he was killed (police checked it out, and it was a complete furphy, but the smear lived on). Local conversations featuring 'Calabria … La Famiglia … Euston crop … mafia … Griffith … ' made many in the Riverina feel that to be Italian was to be misunderstood, and being Calabrian was to be a suspect.

Barbara held the public funeral ten days after Don's death, on an icy, windy Tuesday afternoon outside Griffith Hospital. The Combined Church Thanksgiving Service drew a heap of clergymen, community leaders and 5000 to 6000 locals, about half of Griffith.

Britain's TV star interviewer, David Frost, questioned Mrs Mackay at the Yoogali Club, to which locals were invited. Local State ALP member Lin Gordon was given a rough time – he had been on the radio pooh-poohing talk of Griffith being a big marijuana town at the very time Mackay was gunned down, and Liberal candidate Mackay's preferences had nearly toppled him at a recent election. But Griffith reserved its sharpest contempt for Al Grassby, the premier's Special Consultant for Community Relations. He was booed as he went into bat for 'honest Italians'.

Mackay's death, called a 'disappearance' in all official refer-ences for years, forced the government to do something publicly. Premier Wran promised a royal commission into drug trafficking less than a week after Mackay disappeared. Justice Phillip Wood-ward's team visited Griffith for in-camera hearings and then three days of public sessions. The commissioner's party stood outside some of the overblown houses Mackay and others had called 'grass castles'. Legalistic arguments about wild marijuana and the hemp rope industry were swept aside. 'The Mackay Bill', so-called because it was the main plank of the petition Don was involved in, outlawed marijuana growing in New South Wales, the last state to do so.

With Don Mackay out of the way, it was back to business for Bob Trimbole. He continued to move marijuana – mostly grown far from the Riverina by 1978. But he was less and less interested in that greasy kid stuff. The high-quality smack Terry Clark and his pals moved was the future, and stashing money safely took more and more of his time. There were important race meetings to go to, for a punt, to meet 'by chance' people who could intro-duce him to Terry Clark, to be on the lookout for horses' connec-tions and jockeys he could buy to help with his lucrative hobby of fixing races. But by early 1981, of course, Trimbole would be too hot to handle, and so flee the country after being tipped off that a royal commission was about to put him in the witness box.

Trimbole wasn't the only Riverina rogue to have his reputation shredded. The 1980s would see Al Grassby's reputation trashed, too – mainly as collateral damage because he allowed himself to be too close to the Calabrian figures behind Trimbole.

Playing his self-appointed part as the 'Father of Multicultur-ism' and 'social justice campaigner', the nation's noisiest enemy of racism continued to speak out against the way his Italian ex-constituents were being tarred with the mafia brush because of the activities of a tiny minority. Grassby's shrill pitch was that all the 'grass castle' allegations demeaned Griffith's vibrant multicultural success story, and people talking of 'mafia' had been watching too much late-night TV. He made an inviting target for political enemies.

In August 1980 a Sunday tabloid ran an article headed NOT THE MAFIA. The article was reminiscent of the tired and malicious 'Other Woman' rumour, but with a domestic twist, implying Don Mackay's disappearance might have a lot to do with Barbara, son Paul and family lawyer Ian Salmon, the man who had found Mackay's van. The article prophesised that a document, supposedly written by two policemen, would be tabled in the New South Wales Parliament, where it would be safe from defamation suits. And it sourced the document to Michael Maher, a backbencher of the Wran Labor New South Wales government.

Most of the document was concerned about stereotyping Riverina Italians and Grassby banging his usual multi-cultural drum. The original four pages were never found, but from photocopies of them police concluded it was typed on Jennifer Sergi's typewriter on paper supplied by the New South Wales Government Printing Office. But typewriters leave no clues to when they are used, or who has done the typing. Armed with copies of this scurrilous document, Grassby went to a lot of trouble to get it read in parliament. He approached three parliamentarians with lots of Italians in their electorate: Chris Sumner, Michael Maher and Giovanni Srgno, a Calabrian who wisely rejected him outright. Grassby had phoned Maher and asked him to call on him. At Grassby's office two brothers called Sergi, he thought, from Griffith, and the wife of one of them, were present. Maher was 'bluntly' asked to read it in parliament but he explained that even if he wanted to, as a junior backbencher he could not. Grassby disagreed. Maher claimed he never read it at all but sent it on to the Police Minister, asking it be investigated, the day after the newspaper reported it. Maher said he did not give it to the Press. Grassby said he hadn't, either; but the reporter said Maher had given it to him, saying he'd got it from Grassby who'd got it from 'two policemen' never named. A smell lingered over the whole episode.

Two completely different policemen did read it. They were the head of the New South Wales homicide squad, Inspector Harry Tupman, and his boss, CIB Chief Superintendant Ray Goldsworthy, and they discussed questioning the ex-minister about its origin. But Grassby was a VIP, so they ran the idea past their immediate boss, Assistant Commissioner Cecil Abbott. The wily Abbott could see no merit in police questioning Grassby, so he killed the idea.

New South Wales Police mulled over the document again in 1983. The officer in charge of the Mackay murder investigation, Joe Parrington, wanted to question Grassby over it, but dropped the idea. Both Abbott and Parrington would be criticised for their decisions later.

The allegations and implications saw Al Grassby's life publicly dissected.

For an unfortunate start, Al was born plain Grass, and added the '–by' to celebrate his mother's Irishness. His father, Spanish with a touch of Chile, was an engineer on the Southampton docks when he was killed in the Blitz when Albert was a teenager. Grassby was educated 'at thirteen schools in Australia and abroad', worked for British Army intelligence and as a journalist and came to the Riverina as a CSIRO information officer. There he met, and in 1962 married, Ellnor Louez.

Ellnor Louez had been romantically linked with Antonio (Tony) Sergi, a son of the viticultural and winemaking family, some of whom traded as F & J Sergi, a family private company, in the 1970s. Around Griffith, Italians tended to marry Italians. Of 574 such weddings between 1950 and 1967 only 31 brides and

65 grooms married 'out', and the Calabresi married Calabresi. After Ellnor's marriage to Grassby, she remained a good friend of Tony and his branch of the big Sergi clan, and Al became a family friend. As Al grew more prominent in The Area, he became a regular accessory at Calabresi functions. It was Al who proposed the nuptial toast at big Sergi weddings – 2000 to 3000 guests, lavish amounts of food and wine, and two and three days long. At some stage Ellnor had an interest in a workers' pub in Sydney, close to Paddy's Markets, and Tony Sergi stayed there later. Ellnor had supported Tony, proclaimed his innocence, and was happy to pose with her old flame, champagne glasses in hand, for a newspaper photographer.

Al, meanwhile, talked up The Area outside the Riverina and brought visitors to meet the locals. The word soon spread: Al Grassby might not have been everybody's idea of a rural member, he dressed like a funny bugger, dyed his hair and never shut up, but he knew people. He mixed with people high and low, inside The Area and out, and spruiked the Riverina's future and products relentlessly. Pretty soon, Grassby was cemented in as a Riverina booster. Riverina wines were always at hand in his electoral and parliamentary offices. He and Ellnor threw large private parties at home.

Al had been elected on the ALP ticket to the New South Wales seat of Murrumbidgee in 1965. When he took the federal seat of Riverina in 1972, the ALP was astonished. Grassby was in line for an important ministerial post, and Agriculture seemed a natural, but some senior Agricultural Department public servants quietly convinced their masters Grassby would never do. Al confirmed these suspicions by giving his maiden speech in a purple suit. Country Party members called him 'Paterson's Curse' after the purple-flowered noxious weed – 'colourful but useless' the joke went. Al pointed out that farmers also called the weed 'Salvation Jane' when drought struck and stock would turn to it when there was no grass. When the laughter in the House died down, they gave Flash Al immigration and he changed the country. He killed off the last vestiges of The White Australia Policy, abolished the old imperial preferences that favoured British migrants, freed up tourist visas for Southern Europeans and Asians, and made multiculturalism a key plank of Australian policy.

Although his name first brings images of the outrageous wide ties he wore, WASPish taste prejudices did not worry the citizens of the village of Plati, population 4000, when Al, Ellnor and their daughter arrived there in 1974. Grassby wrote a column, a sort of travel diary, for the Griffith paper, the *Area News*. 'Every building and thousands of people carried Australian flags. I have never seen so many Australian flags before – not even in the national capital.' Posters of welcome in English and Italian were on lamp posts. The mayor, Francesco Catanzariti, gave him a gold key to the city and some sort of honorary citizenship. (R. V. Hall visited Plati ten years later and found it 'a mean, homicidal town', most houses abandoned, the few hundred townsfolk with only twenty surnames mainly old people, among them a few returnees from America and Australia.) But to readers in Australia in 1974, Plati meant one thing: it was where the grass castle guys came from, our mafia Honored Society, *L'Onorata*. In Calabrian slang they call the local crime society the *Mal Vita*, Bad Life.

In Griffith they remembered how, when Pietro Calapari was raided and arrested following the shootings in the Melbourne Markets in the 1960s, Al and a local detective, John Ellis, went character evidence for him. Fine: $40. Al scoffed that talking about the mafia showed you were a TV addict, but it was more like *The Godfather*, a big hit in the 1970s, with Australia and Calabria standing in for America and Sicily. Grassby had done a foolish thing going to Plati at all, shooting himself in the electoral foot in a town where mafiosi shot real feet with real bullets. But he compounded his woes with promises he made there.

He granted entry visas for three men called Barbaro, two Domenicos and a Rosario, overruling his department. The three had been refused entry or been deported from Australia in the past. When a Barbaro returned to Italy after his twelve-day trip, he was arrested in connection with the kidnapping of a wealthy Italian man's son, and he'd skipped assault charges when he left. But for the fuss over that, they would have quietly slipped in and out without questions in the House, and their banking deposits here unknown. Grassby toughed it out, and Premier Neville Wran got a cheap laugh by revealing these criminals' record included 'larceny of a goat'. Rumours flew that Al had smuggled 'ransom money' back within his entourage's luggage, allegedly to fund crops. Back home, people were angry with Labor MP Lin Gordon when he took the visiting Premier Wran to meet community leader Pietro Calapari but not Barbara Mackay. Mrs Mackay's decision to stay in town was admired for the courage it showed.

Before and after his grand tour of Italy, Grassby was honoured with grand titles for his work on Italo-Australian relations and social justice: Commendatore Order of Solidarity of Republic of Italy, Knight Military Order of St Agatha, and Grand Cross of Merit.

Ellnor moved into insurance, becoming an agent working from Canberra. It was unfortunate timing because around that time NRMA Insurance found the Riverina had three times the level of road accident claims other regions produced. Investigators found a trend: the third parties injured were mainly farmers, mainly from Calabria, mainly from Plati, and mostly called Sergi or Pangallo or Barbaro. In fact, the Sergis often hit Pangellos or vice versa, 62 times, and the drivers all escaped injury. Claims on NRMA totalled $40 million. GIO Insurance clients were also unlucky on the roads of the Riverina. One out-of-luck driver had 25 front-to-rear collisions in four years. A truck driven by Joe

Trimboli hit a car driven by Domenico Nirta; bit of a coincidence because they were accused of growing the same marijuana crop. John Fahey, then New South Wales Opposition Leader, later reckoned 'the mafia' hauled $140 million a year out of insurance companies' coffers in the 1980s.

By the end of the 1970s Grassby was spending less time with Ellnor in Canberra: work took him to Sydney a lot, and there he met Angela Chan, and it was often Angela who was on his arm at functions. Relations with Ellnor remained cordial and their domestic arrangements were well understood as the 1980s and 1990s rolled by. Al was so multicultural he effectively had two wives – one for Sydney and one in Canberra.

Not so flashy was the grieving widow Barbara Mackay, whose persistence and quiet dignity brought media, community and national support where Grassby's antics often brought contempt. She told reporters about the eerie feeling when she saw a man rumoured to be a top L'Onorata player, possibly one of those who ordered her husband's death, ruffle her youngest son's hair in the street one day. A friend from her congregation, Lesley Hicks, wrote a book called *The Appalling Silence*. A Concerned Citizens of Griffith group pressed the New South Wales government for an investigation of the police investigation itself, which had, it seemed, gone nowhere for years.

And that is what they got: Justice Nagle's Special Inquiry into the Police Investigation of the Death of Donald Bruce Mackay. Ten years had passed since the murder; Justice Woodward had concluded an unknown hit man working for a branch of L'Onorata killed him. The Coroner had declared Don Mackay legally dead of 'gunshot wounds' in 1984. More to the point, Frank Tizzoni was singing. Justice Nagle was critical of much, but especially critical of Parrington withholding Bruce Pursehouse's evidence (of the first attempt to lure Mackay) from the inquest and from Victoria Police. Al Grassby appeared on the stand, and Barbara

Mackay learned more and more about Grassby's vigorous pro-
motion of the four-page document that smeared her.

The Opposition Leader, Nick Greiner, accused Al of trying
to get the mafia 'off the hook', a view many came to share as the
story behind the document emerged. Grassby had no real option
but to stand down from his job when the report was handed down
in December 1987. One sentence of the report buried Grassby:
'The commission makes only one comment – that no decent man
could have regarded the general attacks on the Calabrians as justifying him in propagating the scurrilous lies contained in the
anonymous document'.

Barbara Mackay sued Grassby for defamation and in April
1987 he issued a full, unreserved public apology and paid $5000 to
cover the legal costs she and solicitor Ian Salmon had incurred.

National Crime Authority officers knocked on Angela Chan's
door and arrested Grassby and took him to court in late 1987.
The charges included conspiracy to pervert the course of justice
(the course of the Mackay murder investigation) and criminal
defamation (of Salmon, Paul Mackay and Barbara Mackay).
These alleged crimes originally stipulated 'with Robert Trimbole
and others'. 'Others' would eventually include Guiseppe Sergi,
doyen of the community and father-in-law of the typewriter-own-
ing Jennifer Sergi, who was also charged. Charges against her
were subsequently dropped, mainly because there was no proof
of who had used her typewriter to type the scurrilous document
smearing the Mackays.

The case twisted and turned, bounced up and down from lower courts to higher ones (including the High Court itself), tore off
sideways for rulings and appeals, but all at a snail's pace. For five
years.

The magistrate who heard committal proceedings felt that
Grassby and the Sergis had a case to answer, but the alleged

offences were already seven years cold and the civil court had already dealt with the three defamed parties' 'injuries', as they are called in law, settled with one defendant's apology and payment of costs. The defence moved to stay proceedings and the magistrate agreed. This meant that nothing further would happen, there would be no trial, unless something new came up. Grassby was delighted but the prosecution appealed, maintaining the magistrate had no power to do this, and a judge agreed.

The prosecution was ferocious. At one stage they refused to let Grassby's team have copies of court transcripts without money paid up front; Grassby, almost broke, his legal team unpaid for years, appealed to another court; and that court ordered the copies be provided free. Every time costs were awarded to the defendants, the prosecution appealed, clearly hoping the delay would force Grassby to throw in the towel. They froze Grassby's modest assets, and a separate legal action had to be mounted to thaw them. The Director of Public Prosecutions and (behind the scenes) the National Crime Authority spared no taxpayers' dollar for a win. The defence called it a 'vendetta'.

There is little doubt the prosecution would have squashed Grassby if his best mate had not been a barrister, with a nephew who was also a lawyer. Jennifer Sergi's defence was she didn't type the smear document, that her typewriter was widely available to many, and that she wasn't in Grassby's office on the day in question. Also, she wasn't the only Jenny married to a Sergi, a surname more common than Smith or Jones there, a point the expensive Melbourne lawyer Frank Galbally put to the court.

Eventually a trial was forced. If the prosecution couldn't get them on criminal defamation, they wanted attempted criminal defamation as a back up. The National Crime Authority, desperate for a scalp and wanting to justify the high salaries that the state police resented, had been busy. They had found two witness, a 'Mr Smith' and 'Mr Jones' whose real names were suppressed.

John Foley, reading the brief of evidence in bed before the pre-trial started, was impressed with what his adversaries had. Mr Smith had worked for Ellnor's Trades Hall Hotel, but he was also Bob Trimbole's man. And at Paddy's Market, close by the pub, he had twice delivered bags with $20,000 in them, and seen Flash Al scuttle off, bag in hand. Mr Jones was cellarman at the Trades Hall. He said he'd driven marijuana from Canberra to Sydney for $500 for Flash Al, had taken delivery of wine boxes full of grass at the pub, and been present when Bob Trimbole and Al talked, noting how Al treated Bob 'like a god'. But it was all a bit good to be true.

Eventually, the evidence of both was ruled inadmissible, and questions were asked about where the NCA had dug them up. Mr Smith was a convicted heroin trafficker and briber of police. Mr Jones, too, had 'a long criminal history' and the magistrate, using Mr Jones's own term, called him a 'rip-off merchant' and an 'immoral opportunist'. In other words, hardly reliable witnesses.

The resulting trial – R v. Grassby, Sergi & Sergi – was highly technical and tedious. Ex-prime minister Gough Whitlam talked of his affection and respect for Grassby and said he was universally liked and had dismantled every vestige of White Australia policies. The jury was sent out, but it returned after eight hours to say its members could not all agree. They were encouraged to give it another try, and two hours later, returned verdicts of not guilty to defamation, but guilty of attempted defamation. Because criminal defamation charges are seldom laid, the sentence could have been anything from a slap on the wrist to three years in prison. The judge fined Grassby $7000, suggesting Grassby's motives as more misguided than calculated, and said he accepted he did not mean to cause harm.

An appeal was certain, and, in 1992, the Court of Criminal Appeal quashed the verdicts, saying they looked like compromises rather than verdicts, did not make logical or legal sense, and there was 'a gap' between the Crown evidence and their line of reasoning. Grassby was awarded costs of $180,000, contested of course.

More than five years of litigation had not crushed Grassby's spirit. He showed his tie for the cameras – a lucky shamrock pattern. It had beaten his wallet around and the shame of the charges meant employment was difficult, but he had a role in the administration of the Racial Discrimination Act and on ethnic radio. He wrote books on battlefields – military history an enthusiasm arising from his days as a junior British Army intelligence officer at the close of World War II, and on multicultural, republican and political themes. An Order of Australia, Italian government honours and a UN peace medal were conferred on him during the time of his dark cloud and after it cleared. He continued to spend most of his time with Angela Chan in Sydney, but never severed ties with Ellnor in Canberra. He eventually died of heart failure while ailing with kidney cancer, in a Canberra hospital in 2005, aged 78.

There were two funerals: a state funeral at St Christopher's Cathedral in Canberra with an Irish piper playing and his 'official wife' Ellnor as chief mourner, and civil libertarians and political friends and co-workers. The following week, another funeral was held at St Patrick's Cathedral in Sydney with a flamenco guitarist and writers, actors, journalists and Sydney friends. Chief mourner at this one was his companion of 25 years, Angela Chan.

As if two funerals weren't enough, Slippery Al also left two wills – and headaches and heartaches for the two wives in his life. For although he left little – 'half a house, an old VW and his army uniform' his lawyer guessed – both women had claims. In

Sydney, Grassby had signed a will in February 2005 thought to be in Angela Chan's favour. But in March or April, the month of his death, he had made another that might have gone the other way.

In death, as in life, Al Grassby was flamboyant, weak and shifty. All the things Don Mackay wasn't.

Postscript

Many Griffith residents wanted Mackay to receive a posthumous Order of Australia to acknowledge that he had died trying to do good and to counter the false rumours started by Grassby's criminal connections. But this was against official protocol.

In 1986, a senior Victorian police officer spoke at a public meeting in Griffith. He called on concerned citizens to fight to ensure that Mackay's campaign did not die with him. He suggested they raise funds for a special scholarship in his name to promote the study of organised crime. The Donald Mackay Churchill Fellowship has been awarded annually ever since, usually to a police officer to study overseas. The officer who made the call was Fred Silvester, first head of the Australian Bureau of Criminal Intelligence.

MELBOURNE

THE HOME OF
THE GUNMAN

5

PRE-EMPTIVE STRIKE

DEATH OF A PAINTER AND DOCKER

'Thank Christ it's you. I
thought it was the Kanes.'

LESLIE Herbert Kane might have been the toughest and wild-
est of three brothers who made their living scaring people, most
of them other gangsters. But to the woman who loved him, and
maybe still does, he was a man of contradictions: he ran with and
fought against some of the toughest crims in the country but he
(and his older brother Brian) didn't have tattoos, didn't smoke,
kept fit and were natty to the point of vanity. And both brothers
could be impulsively kind, especially to priests and children.

Judi Gay would become Les's second wife. He already had
two daughters with his first wife Pat when he met Judi at the
Winston Charles nightclub in Toorak Road in 1970. She was an
apprentice hairdresser and a keen sportswoman – she had played
for Victoria in under-16 netball (and would play the game at a
high level until her early 40s). She came from what Les called a
'squarehead' family: her father was a hard-working foreman mechanic at the Yarra Falls knitting mill in Abbotsford until the mill
closed, then a cleaner at the St Kilda Road army barracks.

At 21, Judi's good looks and physical vitality turned heads. At 25, Les Kane turned heads too, often by kicking them. He was a lean man with a strong nose and blazing cobalt blue eyes that contrasted with the tanned, olive-skinned features. It was a fierce and fearless face of the fighting Irish variety: it could belong to a prize fighter or an IRA terrorist. He combined a bit of both on the docks and in the pubs and nightclubs.

Judi was initially wary of the hard man with the intense gaze and the cocky self-assurance of one who backs himself as the toughest man in the room. Her first instincts might have been right but she was young and her heart over-ruled her head when he refused to take the hint and kept chasing her.

'I gave him a bodgie phone number to begin with. I didn't want to get mixed up with him,' she would recall. But he sought her out the following week, and rebuked her over the bogus telephone number. She made a weak excuse, pretended she'd made a mistake. This time, half flustered and half flattered, she gave him the right one. And in that careless split-second she changed her life.

Because, of course, he called her, suggesting a quiet meet at Pelligrinis restaurant in the city. And she went. She didn't like the fact he was married but he told her he was separated.

Within months they were living together in an apartment in East Melbourne. She liked it, she would say later, smiling at the memory of the carefree, animal joy of a new relationship with a man who seemed to have plenty of money – and spent it freely – and who apparently feared no one and nothing except boredom. They could walk across the Fitzroy Gardens to the city to theatres, restaurants and, inevitably, nightclubs, which was where the trouble happened. She recalls her new man being 'hounded by coppers' in the clubs, the Top Hat and the Galaxy.

'Brian didn't drink much at all but Les liked a drink and when he was drunk he was wild,' Judi would recall almost 40 years on.

'Most of the painters and dockers drank all the time and that led to a lot of the trouble. There was a lot of animosity with the coppers – like cowboys and Indians, really.'

She says quietly that Les was 'the most violent man in Australia' but that he could be impulsively generous. And there was something dashing about him and his brother Brian that some women found irresistible and some men admired. Other people were just intimidated by them. Of course, as the Kanes would find out, a reputation is just about the most dangerous thing you can have in the underworld. The brothers started building theirs early, from the time they went to St John's Catholic Primary School in East Melbourne to Collingwood Tech, known in the 1950s and 1960s as 'Pentridge Prep.'

Their father, Reg Kane, was a hard-drinking scrap metal merchant in Collingwood. The saying 'meaner than a junk yard dog' fitted him. He dealt in scrap and got into plenty, and he brought his boys up to fight his battles for him. As teenagers, they were urged to fight and got a taste for it. No wonder all three of Reg Kane's sons grew into violent men: Brian the fit, disciplined Golden Gloves boxer who became a high-level standover man; Les, for a time the most feared street fighter in Melbourne, and Ray, nicknamed 'Muscles', who lived a less public life of crime than his notorious older brothers but was whispered by some to be a more lethal gunman than either of them. In the end, Ray was the only one of the three to survive, though he served a sentence for murder.

Les, the second son, was born in Carlton on 1 December 1945, and joined Melbourne's traditional criminal breeding ground – the Painters and Dockers Union – at just fourteen.

Soon he and his brothers were making a tidy living from the docks, but not from hard work. They soon had a slice of the secret payment system that ensured the docks continued to function – at huge cost.

It was a brutally simple standover tactic where wages were paid to non-existent employees – or 'ghost' workers – in exchange for promises of industrial harmony. Les (like most 'dockies') picked up two pay packets every week. 'The foreman got four!' laughs Judi Kane.

It was straight out graft and corruption, as would later be revealed by Billy 'The Texan' Longley, but no one complained. Those who made waves could find themselves under them – somewhere in Port Phillip Bay. Men went 'on the missing list' and were never seen again. Such as Alfred 'The Ferret' Nelson, whose car was fished out of the water near South Wharf but whose body was never found.

It was in this environment that Les Kane excelled. He was physically brave, ruthless and reckless. But his strength was his weakness. When the fit took him, he was capable of almost anything. And 'fit' is a good word because violent rage would erupt in him as if something had short circuited in his brain.

His violent temper made him feared but it also landed him in court many times when he could have easily avoided trouble. It also meant he would make enemies with long memories and short fuses.

'Brian had a bit more decorum because he was Golden Gloves and everything but Les was "all in" and barred nothing,' recalls his widow Judi Kane, the handsome, much-respected woman who nurses memories – good and bad – of the man who gave her a rollercoaster ride and two children who are now successful adults.

'Les was fearless and had a terrible temper. He had bright blue eyes that flashed when he was angry ... he and Brian were fearless and they would pick up a gun. Les would just smash 'em. All his criminal record is for assault.' As far as she knows, he only ever did the one robbery – 'but it was a good one.'

A policeman who regularly locked up Les Kane says he was 'psychotic' and 'had a target on his head from an early age'.

One example of many, the policeman says, was that he 'stabbed his neighbour's dog, (belonging to) a nice Polish lady, and then wanted to carry on when I got there. I told him we could do this the easy way and he could come along – or I could call the posse and it would end badly. He decided to come along.'

By the time Kane was in his early 30s he had appeared in court 27 times – almost all for crimes of violence.

When Kane was just 21 he was asked to leave a Collingwood hotel. He responded by throwing two glasses of beer over the publican, a Mrs Irene Bennett. When another man intervened, he knocked him to the ground and kicked him in the face, break-ing several bones.

The judge, who sentenced Kane to two years and three months, described him as a 'violent, vicious and dangerous man.'

The judge seemed more outraged by the beer-throwing against the woman than by the male victim being kicked half to death.

Although Kane was considered among the best streetfighters in the Melbourne underworld in the early to mid-1970s, he did lose a bare-knuckled bout with Paul Higgins – a colourful detec-tive who would later hit his own legal hurdles after being charged with serious corruption that would lead to a marathon court case and a lengthy jail term.

The fight between the toughest cop and the toughest (but lighter) crim began in a city nightclub, the Top Hat, continued down three flights of stairs and ended with Kane unconscious in Bourke Street.

The 'hiding' didn't change Kane and, if anything, made him even more dangerously erratic.

In many incidents of that freewheeling era, there is the police record of how things occurred, and the scenario subsequently put in court by the defence. Then there is the hearsay version handed down by various people connected to the main players. Sometimes these accounts vary a lot in detail.

At a Sunday smorgasbord in the giant lounge of the Croxton Park Hotel in January 1971, Les Kane and a painter and docker mate, former boxer 'Frannie' Bayliss, were reportedly pestering two women. It ended badly when one of the pair of knockabouts poured a jug of beer over the women, according to two off-duty licensing squad police who happened to be working on the door and who assisted in removing the 'dockies'. The incident was virtually over when Les Kane turned around and shot one of the policemen in the leg with a pistol he was carrying.

It was as stupid as it was violent.

Judi Kane recalls the incident this way: 'Les shot an off-duty copper in the foot at the Croxton Park Hotel. He and Frannie Bayliss had been at a dockers' barrel somewhere and then went to the Croc. A bouncer wouldn't let them in. He was an off-duty copper. Les shot at the ground but he'd had a few drinks and got him in the foot.

'I can remember he came home and said we had to get out of town for a while. We went to Queensland to cool off and then sneaked back to Melbourne. But Brian Murphy (a well-known police identity) found us at Oak Park and kicked in the door. Frank Galbally got Les off, but there was an appeal and the second time he was sent to Beechworth prison.'

In another incident, Les was stabbed in a vicious hotel fight. Judi recalls it this way: 'A bloke stabbed Les in a pub in Port Melbourne. Les turned around and the bloke stabbed him three times, once in the bottom of the heart.

'"I went to throw a punch," he told me later, "and collapsed." Les's mates drove him to St Vincent's, to the emergency, and he told them to leave him outside on the footpath. They (hospital staff) came out and got him. Brian Murphy (the detective) went and saw him in hospital but Les wouldn't say who'd stabbed him. That was the code. But Brian (Kane) went around to the bloke's house later with a shotgun. The bloke came to the door with his wife in front of him and said there were kids in the house. Brian let a few shots go and left. But I think they caught up with him later.'

The stabber was Cornelius Robert Irwin, but the police didn't know that for some time. Les was in no mood to tell them. Not only had he been stabbed but he was also on the run, having failed to attend court on earlier serious assault charges. When Brian Murphy arrived, Kane's father allegedly offered him $5000 to look the other way. But 'Skull' Murphy declined the offer, identified the glowering victim as Les Kane and the assault warrant was served on him in his hospital bed. Being stabbed in the chest three times can slow you down – but in Kane's case, not for long.

The starkest example of Les Kane's violent streak was the brutal bashing of a young sailor and his mate after a 'road rage' incident.

It happened 5 July 1975, when Kane was in the passenger seat of a car driven by another painter and docker, Peter Aloysius Howard, and they were cut off in Flemington Road by a car driven by a naval rating.

The official story is that Kane and his mate gave chase along the Tullamarine freeway, side-swiping the sailor's car and forcing it off the road near the Glenroy exit.

Not in dispute is that Kane used a panel-beating hammer to inflict fifteen separate fractures to the man's skull, leaving him more dead than alive. His fellow painter and docker, meanwhile, took to the passenger, a clerk from Broadmeadows, punching him to the ground and then kicking him.

By coincidence, the beaten clerk's surname was Prendergast – a name that would later feature heavily in Kane's life and death.

One of the arresting police from the road rage incident said later: 'Les was the most feared man in the underworld and the most violent bloke I have ever come across. He was smooth and charming and then he would snap.'

He said that at the line-up Kane stood passively – until he was identified. 'Then he jumped from the line and physically threatened the witness. He was surrounded by police but he just didn't care.'

Later, when Kane had calmed down, a detective told him he was an idiot. 'I said, "You make a fortune from standing over crooks and from ghosted wages and you never got caught. Then you get involved in this sort of shit. It just doesn't make sense".

'He just smiled. He knew I was right but he was never going to change.

'If he could have controlled his violent streak he would have ended up a rich man. But leopards don't change their spots and the Kanes couldn't change their mean streaks.'

A lifetime later, Judi Kane would probably agree with the thrust of the policeman's thoughts, but she tells the version of the story that the painters and dockers' favourite lawyer, the legendary 'Mr Frank' Galbally, used to fight the charge in court.

'Les and his workmate Peter were coming home after work after having a beer at the Ivanhoe Hotel in Collingwood. Peter was a lovely bloke and never in any trouble. His wife was a nurse and they had five kids. He drove an old FC Holden wagon, which was slow. Peter was older than Les, and wearing his glasses. It was about 8 o'clock at night, and the seats in the old car were worn-out and low so Peter and Les looked small and old. Along come these hoons in a car and start yelling at them to "Get off the road, you old bloke!" They supposedly threw a can at the FC. Les got Peter to roll down the window and he spoke to them. Then they stopped ahead and waited. Les said 'pull over' to Peter. He grabbed a hammer and battered two of them unconscious. He nearly killed them. I saw the (police) photographs later.

'Peter had put his glasses in their case on the roof of the car. When they drove off, the case fell on the road. It had Peter's name and address on it. That's how the coppers knew who to look for. Next night the police came for Les.'

The case was beyond even Galbally's powers of persuasion. On 1 November 1976, Kane was sentenced to five years prison with a minimum of three and a half for wounding with intent. His mate Howard got six months for assault.

The constant threat of violence eventually became too much for Judi. Once, Les fired shots over her head, trying to 'ping' some new enemy he'd made in yet another pub in Port Melbourne. It got so she didn't want to go out with him because he had too many fights that would end in bashings or shootings.

'I was living with the most violent man in Australia,' she admits. 'All his convictions were for assault ... He'd done a total of seven years for assault before I met him. He'd say to me he was the skinny bloke on the beach and that there was always someone who wanted to kick sand in his face.'

Those who followed in the Kanes' violent footsteps years later failed to learn the lessons of history.

Another gangster with a short fuse who liked to show how tough he was by terrorising weaker people was Jason Moran – who would be gunned down in June 2003.

In the late 1990s, Moran was cut off while driving along Punt Road. In the car with him was Russell Warren Smith, who later described how Moran had grabbed a wheel brace, smashed the other motorist's windscreen, dragged him from the car and beat him severely. No one stopped to help.

'Jason got back in the car and was laughing,' Smith said later.

Moran's actions were so similar to Les Kane's you would think they were related by blood. Close – but no cigar. Moran was Les Kane's son-in-law: he married Trish, Kane's daughter by his first wife, Pat.

In between court appearances, jail and the docks, Kane built a reputation as an underworld hard man. He wasn't the only one.

Raymond Patrick Bennett, also known to many by his boyhood name of Ray Chuck, was tough, cool and violent. 'He was more professional than Kane. He was less likely to fly off the handle and better with a gun. You could talk to him and you knew he meant what he said,' one policeman recalled of Bennett.

While the Kanes liked to take a percentage of other gangsters' work, according to police, Bennett was the independent type who preferred to set up his own jobs.

The Kanes and Bennett's crew had known each other for years and had co-existed well enough until there was a fatal clash of greed, power and ego.

As Judi Kane was to recall: 'Brian and Les would kill you. They got sick of it in the end but unfortunately they reaped what they sowed.'

TRAVEL broadens the mind. Ray Chuck, later known as Bennett, the kid from Chiltern in north-east Victoria, had moved to Collingwood as a teenager. By the time he was a fully-grown bank robber and gunman, his horizons had broadened.

While the remorseless Kane brothers dominated their hometown, the restless Bennett moved on. In the mid-1970s he went to Europe for a working holiday. Like many 'good crooks' from Sydney and Melbourne, Bennett and his great mate Brian O'Callaghan joined the notorious, 'Kangaroo Gang' that robbed jewellery stores and other ripe targets in the UK and on the Continent.

For Bennett, his criminal ventures overseas were like a finishing school: he learned new techniques to try back in Australia. By the time he was ready to fly home he had virtually completed a master's degree in world's best practice stick-ups. It was as if he had compiled a 'robber's rulebook' – a how-to guide for what the English called armed 'blags'.

He was particularly impressed with the Wembley Mob – a gang of East London crooks who carried out at least a dozen major armed robberies over four years. Their methods involved meticulous planning, gathering intelligence through cultivating insiders, specialised training, recruiting a close-knit team that wouldn't break ranks and devising schemes to launder funds. (Ironically, they were brought down when a key member turned into a 'supergrass'.)

No one knew it at the time but the first clue that Bennett was planning a triumphant return to the armed robbery business in Melbourne was when he was spied by an alert policeman in the Moonee Ponds area one day in late 1975. It turned out that he was on a flying visit – literally. He had flown in for a few days to scout the scene while on pre-release leave from prison on the Isle of Wight. He then flew back to finish his sentence – and plot his big move.

When Bennett returned again he was ready to execute the job that other armed robbers, including James Edward 'Jockey' Smith, had reputedly considered but decided was too risky.

Bennett recruited a team of nine for the Bookie Robbery and all of them had specific jobs, including organising stolen cars, checking the escape route, setting up laundering methods, organising guns and cultivating an inside source.

The team was said to include Vincent Mikkelsen, Laurie Prendergast, Ian Revell Carroll, Anthony Paul McNamara, Dennis William Smith, Normie Lee and two brothers who had done plenty of stick-ups.

Bennett also consulted an outsider, a time and motion expert with no criminal record who had helped plan armed robberies in Melbourne, Sydney and Perth.

The team was broken into an assault group of six with a back-up unit of three.

Bennett took the crew on a mini commando course in the bush in central Victoria, ruling that there would be no drinking and no women. To the team that was more a guideline than a rule and, as footballers and soldiers have done in similar situations, they broke out of boot camp to 'play up' at a nearby town.

The target was the Victorian Club, then in Queen Street, where bookies settled after race day. Bennett chose the date – 21 April 1976 – the first settling day after Easter. He knew the bookies would be settling not for one, but three race meetings. Some suggest that an old bookmaker had pointed out this tempting target, later described by a senior policeman as 'an over-ripe plum waiting to be picked.'

Police were later told the team had a dry run in the deserted building during the Easter break. When the time came for the real thing, the gang, armed with sub-machine guns, made their move on the bookies. All went to plan – or nearly. One security guard bravely but unwisely went for his .38 revolver and was smashed to the floor with a gun butt.

Normally, three members of the police Consorting Squad would turn up at lunchtime on settling day to act as extra security. But on the day of the robbery, the 'consorters' were ordered to Frankston by a senior officer on what would turn out to be a wild goose chase. Some in the squad still believe that Ray Bennett had the senior officer in his pocket and that he had deliberately nobbled the squad with the bogus Frankston job to make it easy for the robbery team to pull off the robbery unopposed. In any case, it probably prevented a gun battle that could have ended in a bloodbath.

After the money was delivered to settle for 116 bookmakers, the gang took just eleven minutes to commit the robbery.

They grabbed 118 calico bags filled with cash. The total stolen will never be known. The official amount was declared at $1.4 million, although wild guesses that it might have been more than $10 million have been thrown around because of unrecorded cash bets made 'on the nod' with trusted punters. Those most likely to know, bookies in the building that day, privately suggest the total was perhaps up to $2 million, still a staggering sum at a time when a house (now worth $2 million) could be bought then for $50,000.

There are two theories on what happened to the money. One was that the gang had rented an office in the same building and hid the cash there for weeks. The other, accepted by the police, was that the money was put in a stolen laundry van and driven away by Dennis 'Greedy' Smith.

The van was well-chosen, as the cash was delivered to people who laundered it as part of the master plan. Some was laundered through a female real estate agent in Sydney who bought property in New South Wales, Queensland and Victoria. Some was sent to Manila via Canada and was used there to set up Smith's vice club, the Aussie Bar, later used as an offshore safe house by gangsters from Melbourne and Sydney. More of the cash was laundered through bent lawyers' trust accounts.

Shortly after the robbery, Bennett's mother collapsed in a lawyer's office with a fatal heart attack. When ambulance officers removed her outer clothes in a frantic effort to revive her, they found $90,000 cash in her undergarments. She had discovered that you can have too much of a good thing – that while thermal underwear is one thing, several kilograms of hot banknotes is not what the doctor ordered.

Normie Lee, one of the conspirators, was like a brother to Ray Bennett and he promised him he would never talk to police. He was as good as his word. One of the key money men, Lee once took $60,000 to his lawyers in a plastic garbage bag, which was more comfortable than trying to hide it in his jocks and socks. But though police had good reasons to suspect the inscrutable Lee, they could never get him to say anything.

Lee was eventually charged with receiving $110,000 of the proceeds of the bookie robbery. Police claimed he used his share to buy new equipment for his dim sim factory.

Detectives seized his office safe but he refused to give them the keys to open it. Even when they took the safe to the Russell Street police quadrangle and hired a safe expert to cut it open, he stayed silent. So the expert fired up the 'oxy' torch and destroyed the safe to get it open. It was empty. But Lee had not said a word or offered a key to save it.

Police weren't the only ones looking for the bookie robbers. One crew made contact with the insurance company wanting a reward for 'shopping' the bandits. And the bookie robbers reputedly received the undivided attention of the Sydney 'Toecutters', so named because they would torture fellow criminals until they gave up their stash of cash. And police believe that the Kanes wanted a share, although this is disputed in some quarters.

As part of his planning, the canny Bennett had instructed his men to keep a low profile and not to splash cash around after the robbery in a way that would attract attention. But a chance remark during the robbery put them in the frame – and under the gun. When the masked men ordered all 31 present in the club to lie face down, one masked gunman said to the then well-known boxing trainer Ambrose Palmer, 'You too, Ambrose.'

The robber instantly regretted his half-friendly throwaway line. He had once trained at Palmer's gymnasium (as did world champion Johnny Famechon) and knew the old man might recognise his voice. Palmer naturally forgot to mention this to police, the story goes, but accidentally let slip the robber's identity to people connected with the Kane brothers and other painters and dockers, who were well known in boxing circles. Word soon got around, and members of Bennett's gang became targets for opportunists who wanted a share of the bookies' cash.

It was an ideal scenario for gang warfare. And that war was declared in a Richmond hotel in mid-1978, when Vincent Mikkelsen – a friend of Bennett's and once a friend of Les Kane – refused a drink from Brian Kane and tossed out an insult about not drinking with 'old men'. That was bad enough, but Mikkelsen committed an even graver social indiscretion by biting off part of Brian Kane's ear in the resulting fight.

Both men were so injured in the brawl they needed hospital treatment but the damage to Brian Kane's ear was a daily reminder that he had been successfully challenged as the toughest man on the block.

Musing much later about Kane's reaction to his humiliating disfigurement, Bennett's lawyer Joe Gullaci (later a respected judge) said: 'It's hard to be the number one standover man in town when you've got a piece bitten out of your ear.'

That mouthful of ear was eventually to give Melbourne's underworld heartburn and put the wind up the police force. But all Brian Kane knew then was that it was bad for his reputation – and that wasn't good for business, let alone his ego.

Mikkelsen came to expect massive retaliation. Bennett suggested Mikkelsen's life be spared, and was warned: 'If you stick your head in, it will be blown off.' If war had not been formally declared before that, now it was on. And there was no Geneva Convention.

JUST four years earlier, when Les had been in jail at Beechworth for shooting the off-duty policeman in the foot at the Croxton Park Hotel, Vinnie Mikkelsen and his wife Flossie had lived in the same neighbourhood – 'just around the corner in Broady', as Judi

Kane remembered it. If the Mikkelsens weren't close friends with Les and Judi then they were close to it. Judi was heavily pregnant with her second child, and when her waters broke she rang Vinnie Mikkelsen to help. 'And he drove me to the Royal Women's' where she gave birth to her son. Les's parents, Reg and Alice Kane, who had moved in while Les was 'away', stayed home to look after Judi's two-year-old daughter.

'Four years later it had all turned nasty,' she says. She thinks the notorious fight in Richmond that led to the feud was orchestrated by Ray Bennett and his supporters to bring festering resentments to a head.

'The night Brian had a fight at PA's, the pub in Church Street near the river, they'd been following Brian. I reckon it was a set up,' she told the authors.

'Les and Chuck were both street fighters, and had been friends in the old days. The trouble started at a barrel behind St Ignatius in Richmond. Brian was there. He thought Chuck was arrogant – he'd been knocking people off – and Brian might have said something like, "Don't think you're going to do that to us." Of course, he had to take up the challenge, and that's how it started, really.

'Chuck was deep and dark, don't worry about that. Smart at what he did. We think he stewed on it. Got Vinnie on his posse, sort of thing.'

Specifically, Chuck had knocked off 'Wingy', a painter and docker with a withered arm and what some contemporaries unsympathetically called a big mouth. Whatever the reason, it had caused him to go on the missing list – and heightened the tensions between the two camps.

AFTER most of Brian Kane's left ear went missing the threats flew on both sides. And each side knew such threats were neither idle nor boastful. It was a case of who would get in first. Blink and you were brown bread.

Les Kane was an inner-suburban boy, well-known in Collingwood, Richmond and Port Melbourne and later moving to Broadmeadows and, ultimately, to the distant eastern suburbs to avoid his enemies.

By 1978 it was clear the Kanes and their allies – including Graham 'The Munster' Kinniburgh, Wally Russian and the Morans – were worried about the brothers' safety. Les tried to make himself a less obvious target – moving Judi and their two young children to a nondescript unit in Wantirna in the outer eastern suburbs.

Les and Judi had lived together in a de facto relationship for years because Les, although separated, did not finalise his divorce from his first wife, Pat, until three months before marrying Judi in 1977.

Judi was widely regarded as a good woman who fell for the wrong man. She was too loyal ever to say so, but the man she loved often treated her violently. Police were told that he beat her, once hitting her so hard she needed plastic surgery to repair the smashed cheekbone.

The surgeon wrote on her cheek in large letters – 'DO NOT TOUCH.'

It may have been a message for the nursing staff or, perhaps, a stronger one for the guilty husband with the terrible temper.

Another time he put a noose around her neck, tying the rope over a door to leave her hanging with her toes just touching the ground for an agonising ten minutes.

Finally she had enough and shortly after their marriage she took the kids and fled to Sydney. She returned a few weeks later to give the marriage another chance – 'for the sake of the children'. It was a decision that represented the triumph of hope over experience. As it turned out, it wasn't a wise one. They were in too deep to have any chance of living happily ever after.

THERE were two sides to Les Kane. The cunning, careful streak in him prompted him to drive to work at the docks in his overalls in a Morris mini van, so humble and unpretentious and cheap it was almost an in-joke, because anyone that mattered knew that he could (and did) afford much better wheels.

But the other side of Kane – the narcissistic big noter who wanted to be noticed and admired, with his double-header pay packets plus whatever 'good earns' he could pick up from standover, smuggling, robbery, thieving and gambling – meant he could not and would not stay under the radar the way more prudent operators might. The Collingwood streetfighting 'lair' in him made him a sucker for the status symbols coveted by young men who know no better.

So, despite moving swiftly and secretly one night from the western suburbs to the foreign territory of Wantirna, and trying to 'go into smoke', Kane would not part with his loud pink Ford Futura or the purple Monaro that Judi drove. Keeping the distinctive pink Futura was probably a fatal mistake.

Although the move was for their own safety, Judi couldn't help resenting it. An accomplished netballer, she'd had to give up playing A-grade with her own team in the western suburbs. Her brother-in-law had said not to worry because she could play with a local team at Wantirna but it wasn't the same for Judi, playing with a second rate side after playing at the top level.

Life went on. Until 19 October 1978, a Thursday, when Les took his family to dinner at his sister Valetta's house about 5pm, driving the pink Ford.

When they returned just over four hours later, he backed the Ford into the driveway next to their rented three-bedroom unit on Mountain Highway.

When they got there, the family's miniature long-haired dachshund, Simon, which Les had bought for Judi in Beaudesert in Queensland, was sitting on a seat on the porch.

Judi would later say everything seemed normal – but it wasn't quite, as she would realise too late.

After Les opened the door and dropped the keys on the kitchen table, Judi picked up the dachshund and carried him down the hall. If she had put the little dog down inside, she would later tell herself, perhaps it might have ended differently. But she had no reason to, and didn't. She went to the back door and put the dog in the back yard, where he had a kennel, and never gave him a thought until later.

Judi put Justin, who was four, into bed in his room, near the front door. Les put their six-year-old daughter Martine to bed in her room and turned off the heater and lights. As Judi walked past to fetch some ironing from the hall table, Les was tucking Martine into bed.

As Judi returned with the ironing – fresh sheets to make the bed in the main bedroom – she saw Les in the bathroom, with the door open. He was using her eyebrow tweezers to pluck stray grey whiskers from his Zapata moustache. 'So vain,' she would recall, allowing herself to relive the worst moments of her life.

She went into the main bedroom with the sheets. She turned on the light and they were there, waiting: three men, each armed with a long-barrelled firearm, silencers attached. She immediately recognised Bennett and Mikkelsen and screamed, 'Les, look out!' She would later recall that the third man was wearing a ski-mask but it did not disguise him very well. She would later describe him in court as having blond, shoulder length hair and a fair complexion. In fact, she knew him. It was Laurie Prendergast. He grabbed her by the throat and pushed her back into her daughter's room. She instinctively lay over the little girl to protect her.

She heard her husband cry out, 'Oh, no!' as the two gunmen forced their way into the bathroom. He knew what was coming. So did they.

The man in the bedroom was telling Judi, 'Sh, Sh,' but she heard the barrage of muffled shots. Judi leapt up, her mother's instincts roused, forcing Prendergast back and yelling for her little boy: 'My son!'

Ray Chuck grabbed the toddler from his room and thrust him at Judi and shut the door. Exactly 30 years later, by now a father himself, Justin would recall being carried upside down by the strange man, remember his mother's anguish on that terrible night.

'What have you done to my dad?' six-year-old Martine yelled. The masked man Judi later identified as Prendergast, left the room and she was able to look out the door, down the hall. She saw Les's body lying on the mat near the front door. He made a groaning sound but it wasn't speech, just air escaping from his lungs.

'I called out, "Les!" twice … As I approached his body I saw blood all over his face and hair and a pool of blood on the carpet under his head. He moaned as I called his name and this seemed to be his last breath and he was still after that.'

She saw the front door was open and hoped the killers had gone. But they returned and one of them menaced her with a gun and ordered her back into the bedroom. She tried to calm the children.

She heard the Ford's motor start, the boot slam and then … silence.

When she came out Les's body was gone and so was his car. Neither would ever be found.

The killers had torn the telephone from the wall. She didn't go to the neighbours. Why, she couldn't say later. Except maybe that Les had drummed into her that if anything happened to him

130

– and he often said he wouldn't make old bones – then she should go to Brian and do what Brian said. So she stuck to the staunch criminal code of the family she had married into.

She grabbed the kids and jumped into her car and drove to a telephone box. She called Les's parents and stammered her awful story and her father-in-law, Reg Kane, asked: 'Are you being tailed?' He thought the killers might follow her to get at Brian and Ray, the surviving brothers.

Brian came to her. He was crying. He went into the house and saw the scene and came out white and shaking.

He was so sorry, he said. He didn't go to the police and neither did Judi. Not yet.

She stayed with her in-laws. Next day she returned with her brother-in-law, Valetta Kane's husband.

'He and I cleaned the bathroom together,' she would tell the authors. 'Well, I started to and broke down, so he had to do most of it on his own. There were brain particles and blood which covered the whole floor.

'I saw tissue like sinews where Les's head had been lying near the front entrance.

'I sopped or picked them up with a towel.' She used a mop and a bucket to try and clean the blood from the carpet but the stains were too hard to move.

After a few days, when it was clear that the killers had 'gone into smoke', Brian hinted he wouldn't stand in Judi's way if she talked to the law. His reason was at least, that way, he would 'know where they were'. The advantage of this was twofold: while the killers were in custody or attending court, they would not be hunting him. And if he knew where they would be at a given time and place, he might get the chance to 'back up'. Honor, if not survival, demanded revenge. In the meantime, once police knew Les Kane was dead, the case was handed to the homicide squad.

It was only afterwards, when the shock and the adrenalin wore off, that a niggling detail pushed to the surface of Judi's mind: she recalled that she had left Simon the dachshund in the unit when they'd gone out for dinner that night. That meant that when they found the dog outside on their return, it was a sign that someone must have let him out. And that the intruders had put him in the deck chair, because his legs were too short for him to jump up, she thought. It was an incongruously gentle act to an animal by a man intent on murderous violence towards a former friend. But she has no doubt that's what happened.

Judi often wondered later: if she'd let the dachshund run loose in the hallway that night, would it have gone straight to the bedroom door and started barking and warned them of intruders? Given that there were three men, armed with semi-automatic weapons modified to fire like machine guns, it would surely still have been a fatally one-sided confrontation. Les had a pistol in the pocket of a coat hanging up handy. Even if he'd got to it he was unlikely to have stood a chance. Or would he? Superior odds had never frightened him. That's why three men had come for him. And some still whisper there was a fourth, a driver left outside who later helped dispose of the body and the car.

THE men who ambushed Les Kane were so confident that the code of silence would never crack that two of them didn't even bother with disguises and the third was easy to recognize. They had history on their side. In the 1950s, 60s and 70s police drew a blank when pursuing painters and dockers murders because witnesses refused to talk.

The best-known example of this happened on 6 February 1958, after gangster Freddie 'The Frog' Harrison pulled up at South Wharf in his 1953 Ford Customline to pick up his pay and return a borrowed trailer. As he was unhooking the trailer, a man produced a shotgun and said, 'This is yours, Fred,' and shot Harrison in the head.

There were thirty men in the area. Each later said he saw nothing. A dozen potential witnesses declared they were in the toilet at the time. It was a two-man toilet.

The man who was helping Harrison uncouple the trailer was covered with blood. He told police that when he heard the blast he looked right and walked off. The shot had come from his left so, naturally, he saw nothing.

It was part of the culture of the Melbourne underworld that no one talked. And the killers obviously believed that no one would ever give evidence against them.

But after a quiet hint from her brother-in-law Brian Kane, Judi spoke to the head of homicide, Detective Chief Inspector Paul Delianis. And she decided to do something extraordinary in her social circle – to tell the truth to the authorities.

She immediately identified two of the suspects, Mikkelsen and Bennett, and later identified the masked third man as Prendergast.

She had known the three for years. Mikkelsen, after all, had been the near neighbour in Broadmeadows who had driven her to hospital to have a baby when Les was in prison in 1974.

But after the fight between Mikkelsen and Brian Kane, the friendship was fatally fractured.

Les knew that when Bennett became involved it would probably end in gunplay. Bennett and his mates liked guns. His bookie robbers had been armed with semi-automatic rifles modified to fire continuously like a sub-machine gun. The backyard gunsmithing had reputedly been done by the notorious Jimmy the Pom', Linus Patrick Driscoll of the notorious Sydney 'toecutters', so named because they used bolt cutters to torture armed robbers to force them to give up their haul.

When Les told Judi he had been told Bennett was going to try to kill him she couldn't understand why someone she had known so long would become a lethal enemy.

She told her husband he shouldn't take the talk too seriously but he had said, 'Don't underestimate him. I know.'

He was dead right.

But although his body and his Ford were never found, the three murder suspects were.

FOR the first time in years police had an eye witness in a gangland murder prepared to give evidence.

It was years before a formal witness-protection program would be available, so homicide chief Delianis quietly organised for Judi Kane to be cared for by one of Victoria's most respected policewomen – Pat Hunter.

Despite the nature of her work, Pat Hunter did not let herself become cynical. She always tried to see the best in people. She and Judi soon became firm friends. One well-meaning detective warned Pat she was blind to the 'real' Judi Kane – describing her as just a 'gangster's moll.' He was wrong.

Later, when Pat was diagnosed with leukaemia, it was Judi who would nurse her. And the doubting detective later apologised to Judi. 'I was wrong, she was real quality,' he admitted later.

At Pat Hunter's funeral, the front row of the left side of the chapel was reserved for top ranking police – and Judi Kane. She had earned everyone's respect – and never let anyone down.

But back in 1978, she was a rare commodity – an eye witness in a triple murder.

For the three gunmen, the police were the last of their considerable problems. By killing Kane they risked immediate and deadly retaliation. The evidence that they knew this was overwhelming.

Ray Bennett's 11-year-old son had settled well into Keilor Heights High School and was seen as an attentive and cheerful student. So his Year 7 co-ordinator John Shaw was surprised when the boy stopped attending class.

When he asked why young Bennett was missing he was told the boy was sick, but there was no note or doctor's certificate. After a week, the teacher telephoned home and spoke to the boy's grandmother.

'I asked if Danny was sick. She appeared upset and said that Danny was happy at school, he did not want to be away from school but it was not his fault he had not attended.'

Ray Bennett's wife Gail later told Shaw the family would be away in Queensland for a month while their son 'convalesced'. The teacher prepared some tests and even lent his absent student a text-book for his time away.

He didn't see the boy – or the book – again.

The Bennetts did not contact the school again and strangely, no application for a transfer for the young Bennett was ever received.

When police asked Shaw to check the last day Danny Bennett went to class, attendance records showed it was 19 October ... the day Les Kane had been shot dead.

Police documents later released under Freedom of Information stated: '... have no knowledge of his whereabouts. By the 19th December, 1978, Bennett's solicitor could not locate him. He failed to make his whereabouts known to the parties involved in the purchase of a house which he contracted to buy, and subsequently lost a substantial amount of money. His wife and child were last seen in Queensland. The current whereabouts of he and his family are unknown.'

Police would also discover that Bennett would take out life insurance policies – first checking they would be valid in the event of his murder.

For the Mikkelsen family the story was similar. Vinnie Mikkelsen's daughter suddenly stopped going to Meadow Fair North Primary School after 18 October and his son vanished two days later.

No explanation was given. So both the Bennett and Mikkelsen families made themselves scarce as soon as Les Kane disappeared – but before it was publicly known he was missing.

They knew Kane was dead well before the police did.

One of the first calls Judi Kane made had been to the Bowling Green Hotel in Carlton, then frequented by crooks and coppers.

'Les is off,' she told a close associate at the pub. ('Off' is underworld shorthand for murdered).

The three suspects ran but they couldn't hide – for long. On 1 December, the Special Operations Group found Prendergast hiding in a rented flat in Essendon.

By the time homicide Detective Senior Sergeant Arthur Robbins entered the flat, Prendergast was lying on his stomach next to the double bed, naked and handcuffed. It wasn't a good look.

Prendergast looked up and said, 'Thank Christ it's you.'

Robbins asked what he meant and Prendergast answered, 'I thought it was the Kanes.'

Certainly Mikkelsen was even more determined to avoid a chance meeting with anyone connected to the Kanes. He headed to outback Western Australia, where he took up mining – a dirty, dangerous occupation but safer than the one he'd left behind.

Back home in Melbourne, someone left a message that they were keen to catch up. On the same day as Prendergast was arrested, Mikkelsen's Broadmeadows home was firebombed.

In January 1979, Mikkelsen was arrested in Karratha, a small mining town 1600 kilometres from Perth.

Prendergast, Mikkelsen and Bennett were charged with Les Kane's murder and Judi Kane would be the star witness.

Police documents prepared for the prosecution said 'evidence of flight will be relied on to show a consciousness of guilt in the cases of Bennett and Mikkelsen' but said the motive for Les Kane's death was not clear apart from the fact there had been 'some bad feeling ... between Kane and Mikkelsen for some time.'

IN court, defence lawyers savaged Judi Kane. They questioned her about any beatings she had suffered, implying that she had much to gain from her husband's disappearance.

They argued he could have been killed by warring factions in the Painters and Dockers or other enemies in the underworld.

The forensic evidence left little doubt that Kane was dead. The traces of brain matter found on the doormat told them that.

But there was no body, and that is nearly always an advantage to the defence.

Prendergast's barrister Michael Kelly gave one of the best closing speeches ever heard in the Supreme Court, one that had jury members literally sitting on the edge of their seats, and that other lawyers still mention decades later.

The jury acquitted all three. But their real peers – in the underworld – had found them guilty long before. And they were waiting for the chance to pass sentence.

INSIDE JOB

WHO KILLED THE GREAT BOOKIE ROBBER?

Everybody knows he is a target.
Except, it seems, the police
whose job it is to know.

THE man in the dock knows there's a bullet out there somewhere with his name on it. But he doesn't know it's already in the hit man's revolver, and there's an itchy finger on the trigger, counting down the minutes.

He is Raymond Patrick Bennett, also known as Ray Chuck, and has just stepped into the old Melbourne Magistrates Court from the holding cells.

If he's worried, it doesn't show on his deadpan boxer's face, close to handsome despite its broken nose sprinkled with freckles and dark eyes set in a hard gaze. It's a face that doesn't quite match the bold check jacket with the leather elbow patches, which looks a little like something a jackaroo might buy in a reckless moment on a city holiday.

At 31, Bennett could be among the most dashing Australian crooks of his generation, but a reputation like that wins enemies, and he has plenty. So many that, for seven weeks before this day in court, he has pointedly avoided bail, preferring the predictable discomforts of the Pentridge remand yards to his chances on the outside. He's always been game, but not foolhardy.

Still, he ought to feel safe here, in court, surrounded by dozens of people – including lawyers and policemen – and just across the road from Russell Street police headquarters. But he doesn't.

He has told his lawyer, who waits above, that he wants his wife kept away from the public areas of the court. He has taken out a huge life insurance policy, asking if the company will pay if he's 'shot walking down the street'. Months earlier, he sent his young son overseas to keep him out of danger. In one of the court cells reached through the door behind him is a message freshly written on the wall: RAY CHUCK, YOU WILL GET YOUR'S IN DUE COURSE YOU FUCKEN DOG.

Everybody knows he is a target. Except, it seems, the police whose job it is to know.

Bennett is in court for committal on armed robbery charges over a $69,000 payroll heist in Yarraville. A magistrate has to weigh the evidence to judge if he should be tried in a higher court.

Like all prisoners in custody who have to front a magistrate, he has been brought in through the Court One dock. Committals are automatically adjourned to one of the two courts upstairs, in a double-storey extension behind the main court.

Depending on who's telling the story, three – or perhaps two – detectives escort Bennett past the crowded bench seats and people standing at the back of the room, and into the open courtyard for the short walk to the stairs leading to courts ten and eleven.

Certainly more than one person was interested in Bennett's court proceedings that day. At 8.50am Clerk of Courts Mary Bourke received a call from a man who said, 'What court is Chuck in?' when asked who was calling, the man said he was the accused's brother. She told him it would either be Court 10 or 11.

By coincidence, there is a union demonstration at Trades Hall a block away and 167 officers have been called out, leaving Russell Street short of the uniformed police who usually escort prisoners. Which is why, it is later explained, two consorting squad detectives called Glare and Strang are asked to help an armed robbery detective, John Mugavin, to escort Bennett.

The consorters are tired and irritable. They have been entertaining interstate detectives down for the Spring Carnival for weeks and are deeply hung over. They have gone to the court to check dates for four upcoming cases and to buy milkshakes to line their tender tummies.

They don't want to be in court doing escort duties. They want to do it quickly but there is a delay. Bennett doesn't want to walk past the group hanging around outside the court in case he is recognised by witnesses in the case.

Glare checks the scene and spots a man in a suit with tinted glasses, shoulder-length hair and a neatly trimmed black beard. He assumes he is a solicitor. 'It's all clear,' he tells the escorting police.

As Bennett and his escort walk past, a young constable waiting to give evidence mistakes the well-dressed robber for another detective. It's easy to see why. The dashing crook is a cut above the crowd in the court-yard.

The nineteenth century court is Dickensian, and Hogarth could draw those waiting their turn in the dock. There are pimps, prostitutes, thieves, vagrants, drunks, louts and lost souls from the seedy side of a big city – the bad, the sad and the slightly mad, all chain smoking in the court yard. Bit players in this depressing daily drama, they watch surreptitiously as Bennett the underworld star is led past, through the doors and upstairs to his fate.

A minute later, three shots crash through the buzz of muttered conversations. There is a clatter of footsteps in the sudden silence. Someone upstairs yells: 'It's a .38. Get a gun!' Then the screaming starts.

A young *Age* reporter in the main court looks at his watch and scrawls down the time. It is 10.17am on that Monday morning, six days after the 1979 Melbourne Cup.

WHEN he heard the shots Constable Chris Carnie jumped up from his bench in the courtyard. So did Constable Alan Hill, who'd been waiting nervously to give evidence in the first case of his new career.

The two uniformed officers ran to the door leading to the stairs. Later, they gave slightly different accounts of where Bennett was standing, but it was probably on the landing between the first and second flight of steps. What neither ever forgets is that he had his arms crossed over his chest, and was bleeding from wounds in both hands. He said: 'I've been shot in the heart.'

Carnie caught Bennett as his legs buckled. He and Hill carried him through the courtyard and into the tiled vestibule outside the clerk's office near the Russell Street doorway. Hill, a former Navy medic, tried mouth to mouth and heart massage. He knew it was no use. A bullet had burst the pulmonary artery; Bennett was drowning in his own blood.

Bennett's lawyer, Joe Gullaci, who would later become a no-nonsense County Court Judge, rushed downstairs with the dying man's wife, Gail. He pushed the stricken woman (he described her years later as 'incredibly brave') into the clerk's office so she couldn't see the wounds. An ambulance came, but police stopped the dying man's wife and lawyer getting in it to go to St Vincent's hospital. They jumped in a police car, but the driver took them in exactly the wrong direction – towards Elizabeth Street.

It was symbolic, perhaps, of the way the whole affair was handled. Except by the gunman, whose timing and preparation seemed almost too good to be true.

A court reporter for *The Sun* newspaper, Julie Herd, had sat briefly on a bench beside the man before going into court ten to wait for the case to begin. She assumed he was a lawyer. He had gold-rimmed glasses, a full head of hair and a beard. He appeared calm and was dressed, she thought, in a dark blue suit.

Glare said the man walked towards Bennett, looked at him and said, 'Cop this, you mother fucker,' as he drew a snub-nosed revolver from inside his coat and fired three shots.

Bennett turned and ran down the stairs. Glare yelled, 'He's off, grab him!' Mugavin chased Bennett, assuming the shots were blanks and that it was an escape attempt, he later said.

Glare moved towards the gunman, who pointed the pistol at him and warned: 'Don't make me do it.' According to later coronial evidence, Glare's colleague Paul Strang was inside the courtroom, where he helped Detective Sergeant Noel Anderson remove a pistol – allegedly used in Bennett's armed robbery – from an exhibit bag.

Ironically not all the bullets fitted the gun – meaning Bennett may have been able to beat the payroll charges. But by this stage he was past caring.

Meanwhile, the gunman had threatened a civilian witness, Raymond Aarons, ('Move and I'll blow your fucking head off!'), then waited to see if anyone was going to follow him and slipped through a side door leading down a maze of back stairs and passages to a tin shed behind the police garage. An inspector, Bill Horman, later to be promoted to Deputy Commissioner and appointed as Tasmanian Police Commissioner, held the door shut, fearing the gunman was trapped and would try to come out. When Anderson produced the exhibit pistol, Horman opened the door and Anderson rushed through.

But, by then, the gunman was long gone – through a hole already carefully prepared in the corrugated iron shed wall. The hole opened into a carpark at the neighbouring Royal Melbourne

Institute of Technology. It was the perfect escape route – and it reeked of an inside job. Whoever did it had an expert knowledge of the court and the police carpark, or easy access to people who did have such knowledge.

By the time Bennett was pronounced dead an hour later, the rumour mill was humming. Frantic reporters with deadlines for the year's biggest crime story quoted unnamed police sources suggesting an 'outside' hit man was paid big money – the mooted sum was $50,000 – to do the killing.

But before the last edition of the now defunct afternoon daily, *The Herald*, had hit the streets a different story was circulating inside Russell Street. At 2pm the head of the consorting squad, Angus Ritchie, took a call from an informer claiming the hit had been organised inside his own squad.

Some squad members jokingly encouraged the rumours in the police club that night. 'We couldn't buy a drink for a week,' recalls a retired detective who still doesn't fancy being named over the incident. 'Half the force thought we did it.'

Within days, the squad members would regret feeding the rumours because one detective was told there was a contract on his life to avenge Bennett's death. He carried a gun for two years.

Detectives, unable to protect Bennett when he was alive, were given orders to guard his corpse. They were instructed to go to the North Melbourne funeral home where the body was lying after police heard his enemies planned to break-in, cut his hands off and send them to his wife.

Meanwhile, the public was still being fed the company line of a contract killer. Details of the more sinister theory, involving police, were not made public until the inquest finally began in March 1981. But that was later.

TO his friends, Ray Bennett was tough, loyal, and good company. His lawyer, Joe Gullaci, liked him – though he admits Bennett and his mates were 'big kids with guns', professional armed robbers who terrified people and wouldn't hesitate to shoot rivals.

'These blokes were pretty good at their trade – in and out quickly (on robberies) and no shots fired and no drugs – unlike the current crop running around using their own product. It seemed to me they were thieves with some honour,' the hard-bitten Gullaci would recall. It was this 'honour' that eventually got Bennett killed.

They were the last of their generation. Gangsters who prided themselves on doing their own dirty work. Already they were a dying breed – in more ways than one. Soon it would be the drug dealers who would control the underworld and they could afford to hire others to do their killings. But back then it was the crooks with the most dash, not necessarily those with the most cash, who were respected.

Bennett's charisma won him friends on both sides of the fence: he once had a steamy affair with a policewoman he met while reporting for bail.

The watch-house of a suburban police station may not be as romantic as a Pacific beach but on a lonely nightshift sometimes a hard man can be good to find.

Consorting between crims and cops was colourful in other ways as well. In fact, the Consorting Squad that was assigned to know what the crooks were up to called themselves the 'Fletcher Jones' boys – because, the joke went, like the clothing store of that name, they could 'fit anybody.' Before DNA testing, target profiling and flow charts, they gathered intelligence in pubs, nightclubs and racetracks.

Their brief was to know what heavy criminals were up to, and to act first to prevent crimes. Their tool-of-trade – apart from sledgehammers, planted 'throwaway' guns, unsigned statements and illegal telephone taps – was the draconian consorting law (now no longer regularly used) that meant if a known criminal were caught consorting with another known criminal both could be charged and jailed. One of the phone taps picked up a senior policeman talking to Ray Bennett.

Squad members worked unsupervised, in small groups. Many socialised with criminals and had their own favourites. They were used as trouble-shooters by some senior police who turned a blind eye to methods used. A new detective would be given an introductory speech, 'You are going to enter a special environment, you are going to work with some very capable men. They may do things you may not like, they may overstep the mark but they will get the desired results.' You were told to fit in or leave. Or something like that.

Some of them found the people they thought were the villains and then either massaged or fabricated evidence to suit their conclusions. Sometimes they were right.

One offender who'd been shot while being arrested – the kidnapper Edwin John Eastwood – had his wounded leg stretched in hospital to force him to talk.

It was an era when some of the heavy squads made their own rules and exacted severe punishment for any outsider who broke them. When Ray 'Muscles' Kane pulled up at the lights, and noticed an off-duty detective with his heavily pregnant wife in a car next to him, he made a mistake that was to cost him several months in jail. Kane wound his window down and threatened the policeman, using a string of profanities. The detective quietly told him he was going too far, but the hyped-up Kane did not see the danger signs.

It was late December when the detective's squad mates caught up with Kane in a St Kilda flat. They presented the criminal with several sticks of gelignite, neatly wrapped in Christmas paper. As soon as he saw the gift he knew the evidence against him would be overwhelming. He didn't need a forensic report to know his fingerprints would be all over the package ... they had taken the paper from a drawer in Kane's flat and gift-wrapped it in front of him.

After he was charged he told a senior policeman, 'I knew I shouldn't have shot my mouth off.' The policeman responded, 'You take one of this squad on, you take all of us on.'

It was around the same time that underworld identity Ron Feeney accepted a murder contract, but police didn't know who the target was or when the murder would take place. To stop the shooting, a detective simply walked in, gave him an unloaded gun and said, 'This is yours, Ron.' He was charged with being a felon in possession of a firearm. The hit was never carried out.

In the interview room a suspect who answered a question with the expression 'no comment' could soon find that it was more an opening statement in protracted negotiations than a concluding remark.

One detective, annoyed that his suspect refused to make a statement, removed his size fourteen boot, claiming it was his shoe phone. He put it to his ear, then turned to the suspect and said, 'It's for you.' – before beating the man around the head with the boot. The suspect then began to answer questions. Every time the answers weren't correct the detective would remove his boot, claiming he was taking another call. The suspect would answer questions again.

In another interview an armed robber refused to talk. Finally, a naked detective ran into the room and hit him around the head. The suspect, possibly more frightened of being confronted by a naked, overweight detective than the beating, confessed readily.

When one suspect wouldn't talk until he had spoken to a lawyer a helpful detective gave him the number for the on-call legal aid solicitor. The suspect was somewhat surprised when the lawyer told him to confess to everything immediately and plead for mercy. He did as he was told – unaware the number he had been given was to another extension in the squad room where a waiting policeman was on hand to provide such advice.

While most squads at the time bent the rules to suit themselves the consorting squad had made it an art-form. Consorters, whose job it was to go to places where criminals hung out, combined business and pleasure for fun and profit. Some race clubs were so grateful to have them on course that they slung them payments paid in plain envelopes ... written off as security payments, which, of course, they were. The money was put in a slush fund largely used to entertain interstate detectives who would always arrive thirsty and hungry.

The consorters didn't like critics. When a former criminal and prison activist, Joey Hamilton, publicly complained about some of their methods, two squad members went to his house in Carlton and blew it up with explosives, a retired detective told the authors. When Hamilton said at the time that police were responsible for the attack, few believed him – but he was right. What he didn't know was that there was a member of the media in the car at the time who chose not to report the incident.

This was the consorting squad before the police hierarchy decided that its dogs of war were out of control and disbanded it. Some consorters acted as judge and jury. The question is: were they also prepared to be executioners?

The circumstantial evidence is intriguing rather than damning. One grievance the consorters had against Ray Bennett came from the fact that they provided unofficial security for bookmakers on settling days at the Victorian Club. But, on the day the Bennett gang struck, the usual crew of armed detectives were not there – they had been sent at the last minute on an errand to Frankston, a coincidence that led some to suspect Bennett had connived with a corrupt senior officer to set up the robbery. It was the same senior policeman who had been caught earlier on illegal phone taps talking to Bennett.

Bennett told police, straight-faced, that he'd taken a call on the night of Les Kane's death to say that Kane had 'gone off' and he'd immediately gone into hiding, fearing reprisals.

He wasn't the only one to fear reprisals. When the case went to trial at the Supreme Court in September 1979, court security measures were extraordinary. There were armed police, marksmen posted outside, and stringent identity and weapon checks on everyone who entered court. Even a prison chaplain, Peter Alexander, was not allowed to visit Bennett.

The three were acquitted, mainly because of the absence of a body. Though pleased with the result, they suspected not everyone was convinced of their innocence. Mikkelsen and Prendergast left Melbourne immediately for distant destinations. And Bennett, still to face charges on the payroll robbery, chose to stay in custody.

Seven weeks later, he was sent to the Magistrates Court for committal. This time, oddly enough, there was no security at all.

So who killed him? And how did he get away with it so easily?

The brief inquest that was theoretically supposed to work it all out when it finally sat, raised more questions than answers.

Despite the public interest, and the time available to prepare the brief, it was a slight document – barely a morsel for the eminent legal talent gathered around the bar table.

Joe Gullaci could not represent Gail Bennett and her family because he had been called as a witness. Instead, she hired a prominent criminal barrister, Jack Lazarus.

Lazarus was aggressive but, on instructions, was not out to lay blame in ways that might fan hostilities and make life hard for the widow and her schoolboy son, Danny. Peter Alexander, the knockabout priest who buried Bennett, told the authors that Lazarus's brief was to defend Bennett's reputation for the sake of his son – not to lead a murder investigation.

With Lazarus choosing his punches carefully, no-one else was swinging wildly, either. The result was a predictably thin account of facts already run in the media – except for one thing.

The brilliant advocate representing the police – John Phillips, QC, later to become Chief Justice – was forced to air rumours claiming that two detectives were implicated in the murder. Given that Lazarus didn't directly accuse anyone, it was the only way that Phillips could try to put such rumours to rest.

The men Phillips named, albeit gently, were Paul John Strang and Brian Francis Murphy.

Strang, a popular consorting squad detective later dismissed over a minor matter, was one of the three detectives supposed to be escorting Bennett, but happened not to be standing near him when the shots were fired.

Murphy, then with the new Metropolitan Regional Crime squad – nicknamed 'Murphy's Marauders' – had no official reason to be at the magistrates' court the day Bennett was killed. He arrived from his North Fitzroy office after the shooting, and said later he'd thought the activity outside the court was a demonstration. Extraordinarily, although named at the inquest as a rumoured suspect, Murphy was never interviewed nor called to give evidence. It was that sort of inquiry. Underworld murders are rarely solved, and this never looked like being the exception.

Even the counsel assisting the Coroner submitted there was no evidence the police knew of threats to Bennett beforehand, and blamed the media for airing matters 'improperly put in court and never substantiated.' So solicitous was he about the perception of unfairness to the police involved that the police's own QC was scarcely able to lay it on any thicker. He claimed it had been a bumper week for rubbishing the police, and called on the media to give full coverage if the Coroner found that Murphy and Strang were not involved in the shooting.

Which, of course, is what the Coroner did. But not even he, a policeman's son, could swallow his own assisting counsel's preposterous suggestions that the police didn't know beforehand of any threats to Bennett's safety.

While the Coroner found who didn't do it, he didn't get close to naming who did. But time has loosened tongues. The women closest to the Kane brothers say, independently of each other, that Brian Kane got his revenge that day for Les's death in 1978. And several detectives involved in the case suggest independently that they've always believed the gunman was Kane. But, they say, it would be extremely unlikely that a criminal as well-known as Kane was, could prowl the court precinct to set up his escape route.

One former detective says matter-of-factly that two former colleagues removed four roofing nails and levered open the tin fence escape route days earlier. Interestingly, an RMIT gardener recalled seeing a man dressed in new overalls and digging with a new garden trowel next to the fence at 6.45am the week before the murder – possibly on the morning of the Melbourne Cup public holiday when the area would have been almost deserted. This man had a similar moustache to Brian Kane but it was an era when moustaches were fashionable – particularly among squad detectives.

The truth went to the grave with Brian Kane when he was shot dead in the Quarry Hotel in Brunswick in November 1982, almost three years to the day after Bennett's death.

Twenty years on, Brian Murphy was on a short motoring holiday with his wife in Tasmania when contacted by the authors. He said he remembered distinctly the events of late 1979.

So who was the bearded hit man?

'It was Brian,' he said. 'But not this one.'

The strange thing, he added, was that he'd seen a man who looked very like Brian Kane in Lygon Street the night before, and noticed he had grown a beard.

Nearly 25 years later another underworld figure was ambushed. It was Jason Moran who was related by marriage to the Kane family.

One of the first men on the scene was Phil Glare, who worked at a scrap metal yard across the road from the North Essendon football ground where Moran was shot dead.

The same Phil Glare who was on escort duty when Bennett was gunned down.

It's a small world, after all.

7

SHOT IN THE DARK
HOW MARRIAGE GOT A MAN MURDERED BY MISTAKE

> The killers probably didn't see
> his face in the dark as they
> approached from behind.

NORMAN McLeod was a good man. But that didn't help him avoid a murder contract meant for somebody else.

McLeod's only 'crime' was to be driving a car that had previously belonged to his brother-in-law Vinnie Mikkelsen, a gunman whose deadly but dumb enemies killed the wrong man because they didn't do their homework.

Mikkelsen was one of a family of fourteen children. The odds were that one of them would run off the rails, and Vinnie was the one.

McLeod had known the Mikkelsens most of his life and had knocked around with Vinnie, who was a year younger, when they were kids. Later, in the spring of 1969, he had married one of Mikkelsen's seven sisters, Lynette.

But McLeod proved a good worker, father and husband, and police never had any reason to link him to the criminal activities of his tough-guy brother-in-law, who was quick with his fists and reputedly even quicker with a gun.

When Vincent started to associate with some of the local tough teenagers such as Laurie Prendergast, McLeod chose hard work over easy money. He went into the meat business, initially working as a boner after completing year ten in school.

The young married couple knew some of the local gangsters but they didn't fall for the underworld attitude towards work and saving money.

Norman and Lynette had two daughters and continued to save as they chased the suburban family dream of owning their own home. It took them ten years to put together the deposit for their first brick veneer house in the then new estate in Rockbank Court, Coolaroo, in Melbourne's northern suburbs.

McLeod, 33, had a reputation as a good toiler and after the meatworks folded he soon got a job as a storeman at Berger Paints in Coburg. He was popular at work, a member of the social club committee, and organised many of the staff's after-hours activities.

He had a small share in a trotting horse called Perfect Call, paying $10 a month to be in it with friends. The horse did not live up to its name, as it never raced.

McLeod's only other outside interest was a monthly visit on a Saturday afternoon to the First and Last Hotel to have a few beers with his mates. This would happen only if he worked over-time in the morning and when he went to the pub, Lynette would pick him up around 5pm. For a pair of honest battlers, it was close to suburban bliss.

Vinnie Mikkelsen kept in regular touch with his sister – usually visiting the McLeods every few weeks. But then, in 1978, the visits suddenly stopped. He had more pressing matters on his mind.

Mikkelsen had plans to disappear to the other side of the country – a decision that coincided with the disappearance and murder of Les Kane.

He took his two children out of school in October 1978. In January 1979, Mikkelsen was arrested in Karratha, a remote mining town 1600 kilometres from Perth, and charged with Kane's murder.

In September 1979 Mikkelsen, Bennett and Prendergast were acquitted of the murder. But friends and relatives of Kane were keen to carry out their own homegrown version of capital punishment despite the jury's verdict.

On 12 November, Bennett was shot dead in the Melbourne Magistrates' Court as the first part of the proposed payback. Within three weeks Mikkelsen decided to sell his four-door Mazda sedan with the distinctive number plates, ML 737.

The McLeods were paying their way but they were not so flush with funds they could ignore a bargain. So, when they had a chance to pick up a cheap and reliable sedan from a relative, rather than a shonky car dealer, they jumped at it.

Right car, wrong relative.

Like most families, the McLeods had a predictable routine. By 6.30am Norm would be ready to go to work. Lynette would drive him to the factory less than twenty minutes away and then drop their daughters at the house of a woman who would take them to their local primary school.

Lynette would then head to work at the Coles Supermarket in Sydney Road, Coburg.

Around 5pm they would retrace their steps and drive home together. Regular, steady and safe. And only too easy to follow.

On Tuesday, 15 July 1981, their elder daughter had a throat infection and had to stay home from school. Lynette stayed with her, leaving Norm to make his own way to work.

He drove the Mazda to the factory – the same car they had bought from Vinnie Mikkelsen nearly two years earlier.

The following morning the little girl was still sick. Norm was running late and had to skip his usual shower. While he dressed, Lynette made him sandwiches.

'At about twenty to seven, he said goodbye, gave me a kiss and told me he would ring later that morning to see how (their daughter) was,' Lynette later said.

It was still dark and the outside light was not working. This meant the two gunmen hiding outside would not have been able to identify McLeod's physical features or see his distinctive bushy beard.

He walked out to the kerb where the car was parked, slipped behind the wheel and put his portable AWA radio in the passenger seat next to him.

Lynette went into the kitchen to put the kettle on for an early morning coffee. She looked out the window and saw fumes coming from the exhaust as her husband started the car.

Just about this time I heard about four really loud bangs. I thought it must have been an explosion. I went to the lounge window, pulled back the drapes and had a look at what had really happened. I immediately saw two people running really fast.'

She went outside and saw her husband still sitting behind the wheel. The driver's side window had been smashed. Instinctively, she would say, 'I opened the car door and turned off the ignition.'

She realised her husband was injured because he didn't move and didn't speak, but she still hadn't grasped what had happened. Then the school caretaker from across the road came over and said to her: 'Sorry love, there was nothing I could do – they had guns.'

It was only then she realised her husband had been shot. She collapsed, screaming.

Police later established that McLeod started the car and because it was a cold winter morning let it idle to allow the engine to warm.

In those few seconds, two gunmen approached from behind and fired two shots through the driver's side window followed by three more.

McLeod was shot in the head, neck and chest. He died where he sat. The killers probably didn't see his face in the dark as they approached from behind.

The gunmen then ran to the school opposite, through some vacant land and along Yuroke Creek to another road where their getaway car was waiting.

Later, the Coroner said Norman McLeod had been 'callously murdered in a well-planned operation by two assailants who have not been identified despite extensive police investigations.'

Often, when police probe the background of a murder victim, hidden secrets emerge. Happy marriages can turn out to be shams, seemingly successful businesses can be on the verge of disaster and seemingly healed wounds still fester.

But a protracted police investigation found Norman McLeod to be exactly what he seemed: a good bloke, a devoted family man and a hard worker with modest tastes and realistic dreams.

Detectives found, 'The deceased was happily married and he does not appear to have been involved in any criminal matters. He has never been charged or convicted of any criminal offences or has never been interviewed for any matter. He was not in any extreme financial difficulty or has any financial problems known to police.'

He was, they concluded, simply driving the wrong car and so had been followed and killed by gunmen too stupid to make sure they had the right target.

8

THE LIFE OF BRIAN
THE BITE ON THE EAR THAT STARTED A WAR

> They had reputations for
> rarely missing and they
> wouldn't that night.

BRIAN Kane knew he would die young and violently. It was just a matter of when and where. All he knew was that it wouldn't be in his sleep.

'He was convinced I would outlive him,' said veteran prison priest Father John Brosnan a few hours after burying the man with the reputation as one of Australia's toughest.

The wily old priest was sorry to lose Kane for more reasons than one – his onetime school pupil had been a generous donor to Brosnan's favourite cause, shouting him a trip to Ireland and even a car to get around his parish.

Kane had plenty of reasons to stay on side with God's gang. In the early 1980s, he was in the middle of an underworld war that had already claimed three lives and was still going strong. He needed all the help he could get, the more Divine the better.

Kane made a comfortable living by frightening fellow criminals, among others, and was well qualified to demand a share of the Bookie Robbery funds. He was not accustomed to taking no for an answer.

For years he had collected money from illegal gambling in Chinatown and he had a slice of Melbourne's biggest and busiest two-up school and was a regular at various illegal gambling venues in Carlton as well as collecting debts for SP bookmakers.

But there was another steady and more lucrative source of income. For as long as anyone could remember, 'ghost' payments had been made on the Melbourne waterfront. Workers who did not exist were listed as dockies and wages were paid in their names – effectively as a bribe in return for industrial peace.

Unlike armed robberies and standover rackets, it was a regular, safe stream of cash. Police were too busy dealing with violent crime to worry about the rorts on the docks and the employers didn't complain because a dock strike was more expensive than ghosted wages. It was part of the overhead expenses that made Australian ports among the most notorious in the world.

It took the Costigan Royal Commission into the Painters and Dockers Union to expose the practice as part of a complex, interconnected web of organised crime that included the lucrative bottom-of-the-harbor tax scheme and a string of unsolved murders.

Frank Costigan, QC, listed the murders of the Kanes, Bennett and McLeod as connected to dockland activity without publicly identifying a motive.

He declared Bennett to be a hit man: 'Bennett was believed to have been a person who murdered on the payment of money.'

According to one investigator from the time, 'The new breed came in and the bad blood was over the percentage of the ghosting down the wharves. There was always a percentage of wages paid to phantom workers on the wharf and the Kanes controlled it and divvied it out. It was big business and linked to organised crime.'

According to fellow standover man Mark Brandon Read, 'Brian was a violent, cunning criminal who had the bulk of the criminal world and the waterfront bluffed, beaten and baffled.'

He once sat in a coffee shop with a policeman who had earned a national fearsome reputation. An underworld figure recalls: 'The copper said, "If you look under the table there is a .38 pointed directly at your guts." Brian just smiled and said, "There's a .45 pointing at your knackers".'

So Kane was tough. But a man like Bennett wasn't easily frightened, either. He also had a reputation and, like the Kanes, was well connected in the Painters and Dockers. He was not going to pull off one of Australia's biggest crimes and then hand over the profits.

Brooding dislike had erupted into bloodshed after Kane came off second best in a brawl in a Richmond hotel from one of Bennett's mates, leaving him without part of his left ear.

Brian Kane's brother, Les, vowed revenge. 'Brian was dangerous but measured. Les was a psychopath,' said a Melbourne underworld figure, voicing a widespread opinion.

Bennett, the man they called 'The General', reasoned that he couldn't reason with Les Kane and decided to hit first.

When Bennett, Prendergast and Mikkelsen were acquitted of Les's murder, big brother Brian became obsessed with a payback.

He saw Mikkelsen's barrister at a nightclub after the acquittal and told him he was 'going to cut your client's head off and leave it on your front door step.'

Another time when he found the lawyer in a bar he pulled a gun on him as a reminder that not all was forgiven. One of Kane's best friends, Graham 'The Munster' Kinniburgh, knocked the gun out of his hand. After Brian's death 'The Munster' began to associate with colourful characters such as Alphonse Gangitano (shot dead in 1998) and Mick Gatto. Gangitano had hero-worshipped Brian Kane and did his best to take over his mantle as Melbourne's premier standover man.

It was said that Kinniburgh, a master safebreaker and professional burglar among other interests, had business as well as social links with Gatto.

Kinniburgh was to excel in his role as underworld peacemaker until he was shot dead in December 2003. But that was half a lifetime later.

Kane's moment of vengeance came in November 1979 when Ray Bennett was shot dead in the City Court while being escorted by police to an armed robbery committal hearing.

Brian Kane was the man who killed Bennett, although it has become part of underworld folklore that he had a little unofficial assistance along the way from rogue police with their own reasons to side with him.

While Kane was desperate to avenge his brother's death he remained a reluctant gunman. According to one notable underworld source, Brian Kane hated firing guns. He usually carried one and was known to have pistol-whipped a man into a coma, and would insert the barrel into a victim's ear and twist it, but he wasn't a great one for pulling the trigger. Kane kept a low profile after Bennett was murdered but Ray had been popular in some circles and Kane knew he was living dangerously.

The harsh economic fact of life was that Kane could not afford to disappear for long. A close woman friend of his has told the authors that he and his younger brother, Ray 'Muscles' Kane, flew to Perth to cool off straight after the Bennett hit. But he was Melbourne bred – and that's where the bread was. Standover men can't work by sending stern letters of demand: they have to turn up in person sooner or later.

Men like Kane made a living by appearing to be bulletproof even when they knew they weren't.

Kane was a professional, so he suspected it was only a matter of time. The Painters and Dockers motto, 'We catch and kill our own', meant that enemies would wait years before they grabbed their moment.

But Kane was not without friends – and some of them were in influential positions in the CIB. In fact, when the gangland war broke out a core of experienced detectives decided to back the Kanes against the new breed led by Bennett.

As one detective, now retired, explained, 'The centre of the older style criminals was in the streets of Richmond before it became trendy and the Kanes were entrenched in the area.

'These people who came along lived in the spacious newer developments around Keilor.

'In those days Bennett's house was one of the first to have video surveillance. The older crims didn't have that sort of thing because they knew that enemies wouldn't come to your home. When Les Kane was gunned down in the bathroom of his own home with his wife and kids there it changed everything. It was a horrific event to kill a man in front of his wife and kids and then take him away and deprive the family the right to bury their own. That man and his car have never been found to this day.

'There was a massive division among the criminals. The older crooks took the side of the Kanes and the young dashing criminals took the side of the Bennett group. People in nightclubs were challenged to take a side. At times people were declaring their loyalty to both sides.

'We felt that it was about to get fully out of control with shootings in the streets. If they were prepared to machine gun a bloke in front of his family we thought that all the rules were out the window.

'We decided to stick with the Kanes, not because we liked them but because the established older style criminals were predictable. They had rules – they caught and killed their own; they looked after their own.

'I had many dealings with Brian Kane. He was an enormous source of intelligence to me; not that he was informing, he was feeding me intelligence he wanted me to know and I was feeding him information to try and keep him alive.

'After the death of his brother he kept very much to himself and trusted no-one. I was told that I had to do whatever I could, within reason, to keep that man alive.

'He would say when he had been followed by a car and I would have it checked to see if it was a police surveillance unit. If it was, he wasn't worried.

'Brian was only concerned with staying alive and avenging the murder of his brother.

'After he killed Bennett – Kane kept on the move. Brian never kept appointments, he was very elusive,' the former policeman said.

He could have moved interstate, or he could have used his waterside connections to disappear overseas. But the former amateur boxer did not build his fearsome reputation by running away.

He did, however, use all the lessons he'd learned in the ring: to avoid being hit was as important as landing a punch. More so when guns came into play.

Brian's widowed sister-in-law, Judi, was one of the few people he trusted after Les's murder in 1978. But proof of how close he played to his chest was that even she was not told everything, just in case. She knew it was not so much to protect him but his estranged wife Robyn and his three children.

Robyn had finally kicked Brian out of their Camberwell home – near St Dominic's Catholic Church – after Les's murder. It was too nerve-wracking to live with a man who was, it stood to reason, next on the hit list.

'None of us knew where Brian lived,' Judi told the authors. 'He was very paranoid for good reason. He used to visit me and the kids in Balwyn, maybe once a week after Les was killed.'

Once, when Brian had been living away from the family home in Camberwell to draw the heat away, his wife Robyn invited Judi and her children to visit her on the quiet – that is, without Brian knowing. Before that Judi's two kids had often asked about visiting their Aunty Robyn and their cousins and he'd joked: 'No, you can't because there's a moat with crocodiles in it!' But after visiting their cousins' house, the kids knew better. So next time Brian came to visit the kids said, 'There is not a moat with crocodiles,' and Judi had to admit they'd been there.

It was a humorous take on a deadly serious situation. Kane was engaged in a war of nerves with men who wanted to kill him before he killed them.

After he left home, he struck up a close relationship with an attractive divorcee called Fran Kear, who was later able to give the authors an insight into the soft side and secret fears of the hard man.

Another policeman remembers seeing him in The Galaxy nightclub. 'He gave me a false name and when I said I knew he was Brian Kane he wanted a fight. I told him to settle down. In the end, I could talk to him but if you asked the wrong question he would just stare through you and say nothing.

'Les was more volatile but Brian was more respected. He would help out local football clubs and loved Father Brosnan. He would always give him some cash because the old Father loved a punt.'

Brian Kane was more cunning than his volatile brother, Les, but just as dangerous. While Les was often before the courts for crimes of violence, Brian's criminal record was modest. In 1972 he was fined $30 for hindering police and he had a few early convictions for stealing and assaults.

He was considered one of the most influential men in Melbourne's underworld for years – but he wasn't the only crook with a gun and a ruthless streak.

He knew someone would be coming for him eventually. Three years later, they did.

FOR Brian Kane it was a day like any other. He had his worries but one of them was not having to do regular work. On Friday 26 November 1982, he was looking forward to a long lunch.

At 40 the former boxer might have been beginning to slow down a bit. But photographs taken of him only a few days before show that he was in good shape – and still a man to be reckoned with.

He met a mate, Sandra Walsh, at a coffee shop in Grattan Street, Carlton, and then they went for lunch in nearby Lygon Street.

Around 4.15 pm the pair left the restaurant for some fresh air and some shopping. Kane liked to make sure he was seen in the Lygon Street strip. It was good for business to be spotted there regularly, as his standover beat included the illegal gambling spots hidden above the popular restaurants and cafes.

Brian became bored and stopped off for a quick haircut before the couple headed to the Tramway Hotel in Fitzroy for a few gin and tonics.

Around 8.30 pm they moved on to the Quarry Hotel in the northern stretch of Lygon Street, in Brunswick. It was a semi-regular drinking spot for Kane, who was popular at the pub. He was the first to chat to anyone in the hotel and the first to put his hand in his pocket for a raffle. He could afford to.

'He was really well liked and made the effort to portray an image as a good guy gangster,' one detective said.

He spoke to an older woman in the lounge, asking how the television he had bought her was working. Then he bought a round of half gin and tonics before settling in next to the jukebox.

Police believe the gunmen knew they would find Kane at the Quarry. Whether they were tipped off that day where he would be or whether they had been told the hotel was one of his regulars is not known.

Earlier, a mutual friend had borrowed Sandra's distinctive V12 Jaguar and Brian told him to drop it back at the Quarry after 8pm.

Anyone looking for Kane would have been able to spot the big Jag outside the pub. And the people hunting him were experts at picking their moment.

As Kane sat down with Sandra and another associate, Trevor Russell, two men wearing balaclavas burst in and began firing from .38 snub-nosed revolvers – the same type of weapon Kane used to kill Bennett in the City Court three years earlier.

Kane leapt to his feet, tipping over the table and pushing Sandra Walsh down as he did so.

Legend has it that as the first shot hit Kane, he was diving for his gun hidden in Sandra's handbag. (Because he could be jailed for carrying an illegal pistol, he regularly used women to 'carry' for him.)

He didn't make it. He was shot in the head and chest at point blank range.

Sandra Walsh told friends later that the table was obscuring her vision when the two shots went off next to her. She thought to herself, 'That's Brian and that's Trevor – I'm next.' But she was wrong. Both shots were meant for Kane. She cradled the dying man while Russell bolted through the hotel kitchen.

Police said that when they arrived Sandra was yelling: 'He's been shot, he's been shot. Do you know who he is? Do you? It's

Brian Kane.' Asked what had happened she said, 'He was shot and that's all I'm saying.'

Kane was taken to the Royal Melbourne Hospital but died on the operating table.

Typically, the homicide squad was confronted with the usual blank looks and silence from those who could have helped solve the murder. Those who didn't know, speculated. Those who did, said nothing.

There was a short list of suspects. Some were obvious while some were less so. Top of the pops were the obvious two – Vinnie Mikkelsen and Laurie Prendergast. After all, they had been charged with Bennett over the murder of Brian's brother Les and, although acquitted, no one on either side of the law thought there were other suspects for Les Kane's death. In a direct sense, Mikkelsen and Prendergast had most to gain from Brian's death. For if Brian had killed Bennett in the City Court to avenge his brother's death, it would be a fair bet he would eventually try for the hat trick by nailing the other two.

But, despite the theories, there was nothing directly linking the pair to the Quarry Hotel hit.

The head of the case was Victoria's then most experienced homicide investigator, Detective Senior Sergeant Jim Fry.

He said the obvious motive for the murder was a payback for the Bennett killing. 'Whoever did it was either very professional or very lucky because they got away with it.'

But there were other suspects. One was hit man Christopher Dale Flannery, who was living in Sydney at the time but was a local boy, and a close friend of Prendergast so was seen as an enemy of the Kanes.

Later, when there was an attempt on Flannery's life he wrongly blamed the last of the Kane brothers, Ray, for the attack.

Certainly Flannery was responsible for killing a Kane ally, Les Cole, just two weeks before the Quarry attack but it was unlikely that Kane's enemies would have needed to sub-contract the deal and Chris Flannery wasn't into contra deals. He was more a cash man.

The smart money has always been on two other killers. Both were calculating loners who would occasionally team up with others for a few jobs before moving on.

One was a man known as 'The Duke', a ruthless gunman later implicated in paid hits during Melbourne's underworld war between Carl Williams and the Moran clan. He was an armed robber and rumoured contract killer. Even the hardest of underworld hard men feared The Duke.

The other was Russell Cox, who had escaped from New South Wales' maximum security Katingal Division in Sydney's Long Bay prison five years earlier.

Cox was living with Ray Bennett's wife's sister and had a vested interest in backing-up for the Magistrates' Court killing.

Bennett and Cox had teamed up to commit armed robberies in Victoria and Queensland and were loyal to each other.

Cox and The Duke were close associates in the early 1980s and were both friends of armed robber Santo Mercuri. Just three months after the Quarry Hotel hit, police received intelligence that The Duke had committed another shooting – this time in Reservoir. The report said The Duke was, 'An associate of Sam Mercuri and believed running with Russell Cox.'

Certainly Cox and The Duke were seen chatting and having coffee in Hawthorn in the months preceding the hit.

For a major player in the underworld, Kane's estate was surprisingly modest. But that was before illegal drugs became the currency of crime.

Kane was respected, not because he was rich, but because he was tough. He was one of the last suburban gangsters – the next generation would be national and international.

Brian Kane and his generation of gunmen were fighting and killing over a dying world – dinosaurs battling at the start of the Ice Age.

They didn't know that the armed robbery and illegal gambling were rackets well past their best. Pills and powders were where the real money would be made in the future.

Gunmen would become a penny a truckload while self taught chemists who could brew a batch of speed were prized recruits.

According to Father Brosnan, Kane knew that in his line of work his enemies would eventually find him.

'I don't think he knew he was going to die like this but he was a realistic man; he knew what was possible. The best thing about him was that he wasn't a hypocrite.'

Father Brosnan taught the three Kane boys at St John's School 25 years earlier. 'I taught them how to fight. I didn't do a bad job, did I?'

Well, two were dead and the other would be jailed for many years so the Father's record was not up there with Angelo Dundee. One policeman said after Kane was murdered that he would 'be no great loss.' He was wrong. There were 169 death notices placed in *The Sun* – including a handful from star footballers – in the week after his death.

Many were from women. Brian was a ladies' man as well as a man's man – once having a torrid affair with another underworld identity's wife.

Some of the death notices were placed by the men who would fill the power vacuum left by the Kane murders. Mick Gatto and Alphonse Gangitano were to pay their respects, while one notice to 'Uncle Brian' was signed by 'Your little mate, Jason Moran.'

9

A MATTER OF TIME

ANOTHER BOOKIE ROBBER BITES THE DUST

'Prendergast is no doubt
one of Australia's most
notorious criminals.'

AS a professional punter and career gunman, Laurence Joseph Prendergast must have known the odds of him living to normal retirement age were slim to none. He was right: the closest he came to a gold watch was scoring a 'hot' one from another thief.

Police have at least three strong theories why he was murdered. But what they haven't got is a body, or a suspect, or a murder scene, or an informer, or a lead. Apart from those small problems the investigation is proceeding well – and has been for more than twenty years.

Even as a child Prendergast was bad news – and age didn't improve him. He first came to the notice of police at twelve years old when he became an apprentice housebreaker and thief working with his older brother.

Laurie was the second of nine children from a dysfunctional family that included another two stepchildren. In desperation, authorities placed him in the St Augustine orphanage for two years to try to straighten him out.

It didn't work. It was already too late.

While the young Prendergast had a good relationship with his father he said once that his alcoholic mother had beaten him for as long as he could remember.

It left him with a chip on his shoulder and a desire to square the ledger. As is often the case, those who are bullied look to bully others and young Laurie progressed quickly from fists to rocks (he was charged with throwing missiles to endanger persons when he was a child) and then to guns. He was charged with discharging a firearm from a car when still a teenager.

He went to four schools, leaving in year eight with a reputation as an average student with an above average temper.

A schoolmate remembers, 'He was really cool and stand-offish. He only had about five or six close friends and they all ended up gangsters. He was a tough bastard and he could fight.'

Prendergast became an apprentice butcher, a storeman and a labourer and while he had held twenty jobs, few lasted more than two weeks.

His love was sport, the more violent the better. He was a good footballer, won two amateur wrestling titles and was a handy amateur boxer. But it was his expertise at using violence outside the ring that gave him his fearsome reputation.

His criminal record shows that he soon moved to sex crimes with violence. As a teenager he broke into a house where he sexually assaulted a 26-year-old woman. He was sentenced to twelve months in a youth detention centre for buggery and burglary.

But while recovering from a car accident he escaped from hospital and was on the run for another year. The accident left him with a fractured skull. The injury did not help his anger management problems.

In 1968 he was sentenced to an adult jail for rape and other offences. His partner in crime was his childhood friend, Christopher Dale Flannery. They would live similar violent lives and would disappear in remarkably similar circumstances.

In 1974 Prendergast was sentenced in the county court to five years jail over an attempt to rob the Bank of New South Wales in Pascoe Vale. Again his partner was Flannery, who was also sentenced to jail.

By the mid-1970s Prendergast was uncontrollable. He was convicted of assaulting a prison officer and later of assaulting a policeman.

In the case where he attacked police he chose a strange place to try and get even. He was in the criminal dock as Senior Detective Kim West was giving evidence on a charge of possession of a pistol. West was a Falstaffian figure and his testimony was always entertaining – Shakespeare meets *The Bill*.

But on this occasion the detective's recollections seemed to disturb Prendergast. When the experienced policeman gave sworn evidence that Prendergast had confessed in the back of a police car, it became all too much for the highly-strung Laurie.

'He jumped out of the dock and ran along the bar table yelling, "You are a liar. You are telling lies",' West recalled.

Senior Detective Ian 'Twiggy' Thomas had to tackle him. He grabbed him in a bear-hug and wrestled him from the bar table. Although he was smaller, Prendergast used his wrestling experience to swivel to face Thomas. Then he head butted and bit the startled detective on the left cheek, leaving a wound that required three stitches. It became infected; leaving a permanent reminder that dental hygiene was not high on Prendergast's lists of priorities.

As he was bundled back into his cell, Prendergast lashed out with a kick trying to make contact with West's groin. In the confusion the cell door was smashed into Prendergast's right leg – the same thigh that was still tender from where he had been shot during a failed armed robbery.

The pistol charges were dismissed but he was sentenced to four months for the assault. Clearly he had bitten off more than he could chew.

On release from jail he teamed up with the gang of armed robbers led by Ray Bennett. Police say he was one of the team that carried out the Great Bookie Robbery.

And when Bennett fell out with the Kane brothers, Laurie was quick to back up. He, Bennett and Vinnie Mikkelsen were alleged to have machine-gunned Les Kane to death in late 1978.

Prendergast knew the consequences of taking on the Kanes. Two months before the murder, he obtained a false passport after stealing the identity of an associate named Noel Robert Herity.

He was charged in December with the murder and acquitted nine months later.

His police record states that following the acquittal, 'Prendergast has done everything he can to hide his current whereabouts. He lives in constant fear of being shot by the sole remaining brother Ray Kane or one of his associates.'

When arrested for carrying a gun he told police he needed a weapon because of the 'vendetta with the Kane family.'

His police record states, 'Prendergast is no doubt one of Australia's most notorious criminals.

'(He is) considered to be a determined, persistent and cunning criminal with an intense hatred for the police or any kind of authority'.

In 1980 he was spotted in Brunswick, probably doing surveillance on a payroll delivery. He was found to be in possession of a pistol that he said he needed for protection.

When he was taken back to an interview room in the Russell Street police station he turned around and shaped up to the lone detective. Laurie's judgment was slightly flawed as he had decided to take on a policeman training for an upcoming boxing competition. The policeman hit him twice and Laurie wanted to make friends.

'I asked him why he wanted a fight and he said, "I just wanted to test your reflexes, no hard feelings".'

Two months after he was acquitted of the Bennett murder he met the woman he would marry. They were an odd couple, proving that opposites attract. She worked in banks. He robbed them. Perhaps they could have driven to work together.

In May 1981 he married Ursula and they had a child, Lauren – whose godfather, police say, was Russell Cox, the notorious New South Wales escapee and gunman.

In 1982 the young family moved to the outer Melbourne suburb of Warrandyte, where they were building a new house. Even then he tried to make it difficult for enemies to find him. He chose to buy the land in the name of David Carter – one of his many aliases.

'Once Laurie met me we stayed close as a family and tried to keep to ourselves. Laurie didn't really want me to associate with my old friends,' Ursula would tell police later.

In 1985 – seven years after Les Kane was killed, and three years after Brian Kane's murder – Prendergast remained wary. He used disguises, refused to trust strangers and stuck with an old crew of contacts he had known for years. As police said, 'Laurence Prendergast lived in constant fear of being murdered.' It was the only way he knew to survive.

For the moment.

One of his oldest friends, Christopher Dale Flannery, was in his own underworld war in Sydney and had just become a casualty.

Flannery went missing on 9 May 1985. Some suggest Prendergast started to make noises that he would try to avenge Flannery's death.

The theory goes that Prendergast (rightly) blamed George Freeman for Flannery's death and planned to hit the Sydney crime boss.

One theory is that Freeman, a renowned race fixer, decided to fix the situation by getting in first and organising for Prendergast to go missing the way his mate Flannery had.

Certainly, many believed that Prendergast had worked with Flannery in Sydney. Former Sydney detective Roger Rogerson went as far as to claim it was Prendergast who shot undercover policeman Mick Drury in his Chatswood home on 6 June 1984.

About a week before Prendergast went missing in August 1985 his wife borrowed $6000 from a credit company and gave him the money.

She told police that although they were not financially stable, Prendergast acquired a passport in July for an overseas trip.

So just weeks after Flannery had gone missing Prendergast found the need to be able to head overseas. And he needed cash – quickly.

There was another sign that the normally cautious criminal felt he was at greater than normal risk. After years of police raids, he had taken to hiding handguns so that he didn't get charged with being a felon in possession. But shortly after Flannery went missing he began to carry a gun again.

Ursula told police he carried a silver pistol when he felt threatened. She said that in the last month before he disappeared he began to sleep with it under his pillow. He took it from storage just after Flannery disappeared.

On 15 August, the same day she gave Prendergast the $6000 in cash, Ursula took their daughter to the Gold Coast to visit her parents.

Laurie stayed home, because he was scared of flying. Prendergast and his 13-year-old stepson Carl met up with a group of men. The teenager noticed Laurie was carrying a paper bag full of cash. Was this the loan money? If so, what was he trying to buy?

Certainly there were no obvious signs Prendergast planned to disappear. He had invested heavily in his new house and had just commissioned an in-ground pool.

On Friday 23 August Laurie let Carl skip school as it was the last day of term and they had both had a late night. They cleaned the house for Ursula's return. Then Prendergast drove Carl to Doncaster Shopping Town. The arrangement was that the boy would later catch a bus back to Warrandyte then call Laurie from a local coffee shop to get a lift home. When there was no answer he walked home.

Earlier, two builders working on the block next door had seen Prendergast drive from the house in his silver Volvo. There is no evidence that he returned.

When Carl walked in he found two cups and two dirty plates from a meal of baked beans in the sink. There was also half a load of washing in the machine and part in the dryer.

This surprised Carl as it seemed strange to leave the house messy after they had spent the morning cleaning it ready for his mother's return.

That night Ursula called home to say she would be back the next day.

'Laurie was meticulous when it came to punctuality, so it seemed odd to me that he hadn't contacted Carl to let him know where he was.'

On the same day a woman noticed a silver Volvo parked in Cartwell Street, Heidelberg. When it hadn't been moved four days later, she reported it to police.

It was Prendergast's car – parked and locked. The radio was still tuned to 3KZ, Laurie's favourite station. In the car was the remote control to his garage and the Football Record from the previous week's Essendon v. Melbourne game.

Carl would later tell police that when they were at the football Prendergast saw someone he recognised and needed to avoid.

But there was something else in the car – a cigarette butt. Friends said Laurie was not a smoker and did not let anyone smoke inside the Volvo.

When Ursula arrived home someone who understood her concerns picked her up. It was Gail Bennett, Ray's widow.

She went to a lawyer's house that night and contact was made with the major crime squad. The following morning she officially reported Prendergast missing to the Brighton police but she remained so frightened she refused to give her home address.

She would tell police later, with an understandable touch of bitterness, 'Laurie's friends show no concern as to his disappearance or whereabouts.'

Either they didn't care or they already knew what had happened and there was nothing they could do about it.

Ursula told police, 'When I started going through Laurie's things a couple of days after he disappeared, I located that pistol secreted amongst his clothes in his drawer in the robe in the main bedroom. I believe this indicates that Laurie wouldn't have left home on his own accord or that, if he did voluntarily leave home to meet someone, then he trusted the person he was going to meet.'

Certainly she had her suspicions, once confronting his cousin Billy at gunpoint although there was no evidence pointing to his involvement.

Laurie and his cousin Billy were not close but in the months before he went missing they began to socialise again. A witness told police he saw Billy's van near his cousin's home on the day he disappeared.

Billy chose to remove the name Prendergast from the side of his VW van around the time Laurie disappeared. It was probably a wise move.

There were many theories about what happened. One was that he was abducted and murdered in Yarrawonga, set up by the group still loyal to the Kanes. The most popular theory, of course, was that he was killed as a pre-emptive strike before he could move against George Freeman's Sydney forces as a payback for killing Flannery.

As Coroner Maurice Gurvich found, 'In many ways the story that unfolded here resembled the plot of a gangster movie of the genre popularised by the Warner Brothers. There was evidence of deception, aliases, disguises, fraud, strange property and financial transactions, large sums of money in a paper bag, a missing gun and other evidence, all central to the disappearance of Laurence Prendergast. And there were allegations of a cover-up and conspiracy. All this together with the intervention of a clairvoyant make the ingredients of a good B grade screenplay.'

Or could it all be much simpler?

One of his closest – and most violent – friends suspected that Laurie had been making after hours visits to his wife.

So was it the oldest motive of all?

When Kath Flannery was interviewed by the National Crime Authority in Sydney the widow asked, 'How are you going with Laurie Prendergast?'

Detective: *Not good.*

Kath: *I would be looking in his own camp.*

10

COX THE FOX
ESCAPEE WHO WROTE THE ROBBER'S RULEBOOK

The gang was better equipped,
better trained and better
prepared than the police who
were trying to catch them.

NO WONDER there was a rush to rent the neat weatherboard home in the quiet bayside hideaway of Mt Martha, south east of Melbourne.

For a start, it was only 200 metres from Port Phillip Bay, with access to beach and water. And, on the outer fringe of suburbia, it was ideal for someone seeking seclusion at a reasonable price. Many houses in the area were holiday homes, vacant most of the year. The rest were largely occupied by retirees who respected their neighbours' privacy.

Four families applied to take the long-term lease on the fully furnished house. But after examining references and conducting interviews the owners felt they had found the perfect tenants in a couple who introduced themselves as Kevin and Sharon Ames.

And for six months after the couple moved in, the owners had no reason to doubt their choice.

He was a fitness fanatic who went to bed early and she was a stay-at-home type who spent evenings knitting in front of the television.

They were never short of money, paid their rent on time, looked after the property properly and without complaint and didn't throw parties. He was always up and out by 5am for his daily run on the beach with his dog. (Later it would be established that fitness was not his only motivation: he wanted to be out of the house at the time police traditionally carried out early morning raids).

But on 3 January 1983 the quiet tenants had one of their rare visitors. It was a man in his early 40s, driving a flash imported maroon Chevrolet utility.

It was the first week of the New Year, where work traditionally takes a back seat to sun and socializing, but this group of people was self-employed and rarely took a break.

The meeting this day, in the quiet house in Helena Street, was about business and it would end badly.

The fact was that the tenants were Russell Cox, a New South Wales prison escapee and prolific armed robber, and his loyal de facto wife Helen Deane.

Cox was known as 'Mad Dog' although he was one of the coolest criminals around. That's why, while on the run for more than a decade, he was able to blend into the background. And that's why he was known inside prisons in three states as 'Cox the Fox.'

The 'Mad Dog' nickname was given to Cox by one of the authors. It was not one of his career highlights.

Many times Cox was close to capture, but each time he was able to talk or fight his way out of trouble. Once, when stopped by two Queensland police, he pulled a gun, disarmed them and drove off.

A Victorian policeman who had been training at an inner-suburban boxing gym went for a drink in Richmond with a few of his sparring partners. At the pub he was introduced to a quiet bloke sitting at the bar. They had a chat and then the quiet man drifted away. It was Cox.

Once, when overcharged at a Japanese restaurant, he queried the bill then meekly backed down rather than risk a public confrontation.

The restaurant manager might have been less self-righteous if he'd known the quiet customer was almost certainly carrying a gun.

But Cox was extremely violent if he were cornered. He was a much better friend than enemy – as his visitor in the American car was about to find out.

Cox had been serving life for the attempted murder of a prison officer in an earlier escape, then broke out of the top security Katingal division of Sydney's Long Bay Prison in 1977. The division was later closed on humanitarian grounds – not that it worried Cox, by then long gone.

When he was let into the exercise yard he pulled himself up with one arm and cut through the bars with the other with a saw. He then painted the bars to hide the saw cuts until he was ready to go.

Just on lock-up time he said he'd forgotten his runners and slipped back into the exercise yard, through the window, over two football fields and away.

It was a feat of strength and ingenuity. But prison authorities expected he would be back in custody within days. They were optimistic. It took eleven years.

The Chevrolet driver was hot-rod enthusiast and gunman Ian Revell Carroll, a heavy player in Melbourne's underworld for decades.

They were there to discuss future jobs and to split dividends. It had been a good year and the future was looking even better. They had guns, brains and an inside man in a security firm.

It was, for them, a boom-boom economy. They were part of Australia's best ever stick-up crew. The gang included the surviving elements of Ray Bennett's Great Bookie Robbery team, reinforced by hand picked replacements such as Santo Mercuri (who, five years later, would kill security guard Dominic Hefti during an armed robbery in Brunswick) and Cox himself.

The team had lost key players to guns, drugs and prison but they had eager apprentices, including two young men whose underworld careers would blossom until they were shot dead in a later underworld war – Jason and Mark Moran.

For Jason it was an interesting career choice. It meant he was working with the survivors of the team that killed his wife's father – Leslie Herbert Kane.

It also meant he worked side by side with Cox, the number one suspect for killing her uncle (and his childhood hero) – Brian Kane. So while blood may be thicker than water, cash speaks all languages. And a rolling stone gathers no moss and a watched pot never boils – but we digress.

Carroll was another graduate from the Painters and Dockers crime finishing school. He was arrested with Neil Stanley Collingburn in 1971 when police found a set of golf clubs suspected of being stolen in the boot of a car the pair were using.

Collingburn received fatal injuries while in police custody. Two detectives, Brian Francis Murphy and Carl John Stillman, were later acquitted of manslaughter. It was later established that the interview and the fatal consequences were pointless. The clubs were legitimately acquired and not stolen.

Carroll, a former professional boxer, had been recruited by Bennett as a key member of the Bookie Robbery team. While he was supposed to be living as a battler on waterfront wages he had graduated to executive class, driving his Mercedes or one of his eight vintage cars. He put his children through private school and began several businesses, including a computer company and an American car-importing firm.

A posthumous check of his financial records showed he had more than twenty bank accounts, some in false names, and an impressive property portfolio. He was building a luxury home on a two-hectare block in the outer Melbourne suburb of Wonga Park.

In the months that followed the Bookie Robbery, Carroll deposited nearly $450,000 in cash in different accounts. It was unlikely to have come from overtime at the docks.

In the six months from September 1981 until February 1982, Carroll made a series of huge deposits in his various accounts. His income spike coincided with four Melbourne armed robberies that netted the gang nearly $600,000 in cash. Business was so good that Carroll was able to take a 35-day holiday in the US.

Cox and Carroll had become almost inseparable. Carroll's friends and relatives noticed the usually gregarious car enthusiast had become secretive and chose to spend most of his time with the mysterious escapee.

On this day when Carroll went to visit Cox, money was one of the first items up for discussion. As no minutes are kept of such business meetings, police could only piece together fragments of what happened that afternoon.

It was a warm afternoon when a man holidaying with family and friends decided to take a break from listening to the fifth Test in the Ashes series during the tea break. (He didn't miss much. It was a draw. England nightwatchman, the rotund Eddie Hemmings made a stubborn 95 but, again, we digress).

The man stretched his legs and then sat in the back yard and opened a book. It was 3.55pm.

Over the side fence he heard an argument and a scuffle. 'I heard a woman scream, "Don't shoot him!" or "Don't point that at him!"'

When he peered over the fence he saw a man and a woman struggling. The woman had a pistol in her hand and appeared to be fighting a losing battle to keep the gun away from him. The man screamed, 'Give me the fucking gun.'

The witness said the man dragged her away and grabbed the handgun. 'I saw this man raise the gun and fire one shot towards the back fence. I just thought it was a cap pistol or someone playing so I thought nothing of it and went back to reading my book.'

It must have been a riveting read.

About two minutes later he heard another shot and looked over again. 'I saw a person lying on the ground in the middle of the back yard dragging himself along the ground towards the house. He fell to the ground. I presumed he was dead.'

When police were called, the man in the backyard was, indeed, very dead.

Just months earlier the cashed-up Carroll had bought the Mt Martha house from the couple that had rented it to Cox.

So not only did Cox kill his business partner but his landlord.

Dead, Ian Revell Carroll was able to tell police more about the elite team of armed robbers than he ever had when he was alive.

It was clear he had been in a fight before he was shot. He had a bruise on his left shoulder and a bite mark on his left upper arm. His right knuckles were bruised and his left thumbnail was black and bloody. He had cuts and abrasions to both knees.

He was wearing conservative brown corduroy pants and a tee shirt. The only clue that he may have been a gangster (besides the bullet holes) was the gold chain around his neck and the heavy tattoos over his legs, arms and back. Further examination would show old wounds, including one where he was shot in April 1972.

He must have been a slow learner.

Where Carroll was found near the shed behind the house, a trail of blood was still visible on the grass.

In his pocket was a bloodied Seiko watch, indicating he could have used the old street fighter's technique of using it as a make-shift knuckle-duster.

He had been shot twice with a .38 handgun. One bullet went into the pelvis and created little damage. But the second entered the left side of the chest and went through both lungs, causing him to drown in his own blood as he crawled towards the house to get help.

He was found lying on his back in the yard with his head resting against a trellis.

In the driveway were two parked cars – a Ford Escort panel van and Carroll's Chevrolet utility. The driver's seat cover of the orange Escort was drenched in blood and in the back on a mattress was an Able Baby hammerless .22 revolver also covered in blood.

The front bench seat of the Chev was bloodstained, indicating someone bleeding heavily had hopped into the car from the passenger side and slipped over behind the wheel. There was an empty, black holster under the front seat that would have fitted the bloodied .22.

It was what police would find inside the house that revealed the secrets of the armed robbery team that had pulled the biggest jobs in Australia for seven years.

There was a blood-covered green towel in the bathroom and a partly-cooked meal on the stove.

The house was 'clean'. There was not one envelope, note, address book or diary that would point to the real identity of the people renting the house.

But there was a mountain of evidence that showed the real nature of their business.

In the hallway was a bloodstained, orange stool directly under a ceiling manhole that was askew and smeared with blood.

There was a dust mark where an object had been moved. In the ceiling space was a vinyl bag containing a wig, a walkie-talkie and a police scanner. A second plastic box contained silencers, a small radio receiver, a machine gun and boxes of ammunition wrapped in a tablecloth.

It was clear police had found the command centre of the payroll gang. And there was more – much more.

They soon found three large wooden chests originally used to import and export parts for Carroll's car business.

The boxes, about a metre tall, wide and long, were topped with tools to look like tradesmen's boxes. But in carefully-made hidden compartments, police would find what Detective Senior Sergeant David Sprague would describe as, 'One of the largest arrays of weaponry and associated crime equipment ever seized in this state.'

It included machine guns, military semi-automatic weapons, handguns and a pistol stolen from Ireland.

There were stick-on tradesmen signs to use on the side of vehicles during armed robbery surveillance, disguises, security guard uniforms, medical kits that included bandages, painkilling injections, antibiotics and splints.

The official police inventory listed: 'The hidden compartment in one box contained four revolvers, two armalite rifles, magazines, ammunition, handcuffs, balaclavas, bullet resistant vests, false vehicle, personal identification signs and stolen Armaguard uniforms. The top sections of the boxes contained tools and overalls, giving the appearance of being a legitimate tradesman's toolbox should they be searched. Other boxes included items such as liquid ammonia and tennis balls for guard dogs, first-aid kit containing pethidine, morphine, motor vehicle ignition barrels, handcuffs, bullet resistant vests, gas masks, hand-knitted balaclavas, false magnetic vehicle signs, magnetic flashing lights, stolen security company uniforms and false moustaches, hair and skin colouring. Two of the revolvers located in the residence were from an armoured vehicle robbery and an automatic pistol was stolen from a Northern Ireland Police Officer.'

In short, it proved that the gang was better equipped, better trained and better prepared than the police who were trying to catch them.

Detectives also found handwritten notes on armoured car movements in Queensland, Victoria and New South Wales.

The blood in the two cars and through the houses showed that Carroll had managed to shoot Cox in the gun battle.

Cox, they say, was prepared for any contingency, and although badly wounded, climbed on the stool to grab his escape kit from the ceiling that included cash, firearms, false identity papers and first aid equipment.

The blood smears in both cars indicated he had a serious wound to the upper left thigh. Police say he tried the two cars before leaving in a third that was backed into the drive just after the shooting.

A Ford panel van was later recovered in Oakleigh. The previous owner was one Santo Mercuri – an armed robber who would later turn killer.

There was a green towel saturated in blood and a pool under the driver's pedals. Experts estimated the wounded man had lost more than two litres. He was in deep trouble.

Cox's longtime lover Helen Deane was a nurse's aide who could help in the short term but she would have known he needed expert medical assistance to survive.

If the injured man went to a local hospital or medical centre a doctor may have linked him to the Mt Martha killing as the news broke. So he and Deane drove to New South Wales, convincing a doctor in Gosford that the wounded man had accidentally shot himself in New Guinea. Cox told the doctor he chose to fly home for treatment rather than risk the poor medical standards there. As a self-inflicted wound sustained outside Australia, there was no need to report the 'accident' to authorities.

The doctor swallowed the story while Cox swallowed the painkillers. The bullet was dug out, the wound cleaned and the fitness fanatic escapee made a full recovery.

Detectives went through the Mt Martha house looking for clues. Then they returned to the backyard and to a roughly-made shed that was probably once a child's cubby house. Inside, police found two bullets of different calibres, a pair of men's leather sandals, blood on the floor and signs of a struggle, including broken cement sheets that made up the walls. They believed the dispute started in the shed and then spilled into the yard.

Police forensic experts carefully dismantled the shed looking for clues. They found wood, cement sheets and bricks, then a grounding of sand. They dug down – but not deep enough.

The object of the argument was just a few centimetres under their feet – a large plastic barrel designed for home brewed beer.

Six months later police returned and dug again. This time they found the barrel. It was empty. Many years later Dave Sprague, by then a Commander, said he believed the barrel had contained at least $1 million in cash and probably documents such as passports.

'That's what they were arguing over,' he said.

Cox, or someone acting for him, came back to get the money after police cleared the crime scene in January.

Waste not, want not.

THE child who would eventually become known as Russell Cox was born Melville Peter Schnitzerling in Brisbane 15 September 1949, several weeks before he was due. The tiny premature baby was nicknamed 'Tim' by his family.

As a boy, he was in and out of Queensland youth training centres, Boystown and Westbrook, before finally being sent to an adult jail in 1966 for stealing a car in Seymour. In 1972, he started to use the name Russell Cox and began his long career as an armed robber.

In 1974 he was arrested in New South Wales over a string of armed robbery and theft charges and sentenced to eleven years. His co-offender was a Melbourne man on the make – Gregory John Workman – the Preston hoodlum shot dead by Alphonse Gangitano in 1995.

In 1975, after an unsuccessful attempt to break out of Sydney's Long Bay Jail, Cox was sentenced to life for the attempted murder of prison officers during the escape bid. For Cox it was just a hiccup and within two years he had learned from his mistakes. Not by reforming but by refining his escape methods.

On 3 November 1977, he broke out of the supposedly escape-proof Katingal Division of Long Bay and soon teamed up with master tactician Ray Bennett in Melbourne.

How come?

Police were to find much later that the escape of some of Australia's most dangerous prisoners were not one-off events.

The Australian Bureau of Criminal Intelligence completed an investigation, code-named Operation GAP, which found that a nationwide network existed to help prisoners on the run. It found that the group provided escapees with safe houses and fake documents.

The theory was confirmed when it was found that jail breakers and armed robbers Christopher Dean 'Badness' Binse and James Edward 'Jockey' Smith used the same safe house in Daylesford at different times while on the run. Gunman Ian 'Rabbit' Steele was also provided with a fake passport to head to England – a novel twist that sent a convict back to the Old Dart. It did Steele no good. He was later sentenced to life there for murder.

On New Year's Eve 1977, a notorious armed robber was arrested in Northcote in a shootout but a second man jumped from the car and escaped. Police believe it was Cox.

He used forged identity papers to successfully apply for a passport under the name of Gary Nevin, giving his address as Williams Road, Toorak.

In May 1978, prison officers found evidence of an attempt to break *into* Katingal. This was something different. According to police intelligence, Cox and another well-known armed robber had tried to free some mates.

They failed – proving that while you could break out of the 'escape-proof' jail it was too hard to break in.

Cox was to find more than a partner in crime when he teamed up with Bennett. He would find a partner for life.

In 1978 he met Helen Eva Deane, Bennett's sister-in-law, and they became lovers.

The green-eyed, petite Deane was educated at the Prahran Technical School and had become a qualified nursing aide.

She was blood loyal to Cox, nursing him when he was shot and abandoning friends and some relatives to live life on the run.

Late in 1978 they moved to Queensland but he maintained his links with the Melbourne underworld.

He would fly in key members of the Bookie Robbery team for the jobs. But it cost to enlist the best and on one occasion he just broke even after masterminding the robbery of the Strathpine ANZ branch of $5780. He later said it cost him nearly $5000 to fly his handpicked crew (including Ray Bennett) from Melbourne and back.

Other jobs were more lucrative – including payroll jobs from the Prince Charles Hospital ($16,618), Royal Women's Hospital ($62,446), Woodlands ($38,000), Boral Cyclone ($21,348), Queensland Railways ($327,000) and Queensland Bacon ($90,329).

Cox stayed on the run not only because he knew how to commit an armed robbery but when to walk away from one.

In November 1983, Queensland police scored a tip-off that Cox was planning to rob the Brisbane railway yards. The armed robbery squad launched a stake-out operation.

Cox walked into the yards, wandered into the canteen and bought a drink. This was his usual practice before a 'job'. He did his own surveillance, wandering around his target dressed as a worker. He saw two men in railway uniforms but correctly picked the dog with them as a police canine.

When he left, driving an old Valiant, he was pulled over by two members of the squad, who did not know he was their suspect.

Cox was to pull a gun, disarm the two detectives steal their keys, lock the police car and drive off, leaving them unharmed.

While he would have had no compunction about killing police, he knew shots would bring back up – followed by unrelenting pursuit. He knew it was always better to slip away than shoot it out.

COX and Deane lived healthy lifestyles on the run. She was a vegetarian who used herbal toothpaste and he rarely ate red meat.

Standover man Mark 'Chopper' Read once remarked the most dangerous thing about Cox was the vegetarian curry he cooked in Pentridge's high security H Division. He was a repeat offender.

Cox fancied German beer and good wine and the couple loved Japanese food. Living on the run did not thwart their international travel plans. They visited Japan and the Philippines using false passports while being hunted around Australia. He later said he also went to the UK, where he worked as a seaman.

Cox managed to stay at least one step ahead for more than a decade because he was smart enough not to play the tough guy. For a violent criminal, Cox could appear remarkably calm. He became an expert at appearing ordinary in extraordinary circumstances.

Cox and Deane would always rent moderate, furnished homes, which they would share with their black Labrador, Devil.

Cox's brother was a champion surfer who retired in the United States, and athleticism and self-discipline ran in the family. Cox loved the beach and regularly ran fifteen kilometres a day. But he didn't drop his guard. He always had a sub-machine gun under the front seat of his car and had a handgun concealed on his body even when running.

The chatty Deane and quiet Cox passed as perfect tenants and usually provided glowing references when renting a house.

In November 1981 they moved into a small house in Lynette Street, Nunawading, taking a six-month lease at just $75 a week. An armed robbery squad detective rented a similar home just two streets away but did not cross paths with the fugitive.

In January 1982 Cox and Deane made sixteen separate deposits for a total of $30,000 in a building society account held under false names. They travelled around Victoria to make the deposits making sure that none were big enough to raise suspicions.

In February, Cox withdrew $25,000 to buy 80 hectares at Broadford next to a property owned by the Hells Angels motorcycle gang. Police reports suggest Cox and Deane used the small log cabin on their country retreat as an emergency safe house. In March 1983, two months after the Carroll murder, the cabin was found burnt out. Police believe it was either a revenge attack by friends of Carroll's or – more likely – it was torched by Cox himself to remove any evidence he had stayed there while recovering from his gunshot wound.

Detectives say Cox tapped a phone line into a police station so that he remained up to date on the search for him.

During one raid where police narrowly missed the pair, they found theatrical books, which had chapters on make-up. They believed he used actor's make-up, false teeth and wigs to continually change his appearance.

Cox preferred heavy, military-style weapons and kept bulletproof vests and gas masks.

He often used the alias 'Mr Williams', the same name used by his favorite comic hero, The Phantom. Even Devil the dog had an alias: he was known as 'Butch' when they were on the run. In fact, he might not have answered to his real name at all.

After the Carroll killing, Cox moved to Queensland and joined the Royal Automobile Club of Queensland under a false name. He bought two high-powered military weapons from a Brisbane gun shop after producing fake identity papers.

He studied Australian bushrangers, including Ned Kelly and the 'Wild Colonial Boy'. His favourite magazine was *Soldier of Fortune*. He also read non-fiction Australian crime books, contributing in a small way to these authors' meagre income in those lean years.

According to 'Chopper' Read, Cox won $15,000 on Tattslotto while on the run. 'I've shot people for less,' he said.

Read also said Cox had once revealed he'd turned to crime when he won a raffle for a new bike when he was ten years old but because he wasn't present at the draw the prize was withdrawn and raffled again. He was so angry 'he stole a brand new bike and told everyone he had won it in a raffle,' Read said.

Read said Cox was famous in the underworld for his cool head.

'He was pulled over for licence checks and breath tests and was never fazed. Once, when there were police screaming all over the place, he just drove off. The police didn't notice the dog running after the car. Russell just opened the door of the car and Devil jumped in, barking out the back window at the police, who were blissfully unaware.'

Cox was cool under pressure, a loving partner and would try to avoid a fight if he could but, underneath it all, he was a gunman.

IT would be the hardest job in policing: to go undercover and infiltrate the tight knit Bookie Robbery team.

The risks were enormous. This mob killed rivals and would have no hesitation in shooting nosy outsiders.

But Graeme Henderson, a detective who had just returned from studying overseas under a Churchill fellowship, was keen to use the tactics he had learned and there was no bigger target than Ray Bennett.

Henderson recruited Rob Robertson, a Vietnam veteran, who was brave to the point of recklessness, and together they would be the first full-time undercovers in Victoria.

It was nearly two years after the robbery that police found their first way in – and that was only because the gang had no intention of retiring on the spoils from the Victoria Club.

They continued to pull off big jobs in Perth and Brisbane using methods imported from the London team known as the Wembley Mob. In February 1978 they were looking for a new target in Melbourne.

Bennett believed the heat was off them. His best friend, Norman 'Chops' Lee, had been acquitted of charges over the Bookie Robbery and most of the team were free and available.

Again he hand-picked the crew and this time included an armed robbery expert who would never crack under pressure – Russell Cox.

After all, Cox was near enough to family now that he was living with Bennett's sister-in-law.

As usual, Bennett wanted an inside man and on 18 February 1978, a Queensland SP bookmaker made tentative approaches at Flemington races to a part-time worker for the Mayne Nickless security company, the same firm that handled the cash delivered on the day of the Bookie Robbery.

If the security man could provide information on cash movements and payroll deliveries there would be a handsome 'earn' in it for him.

But Mayne Nickless learned of the potential breach through its own security systems and contacted police, who slipped Robertson into the firm.

The operation, code named Osprey, was designed to destroy the million-dollar payroll gang.

Robertson became Brian Wilson – a security guard with a weakness for luxury cars and fast women. And he wanted cash to support his lifestyle.

Robertson (as Wilson) twice met the Queensland man – a skilled armed robber known as 'Bikkie' at a North Melbourne hotel to discuss possible targets.

'He told me they were the crew behind the Bookie Robbery and they wanted another job worth between $8 million and $10 million,' Robertson remembers.

On 22 April Robertson met key gang members at Werribee races. Bikkie introduced him to 'Kelvin'. It was Russell Cox.

'He was super fit and super smart. The consummate professional at what he did,' Robertson said later.

The undercover told the team he had identified a likely target – the Country Roads Board offices in Denmark Street, Kew.

While it wouldn't be a $10 million heist, it was still worth the risk.

The payroll would usually be $600,000 but on 4 May it would be swollen to $900,000 because of back pay.

Embellishing the story as he went, he told them it would be 'a piece of cake.'

The inside man was promised 10 per cent of the takings in funds that would be laundered through Dennis William Smith's Manila bar operations.

He was told he would get $5000 up front and the rest about a week later.

Police planned to take the sting to the line. This was their chance to catch the Bookie Robbery master-minds. But it was uncharted waters. Undercover work in the 1970s was rudimentary – largely 'buy-bust' drug deals at a street level. No police in Australia had tried such an elaborate – and dangerous – ruse.

They fitted out a Mayne Nickless armoured van with James Bond style electronic devices to foil the robbery and the Special Operations Group was briefed. The briefing was straightforward: If the crooks have guns don't hesitate to fire. In other words, police were preparing for a gun battle.

They were simpler times and Coroners tended not to ask too many questions.

On 26 April Roberston met 'Kelvin' and 'Bikkie' at a North Melbourne coffee shop. 'They wanted to check me out. Ray Bennett just wandered past to have a good look,' Robertson said.

Four men, including two identified as Bookie Robbers, followed them to the target for last checks before the job.

Cox authorised the raid but only after doing his own homework. He later told Roberston he had donned a workman's dust-coat to check out the building and found the payroll office was protected by only a plywood door. 'He said they would kick it in and do the job without any problems.'

Once Cox approved the job, the team began to gather, with up to fourteen staying in different motels around Melbourne.

At 8pm on the night before the raid, Cox and Robertson met again in North Melbourne. They were waiting for Bikkie to arrive with the $5000 deposit for the information but the Queenslander was late.

Cox suggested they go somewhere quieter to wait and the undercover agreed. They went to the nearby deserted Victoria Market where the police back-up team couldn't follow without being seen.

One of the shadowers said they knew if they went in they would blow the job but if they didn't the undercover's life was at risk.

'He was an ex-serviceman who was absolutely fearless and a first class operative. Basically, I think he was half crazy. He wasn't that flash at his paperwork but he could think on his feet. We decided to let it run.'

Robertson says he felt fully in control. 'I didn't have a gun and I wasn't wearing a tape. I had a knife in my shoe but that wouldn't be much good against a gun. To this day I don't think Cox had any intention of harming me.'

But as they were standing and chatting, a police car with three uniformed police on board pulled over. One of the police recognised Robertson, but was alert enough to realise it was an undercover operation and continued to perform a routine identity check. Robertson produced a fake licence while Cox produced a real, long-barrelled .38 revolver.

'I have no doubt he was going to kill the coppers,' Robertson said. The undercover started talking, telling Cox that he could solve the problem and there was no need to shoot.

He ripped the microphone from the police car and took their guns, throwing them on the market roof.

Robertson then forced them into a large rubbish bin and placed heavy wooden pallets on top.

'Before Cox ran off he said to me "You're a true Briton, and then fired a shot in the air".'

Robertson ran back to the coffee shop to ring for back-up when another police car arrived. He told the two policewomen in the car he was in the middle of an undercover operation and they should not use their radio but ring the head of Osprey, Detective Chief Inspector Fred Silvester.

Despite the warning, one police officer foolishly used the radio to inform headquarters they were talking to an undercover policeman at the market.

'Cox always used police radio scanners. He could have been tipped off straight away. He had the knack of knowing when a job wasn't right and he would walk away from it.'

Cox ran from the market to the Marco Polo Hotel where he met the team leaders.

Meanwhile the SOG was already in the Country Roads Board building, doing a floor by floor search to check if the bandits had already set up.

Cox told the others their inside man had probably been arrested and was still wearing his Mayne Nickless shirt. They believed that if the police connected him to the robbery he would be able to identify some of them. They decided to abort the job and scatter.

It was just as well – for them. The SOG also had a meeting. They were not going to take any chances. The fact that a key gang member was prepared to kill three police hardened their resolve to shoot first.

But Bikkie did send the undercover $500 with a message that he was sorry the job didn't go ahead. Proof that occasionally there is honour among thieves.

Years later, when Robertson was working at the Consorting Squad, he saw Bikkie at the races, sauntered over and just said: 'How's Russell?'

The Queenslander quickly lost his tan, as he turned white.

'Years later I got some feedback from Russell – he said he thought I had done a good job,' Robertson would recall.

IN the end it was dumb luck that brought down Russell Cox and it was sheer luck that kept him alive.

It was on 22 July 1988 when the crew from an armoured van heading to Doncaster Shoppingtown in Melbourne's eastern suburbs radioed police to say they feared they were being followed.

A local divisional van was despatched to check the scene but saw nothing suspicious and radioed headquarters to say they were leaving the area.

But an armed robbery squad crew in the area, headed by Paul 'Fish' Mullett, turned up and located the car, a Holden station wagon, in the shopping centre car park.

Mullett contacted the armed robbery squad office and three crews, all heavily armed, headed east.

Members of the squad, armed with concealed pistol grip shotguns, wandered around the shoppers trying to see would-be armed robbers.

Meanwhile police opened the back of the Holden station wagon and the first item they saw was a prison library card in the name of notorious gunman Raymond John Denning, who had escaped from New South Wales's Goulburn prison just days before.

The detectives knew they were onto a heavy criminal but they were unaware that Denning had teamed up with Cox.

When Denning had escaped he'd headed to Queensland and made immediate contact with Cox, who told him to go to Melbourne where they would meet in Doncaster. He set Denning up in a local motel and began to plan the next armed robbery.

Armed with a scanner Cox, Denning and a woman were inside the shopping complex where they remained until they heard the divvy van report that it was leaving the area.

But the armed robbery squad was equipped with new, 'silent' radios that could not be intercepted by scanners.

Denning, wearing a brown Stetson hat, walked back to the Commodore and slipped in behind the steering wheel. Then a second man, wearing a black hat, wandered over, opened the passenger door and stood there chatting. It was Cox, not that the watching police knew that.

He sat in the passenger seat but left the door ajar as he continued to chat. Finally, he moved away but returned for a few more words before heading to the car parked next to it – a yellow Ford Fairlane sedan.

They were on the move.

As Denning took off an armed robbery squad car, driven by Paul Mullet, drove straight at the station wagon then stopped, just kissing the front bumper. But to be kissed by this Fish did not involve a quick release.

His passenger, Ken Ashworth, later to win a Churchill Fellowship, jumped on the bonnet of Denning's car and pointed a loaded shotgun at the driver. The escapee quickly realised that the gig – and his hands – was up.

But Cox had spent more than a decade on the run because he could slip through doors just before they shut.

He drove straight at detectives while brandishing a dark-coloured revolver. Police opened fire, yelling, 'He's got a gun!'.

Members of the armed robbery squad in the 1980s were famous for many things, such as bravery and the capacity for marathon lunches. One detective even had the ability to sing the *Robin Hood* theme song backwards. But subtlety was not among their many talents.

What occurred next was more fitting to a John Wayne movie than a staid suburban shopping centre.

Police on foot and in cars chased the suspect, who continued to wave a gun. He drove to the edge of the carpark until he saw there was no exit, then threw a U-turn and drove straight back into what must have appeared to be the Guns of Navarone.

The 'robbers' and local police began to fire – sending more than 80 slugs from handguns and shotguns in his direction and peppering the car. The handgun shots bounced off the windscreen until Cox drove directly at them – then Ashworth blasted it out with a shotgun.

Cox's car hit another vehicle and smashed head-on into a wall. But Cox was still armed and ready to chance his luck until Ashworth fired another shot into the passenger door. Only then did Cox concede his eleven years on the run was over.

Miraculously, despite the hail of lead, Cox was left with just a slight nick to an eyebrow caused by a glass fragment. All the shots had missed him.

Over the following few days, police were to receive reports from people whose cars had been parked in the shopping centre inquiring how their vehicles ended up with 'shrapnel' damage.

Dave Brodie was one of the armed robbery squad that day. He joined the police force in 1977, around the time Cox became Australia's most wanted man. 'I always thought it would be fantastic to catch him one day.'

But when the man in the black hat was arrested, no-one knew who he was. 'He just said, "You blokes will jump through hoops when you know who I am."'.

When they checked the cars, police knew they were dealing with a serious crew. In the Ford they found gloves, binoculars, beanies, three sawn-off semi-automatic rifles and shotgun cartridges.

In the wagon they found maps, bullets and a motor vehicle lock pick, a revolver, hair dye and a manual for a hand-held police scanner.

It would have appeared the visitors weren't there for the Myer winter sale.

Detectives took the mystery man back and it was only fingerprints that established they had arrested Russell Cox.

Cox remained staunch and refused to answer questions but he sportingly posed with members of the armed robbery squad for a team snap. The big-game hunters wanted a record of catching the biggest name in Australian crime.

But most of the pictures were stolen when the police photographer's car was burgled the same night.

While Cox refused to talk, Denning – who had escaped while serving a life sentence for escape, malicious wounding and armed robbery – opened up.

'He said they were following the van "for fun" and had no intention of robbing it – at least not then.' Brodie said.

Denning was a cult figure in New South Wales and was seen as a latter day bushranger. So it was a surprise when he became a police informer.

When Denning gave evidence in New South Wales, a man in the gallery threw a bone towards him yelling: 'You forgot your lunch, Denning – here it is.'

Cox and Denning fell out after another armed robber, Graeme Jensen, was killed by police in October 1988. Jensen was killed when police botched an attempt to arrest him over the murder of security guard Dominic Hefti in a robbery. The trouble was, Jensen didn't do it.

According to Denning, Cox was happy that Jensen was killed, believing the Hefti murder would be wrongly pinned on the dead man.

Denning then decided to talk and he had plenty to say. He listed armed robberies and other crimes he knew Cox had committed.

'Russell Cox told me that this murder and armed robbery committed on Dominic Hefti had been done so by himself with Sam Mercuri and a person named Mark Moran.'

He said that after Mercuri was wounded, Cox planned to kidnap a doctor to tend to his mate. 'Mark then said that wasn't a very good idea and Russell was dirty on him for that.'

According to Denning, Cox acted as a crime mentor to Mark and Jason Moran. He said Cox showed them how to build secret compartments after he went to Jason's flat and saw two kilos of speed sitting in a normal drawer. 'Russell told me that he has given Mark and Jason advice in relation to drugs, money, guns and all that in secret compartments.'

Denning said one of the reasons Cox's mail on armed robberies was always right was that he had inherited a security guard contact from Ray Bennett. He paid the guard ten percent for information and once gave him a video player as a bonus.

But the close connection with Bennett was obviously a problem as the Morans were linked to the Kanes through friendship, business and marriage. The tension would have been somewhat greater because it was suspected that Cox almost certainly killed Brian Kane in the Quarry Hotel in Brunswick in 1982.

'Mark's father wasn't to know that Mark was working with Russell because Mark's father had been close to the Kanes over the years,' Denning told police.

According to Denning, Mercuri and Moran turned on Helen Deane when Cox was jailed. 'Sam Mercuri and Mark terrorised her and drugged her, trying to find out information as to where he had money buried.'

He finished his statement saying, 'I realise that I am in great danger of being killed by any number of persons through what I have informed to the police.'

He was right.

Denning received a shortened jail term in exchange for his co-operation but died of a drug overdose in 1999 that many believe was a hotshot. He died only days before he was to give evidence against Cox.

After Cox was arrested, police found a card for a lawn mowing service and through it tracked the gardener's client list to a property in Bowen Road, East Doncaster.

In January 1988 Cox rented the house directly from the owner under the name Peter John Roberts.

Police found a false cupboard in the laundry, disguises, dust-coats with pens in the pockets, notes on movements of armoured car deliveries, a fake plaster cast for an arm and a list of coded phone numbers. The list was given to ASIO but its experts could not crack the Cox code.

Cox had even cut off the tags on his clothes so that if he had to abandon his safe house police would not be able to work out where he shopped.

Police also found a grappling hook with a rope attached and a rowing machine.

But it took police ten days to find his house and the secret storage cupboard was empty.

But the most sinister find was a single page from a telephone book with one name underlined. It was the name of a woman who had inadvertently been involved in the armed robbery in which the security guard Dominic Hefti had been killed.

Just eleven days before Cox's arrest he had led the team of bandits who jumped two armed guards carrying a cash tin from a Coles Warehouse in Barkly Square, Brunswick.

In the struggle, Hefti was shot in the chest and the leg. He died two days later at the Royal Melbourne Hospital.

But Hefti had managed to fire a shot, hitting one of the bandits, Santo Mercuri, in the hand. Cox and his team, including Mark Moran, fled with $33,000.

The bleeding Mercuri commandeered a car from a woman and drove away, eventually making his way to Cox's East Doncaster home, where Helen Deane tended his wound.

The phone book address found at the house was for the woman whose car Mercuri had stolen. Denning later told police, 'It was decided ... that they try to find her home address and knock her because she was the only one that Sam believed had identified him.'

When Cox was caught Deane and Mercuri saw the police helicopter above the shopping centre and fled. A policeman's mother, who lived across the road, later identified both suspects as having been tenants in the house.

Hefti's murder sparked a spate of killings. Police wrongly believed that armed robber Graeme Jensen was responsible and he was shot during a seemingly clumsy attempt to arrest him on 11 October 1988.

The following day two young uniformed police, Constables Steven Tynan and Damian Eyre, were murdered in Walsh Street, South Yarra, as a payback by criminals who believed the armed robbery squad was shooting to kill.

Much later, Ken Ashworth would be assigned to investigate the Hefti murder and he used groundbreaking DNA technology to link Mercuri to the crime. Mercuri, 47, pleaded not guilty to murder and armed robbery but the DNA and X-ray material was overwhelming. He was sentenced to 25 years with a minimum of twenty. He died in jail in 2000.

Before he became a robber, Mercuri was an outstanding sausage maker. Perhaps he would have been better sticking to smallgoods than small arms.

In September 1982, Helen Deane and Russell Cox were invited to a family wedding by Mercuri. A photo taken at the reception shows a smiling Mercuri and Deane. But between them is an empty chair. Even at weddings Cox preferred to be invisible.

After his arrest Cox was charged with a number of offences, including the murder of Carroll but he beat that charge on grounds of self-defence.

At one of his first hearings, police noticed a demure looking woman in the public gallery. It was Helen Deane. They later found out she was armed with a pen pistol.

Cox was never convicted over the many armed robberies he pulled in Queensland (six between 1978 and 1983), the jobs he organised in Victoria nor the three murders he was said to have committed. He was extradited to New South Wales, where a judge found that Katingal was not a gazetted prison and so he beat the escape charge. His initial life sentence for an earlier escape bid and shooting at guards was reduced to a 29-year minimum but the 11 years on the run were included.

Ashworth went to visit him in the hope he would finally talk. 'He just put one hand up and said, "I've got nothing to say," and then he walked away.'

While in prison he was a polite loner who was popular with inmates and prison guards.

He studied at Grafton TAFE and passed courses in computer studies, numeracy, literacy and youth work and first aid. He was awarded a certificate in hospitality and studied food and nutrition. He became a qualified fitness trainer and boxing coach.

The circle was completed when prison guards pushed for his release, believing him to be fully reformed.

Cox had been a ruthless gunman and a violent man. He terrorised payroll and bank staff and was a killer. But ultimately his coolness, his professionalism and his refusal to turn on others won him the respect of police, prison officers and the underworld.

When he was released from prison in 2004, the loyal Helen Deane was waiting. The crook had finally made her an honest woman and they had married while he was still inside jail.

They refused offers of interviews, turned their backs on celebrity gangster status and disappeared to Northern Queensland.

Police believe they are living a quiet life near the beach – probably on what was left of the money dug up from Mt Martha that had been hidden inside a home-brew barrel.

Who says crime doesn't pay?

11

HOSTILE TAKEOVER
FLANNERY APPEARS, ROGER WILSON DISAPPEARS

> The career criminals could have
> been mistaken for detectives
> in their work suits, which is
> exactly what they wanted.

THEY called him 'Rentakill' and he loved it. Christopher Dale Flannery was always one to believe in the value of advertising. For a while, it worked. But ultimately his reputation would get him killed in a business where publicity is a double-edged sword.

Well before it was fashionable, Flannery began to work from home, involved his wife in their growing cottage industry and grasped niche marketing by adapting the snappy brand name that stuck in people's heads – sometimes along with a bullet or a baseball bat.

For $10,000 he would bash a stranger badly enough that the victim needed hospitalisation. For $50,000 (sometimes less) he would kill – and as part of the deal – dispose of the body.

Flannery was born in Melbourne's Queen Victoria Hospital on 15 March 1949, the youngest of three children of Edward and Noelle Mary Flannery. But Edward senior walked out when Chris was still in nappies. Noelle divorced him on the grounds he beat her. The youngster vowed he would never see his father again and he kept his word. But he loved the rest of his family and even after he became a paid killer he would ring his mum every fortnight and send her a card on Mother's Day. He apparently couldn't see the irony that he left many mothers without their loved ones. He did once say if the price was right he would kill his own mother, but he was joking – probably.

As a schoolboy, Flannery was a champion swimmer who made under-age Victorian finals. Thirty years later his swimming ability couldn't help him when his body was allegedly dumped into the sea.

It would be just one theory. There would be many but they all shared one element: that he died violently at the hands of men he knew.

He went to five schools before leaving at the earliest opportunity at age fourteen. What young Chris wanted to learn they didn't teach in class. His elder brother, Ed, became a successful lawyer and his sister became a schoolteacher. Ed died in Melbourne at a young age from cancer. Chris also died relatively young, but more suddenly.

By the age of twelve, Chris was on the road to becoming a gangster. He started as a car thief and house burglar. By the age of sixteen he was a rapist and had convictions for assaulting police and carrying firearms. He was an armed robber and habitually carried a gun before he could vote.

His sidekick in the rape and attempted armed robbery was Laurence Joseph Prendergast: another Melbourne man with a vicious temper, a lack of respect for human life and a love of guns. Many years later they would go missing just months apart and neither body would be found.

The case of the Crown v. Flannery and Prendergast was such a classic that it has been taught in Victorian law schools for more than twenty years. In fact, the case lasted longer than they did.

Flannery was a poor student who would turn violent at the first sign of a problem – and there were many. He left his last school before he had completed year nine but he was neither stupid nor illiterate.

A boy who grew up with him but would take a different path – he became a policeman – said of Flannery: 'He was a cocky, good-looking kid who made an impression.'

The young Flannery dressed to impress, wearing Cuban-heeled shoes, smart shirt, pressed pants, a white trench coat topped with a black Stetson.

Blond and charismatic, as an observer later commented, he had star quality. Quietly spoken and sometimes charming, his sharp image could not hide his filthy temper. One day in church a much larger Greek boy was mocking the service. Flannery smashed him in the face, took him outside and beat him senseless.

Flannery, the theologian, had obviously failed to grasp the concept of turning the other cheek, although he knew plenty about giving cheek.

He began to step out with a teenage girl with a distinct bee-hive hairdo, a severe face and snappy clothes. She was popular with the young men of Coburg but when she was fifteen she would eventually fall for Chris who was just seventeen. They met at the Heidelberg Town Hall dance where many long-term and more short-term relationships were consummated upstairs in the cheap seats.

Back then she was just a young girl looking for a good time and a little excitement. They went out a few times but drifted apart until years later. When her first marriage was on the rocks she again found Chris, by that time in prison breaking them.

A friend invited her to visit Flannery in jail and this time they stuck – marrying in 1978 while he was still in prison. It certainly saved money on the reception.

To police she became known as Kath 'Kiss-of-Death' Flannery. She was blindly loyal to her husband and just as intimidating.

Much later a New South Wales Coroner wrote of Kath: 'Her relationship with him should not be equated with a "Bonnie and Clyde" degree of association but nonetheless I am convinced she possessed a not insignificant knowledge of her husband's criminal activities and the extent of his contact with the criminal milieu. A number of witnesses who knew the Flannerys suggested that of the two, Kath Flannery had the stronger personality.'

One of his close friends when he was growing up was Michael Ebert, who would become a big player in the Melbourne vice scene until he was shot dead outside one of his Carlton massage parlours on 17 April 1980, reputedly by another career criminal who had designs on Ebert's woman. It was a case of all's fair in love and war, the .38 calibre way.

Flannery taught himself the basics of the human body, not to heal but to hurt. He wanted to know about bone, muscle and vital organs and what bullets would destroy them. He had a book of pathology, which he used as a working text. He also played up to his deadly reputation, famously running barbeques with the beer kept on ice in a coffin.

As a teenager he took up with another young armed robber in Alan Williams and their business dealings much later would change the face of policing.

By 1966 he had graduated to adult courts and later served four years for rape. A year after his parole he and Prendergast were charged with attempted armed robbery. He jumped bail and fled to Western Australia, where he became a buyer with David Jones.

He was not looking for a new start, just fresh opportunities. Suspected of robbing the department store in May 1974, he fled to Sydney. There, he was arrested at West Ryde railway station by one Roger Caleb Rogerson, who described the incident as a 'very violent struggle ... It was a fight to the death, almost.'

Flannery was flown back to Western Australia in an air force transport plane and a straitjacket (thereby missing out on his frequent flyer points and the little biscuits they serve with a cup of tea).

He was acquitted of the Perth crime and immediately extradited to Victoria to answer the earlier charge. Along the way the suburban peacock, failed armed robber and street thug became a paid assassin.

He became a bouncer at Mickey's Disco in St Kilda – a dodgy nightclub frequented by young adults looking for a good time and gangsters looking for a bad one. He began to socialise with people who fancied having a human Rottweiler on tap. People like Ron Feeney, part owner of Mickey's and well connected in the underworld. And like Tom Ericksen, a one-legged private investigator, who tried to play both sides of the fence even if he couldn't jump one.

The evil Ericksen, or 'Hopalong Tom' as he was known in police circles, was a Machiavellian character. He first employed Flannery to bash and hospitalise a well-known book retailer for a real or imagined indiscretion.

From there it all went downhill.

MICKEY'S Disco was a seedy joint, the sort of nightclub where you could get anything for a price. Not that the price affected the off-duty police who drank there beside hookers and gangsters and – even worse – reporters.

Every now and again a 'tourist' from the real world would stumble in for a Bacardi and coke and drink to the disco beat of the latest popular tunes, unaware that this was the black heart of Melbourne's underworld. Crimes were planned, spleens vented, teeth re-arranged and vendettas started on the nightclub's sticky carpet. Off-duty detectives and on-duty gangsters worked side-by-side as heavy-duty bouncers.

And one of the most unpredictable doormen of the whole crew was the well-dressed and slightly unhinged Flannery, who worked under the tutelage of Feeney – a well-known underworld figure and no stranger to violence.

Flannery was ambitious and keen to make a mark (other than the ones he habitually left on the faces of unsuspecting patrons). He didn't want to control the door – he wanted to own it.

When one of the smaller owners wanted out, Flannery jumped at the chance and bought a ten percent share. Feeney still owned 41 percent but maths was never Flannery's strong suit. He started to behave as if he were the boss. And he managed to do what appeared to be impossible: he took Mickey's downmarket.

'After Flannery had bought the shares, things started to go wrong. His wife Kathy came to work there and the takings started to drop,' Feeney would tell police later.

He said Flannery would invite friends to 'his' nightclub, including a young gunman, Alphonse John Gangitano, and an older one, Kevin John Henry 'Weary' Williams.

'There were a lot of fights and Chris and his friends used to belt people up.

'Chris was a very hard man and told me on one occasion that he would knock his mother for five or ten grand.'

One night at the club he saw Flannery in deep conversation with former lawyer turned corporate raider Mark Alfred Clarkson, who was sipping on a scotch and dry.

Feeney later claimed that after Clarkson left the club Flannery wanted some free advice. He recalled the conversation:

Flannery: *If you had to get rid of a body, what would be the best way?*

Feeney: *Take it ten miles out in the bay and dump it.*

Flannery: *No, I reckon, dig a big hole up the bush.*

Feeney: *Why?*

Flannery: *I'm gonna' tell you somethin'. It was just put to me to get rid of a body. I was told to give a price.*

Feeney: *Did you give a price?*

Flannery: *Yeah, I was offered fifteen.*

Feeney: *Shit, you'd want more than that to have to do that. Why? Who is he?*

Flannery: *Ah, some barrister they want knocked off.*

Feeney: *Is that what he* (Clarkson) *was here for?*

Flannery: *Yeah.*

Feeney: *Fucking well – that's not much money.*

Flannery: *What do you reckon? I'll tell him twenty thousand. But he's never to be found.*

Flannery: *There's no hurry; there's no great hurry. It's got to be done in the New Year.*

Feeney: *Are you fair dinkum?*

Flannery: *Yeah, I'm telling ya that's what he was here for.*

If Feeney had any doubts about the malevolence of his former crime apprentice, one incident stood out in his memory.

'One night at my place Flannery had a fight with Gangitano, who bit Flannery on the nose. When the fight was over Chris told Kathy to go and get a gun for him. I thought she would have got a shotgun but she came back with a .38. Just before she gave it to him, Gangitano and others with him drove away, so Flannery smacked his missus across the face and accused her of deliberately stalling so the others could get away.'

Shortly afterwards, Flannery sold his shares in Mickey's and Feeney tried to rid himself of the hit man's malign influence. Then someone fired a shotgun through the back windscreen of his car.

The offender was never identified.

But the message was.

ROGER Anthony Wilson was ambitious, smart and a hard worker.

After studying law at Royal Melbourne Institute of Technology he began practising as a barrister but he soon saw his real talent lay in the world of commerce.

He married his girlfriend Deidre Schultz in 1971 and they had three children – two girls and a boy.

By the time he was 31, Wilson was beginning to be a player in the business world. He had interests in two private hospitals, two farms and manufacturing companies. But while he could make numbers add up, he must have been a careless judge of character or he wouldn't have teamed up with another lawyer-turned-businessman, Mark Alfred Clarkson, a known New Zealander.

In August 1978 Wilson acted for Clarkson in an action in the Queensland Supreme Court and their relationship soon progressed from client and lawyer to business partners.

Clarkson couldn't raise the funds he needed for many of his grandiose plans. He needed the squeaky-clean Wilson to be his front man. Wilson was respectable but Clarkson's reputation was not.

The scheme was for the young barrister to borrow the money so the two could go about taking over companies, stripping them for a tidy profit.

In June 1979 they began a plan to take over Falkiner Holdings. To do this they first bought a major share of an industrial hardware company that had a major stake in the takeover target.

But Wilson lost interest in stripping the company and installed himself as executive chairman of the industrial holding. Clarkson was left with a debt of $557,672 and he believed Wilson had a legal obligation to bail him out. Wilson, on legal advice, begged to differ and Clarkson was made bankrupt.

He wasn't happy and he began to tell others of his distaste for the young lawyer. Business partners fall out all the time without it ending with bullets and hit men, but this time it did.

Roger Wilson disappeared some time between driving from his factory in Footscray to his home on a dairy stud farm in Nar Nar Goon, east of Melbourne, on 1 February 1980. His white Porsche was later found in the long-term car park at Melbourne Airport.

The investigation would expose links between business and the underworld and result in a young female witness joining Wilson on the missing list.

It was the time when Flannery's reputation would change from hot head to cool killer and he revelled in the headlines. But it would eventually lead to his destruction as he began to believe he was bullet proof, a belief not shared by a particular Sydney crime boss, among others.

In the months leading to his disappearance, Wilson was worried. He knew he was dealing with ruthless people and he suspected he was out of his depth.

He was dead right.

ROGER Wilson had always stood out. As a student at De La Salle College, he had been a leader, a dedicated student, commanding officer in the cadets and an accomplished singer. He impressed his contemporaries. One of them remained close after they had left school. They formed a singing group and played for the East Malvern Cricket Club.

The former schoolmate described Wilson as 'level-headed' and a 'determined, aggressive type who had a very strong desire to succeed.'

In late 1979 the two old schoolmates had a meal in Sydney's well-known Bourbon and Beefsteak Bar. While sitting there, Wilson slumped in his seat so he would not be seen by a man who had entered the bar. The man was Mark Alfred Clarkson.

'He told me that Clarkson had threatened his life and that of his family,' the friend would later state. 'He also mentioned that he was concerned that his kids would be kidnapped. I thought this was strange and wondered what Roger was involved in.'

On 30 January Wilson visited his brother-in-law, who later told police: 'He seemed very uptight that night and mentioned that his life had been threatened.'

It was a story repeated by friends, legal associates, business contacts and even his local golf pro. Wilson was frightened but he decided to go it alone. He did not report the threats to police. By the time detectives became aware of the case he was already dead.

THE first day of February 1980 had been a long day for Roger Wilson, even by his standards. Around 8.20pm, he was ready to leave his West Footscray factory for the long drive home. He had been trying to lock in a contract on big-screen televisions but the deal looked like falling short. He had called his wife a few hours earlier and she noticed he sounded stressed. He said he would talk through the problems of the day when he arrived home.

If he thought he might relax at the wheel of his leased Porsche coupe, he was wrong. At the South Yarra end of the South Eastern Freeway he ran into the back of a Peugeot sedan. The Porsche was left with a smashed left headlight and some panel damage. The Peugeot driver exchanged names and addresses with Wilson, who 'apologised several times over the accident' but appeared 'quite calm and not agitated.'

Perhaps he just had bigger problems to worry about than a broken headlight.

Around 9.30pm he stopped at a milk bar at Pakenham to buy a can of soft drink. About twenty minutes later, just up the highway, a man saw a white Porsche pulled over on the side of the road next to a bright yellow car.

The local panel beater knew Wilson's car and was surprised to see it turn down a dead end before the normal turn off. He also thought the driver was hesitant as if he didn't know where the highway narrowed. This also surprised him because Wilson had lived in the area for years. In other words, it seemed unlikely Wilson was driving the Porsche. And whoever was driving it was almost certainly the last to see him alive.

Wilson didn't make it the few extra kilometres to his home at the Clements Jersey Stud that night. Deidre Wilson reported him missing and the car was recovered at Melbourne Airport.

Eventually Clarkson, Kevin Williams and Chris and Kath Flannery were implicated but it was always going to be a tough case to prove. At the time there had never been a successful prosecution in Victoria in a case where no body had been found. Today, through credit card transactions, Medicare movements, mobile phone records, and closed circuit security footage, most people leave an electronic footprint but back then it was plausible to suggest a victim had faked a crime and staged a disappearance.

The jury had to decide first if there had been a murder before examining who might have done it.

At least two witnesses came forward to say they had seen Wilson after he was reported missing. While the Crown had no doubts, the lack of a body and the loss of a key witness fatally wounded the case.

THE life of Kevin John Henry 'Weary' Williams' would have put Sigmund Freud into therapy.

While still living with his wife in Fitzroy, he was taken with his son's pretty and naïve girlfriend, Debra Boundy. So taken that he just took her. It would have made family dinners a touch frosty.

It was two days after her eighteenth birthday. He was 39 and a career criminal. She was unemployed and lived up the road with her parents. It was love at first fondle.

For a few weeks the couple moved from one cheap motel to another. The routine was broken when they agreed to baby-sit for friends of Williams – the Flannerys.

Eventually it was thought better for business if they moved in for a few days with the Flannerys at their home in the bayside suburb of Aspendale, as the men had a job to do together. Debra had no idea what that business was.

It would have been better if she had remained in the dark – in Flannery's social circles a little knowledge could be a fatal thing.

For the first few days she was treated as a guest rather than a friend but eventually (she later said) Flannery told her: 'I'm sick and tired of talking in riddles in front of you. We are going to kill someone and we are trying to work out some way to stop him.'

Welcome to the family.

Debra Boundy said she didn't want to know, telling Flannery her boyfriend 'didn't want me to have any part of it.'

So why was Flannery so forthright? Perhaps he wanted to implicate her so she could never be used as an innocent witness. Or maybe he thought that if she became a problem he would just make her disappear. Or perhaps he was just an idiot.

Flannery was full of ideas – some good, some not so good.

The gunmen carried out surveillance on their 'mark' and followed him to his home. A witness later saying he saw Flannery on the property.

The team, so the police claimed, had already dug the bush grave where they would bury their victim with nearly 50 kilos of lime.

They had taken the contract on the basis the body would never be found so a shoot and run scheme would never work.

An ambush would be the best plan. But how?

Because he drove a Porsche, Wilson could speed away from them if he became suspicious. If they grabbed him at home or at work there would be witnesses. So they needed to make him stop voluntarily on the road.

Later, after Debra Boundy was fleetingly persuaded to become a prosecution witness, she claimed (in a statement tendered to the Coroners Court) that a few days before Wilson went missing she was surprised to see a woman close to Flannery dressed to kill – perhaps literally.

Wearing an apricot dress with a plunging neckline and a crucifix around her neck, she looked like a woman on a mission. 'The material was very light and feminine, like chiffon, and clung to her body.' She wore stiletto heels and make-up, Boundy said. 'It was very dressy for day wear.'

According to Boundy, whose version of events was never tested in open court, the plan was for the woman to raise the bonnet of her car and try to flag Wilson down to help her. Chris thought it would work.

But she said the woman was concerned that Wilson might recognise her because she had met him once when working for Clarkson.

In any case, it didn't matter because it didn't work: Wilson had ignored the damsel-in-distress routine and driven straight past.

Boundy later told police the men rented a canary yellow Ford Falcon – the same type used at the time by traffic police. Homicide detectives would say Williams hired the car from Avis using the false name Marshman the day before the killing and returned it the day after, having travelled 966 kilometres. When Williams was arrested months later, he still had the licence under the name Marshman.

Boundy said that on Friday 1 February she watched Flannery sit at the dining room table and make a fake police sign with white letters on a blue background.

(Much later homicide squad detective Paul Sheridan would make up a similar sign. When he walked into court Williams said to Flannery, 'Fuck, they've got the sign.' The comment could not be put to the jury.)

On the night of the hit, the two dressed like detectives. Flannery was a snappy dresser so it was unusual to see him wearing a plain suit and a nondescript tie. Williams was also dressed as if for one of his many court appearances.

Boundy saw Flannery take a revolver from his jacket and take it with him when they left about midday.

'The only comment I can recall Kathy making was it would be a long day for them.'

It was a long day and a longer night because they weren't back until the following morning. They cleaned the car then Flannery had breakfast, showered and went to bed while Williams 'didn't look too good and went to the toilet.'

Boundy said she and Williams left to move into the Flag Inn at Frankston. 'On the way to the motel Kevin said to me, "He's dead. We pulled him over and when he got out of the car Wilson said, 'It's my unlucky day. I've got pulled over before'."' (He was probably referring to the earlier car accident on the South Eastern Freeway).

Williams told Boundy that Flannery handcuffed Wilson and put him in the fake police car. He said they later dumped Wilson's car at the airport.

Later that day Boundy says Williams met Flannery and returned with $4000 wrapped in a rubber band.

'We stayed at the motel that night and while we were there Kevin told me that Chris shot him (Wilson) in the head and that he ran away and that Chris chased him and caught him. Wilson had run into a fence. They brought him back and there were six or seven bullets put into him. Kevin said that he was dead and they buried him in a hole.

'On Saturday night we bought a pizza for tea.' Details of the pizza toppings were unavailable at the time of going to print.

Two nights later they were at the Flannerys' watching the Channel Ten news when the story broke that Wilson was missing and that police had found his car. Flannery just said, 'I didn't expect it to be on TV so early.'

Kathy then instructed the couple to head interstate.

They met the Flannerys at Surfers Paradise and while sitting in their room Flannery said, 'Things are happening too fast. I hope they don't find him for a couple of years.'

Chris and Kath went back to Melbourne and Williams took a call from one of them. 'When he came back into the room he was most upset.'

They went for a drive and at first Williams wouldn't talk to her but finally revealed that Flannery wanted her dead 'because I knew too much.'

As instructed, Williams rang Flannery the next day to report in that Boundy had been killed. 'Kevin told me that the hardest thing he had to do was keep me out of sight.'

But the suspicious Flannery didn't believe Williams. Within days the couple started to get threatening letters and their car was sprayed with the words, 'Just Married', and 'Dog.' A neighbour told her there was a suspicious car parked in the street. It was mauve with a white vinyl roof – the same type as Flannery's.

It was time to make tracks without leaving any. They went bush where they thought they would be out of Rentakill's reach.

Walter Willgoss was a drifter and a mate of Williams who would eventually travel with the couple, although Boundy barely tolerated him, believing he was just a sleazy old man.

Willgoss later told police that in January, Williams turned up at his house to show off his young girlfriend and to brag he was about to pull a job that would 'make the papers.'

But he said the next time he saw his old mate Williams had lost his swagger. He said Flannery intended to kill Boundy because, 'Debbie knew too much.'

The three left Melbourne in two cars and camped by the Delatite River for a week before pushing on. During their trip Willgoss said Williams was crooked on Flannery and believed he had not been paid enough for the job. He believed his share should have been $25,000 and he had got only $10,000. 'He said Flannery was trying to lash him.

'Kevin said it was quite funny how it happened. Everything had gone wrong.

'He said we took him up to where the hole was and Flannery shot Wilson in the head and Wilson said, "What's going on?" and started to run. He said that they had previously handcuffed him behind his back and when Wilson was running across the paddock with Kevin and Flannery chasing him that Kevin twisted his leg and his cartilage slipped out. It was his left leg. He said that Wilson ran into the fence and bounced back and fell down and they jumped on him and grappled with him. He said Flannery went mad and emptied his gun into him.'

When Flannery arrived home after Wilson was killed, the observant Boundy noticed Flannery had a small three-cornered tear in the left leg of his pants half way up the thigh. Could he have caught his leg in the barbed wire fence while he wrestled with Wilson and is that why Flannery 'went mad'?

Or perhaps he was a little mad to begin with.

A police surgeon later examined Williams and found he had cartilage damage to his left knee.

Willgoss said Williams told him they had followed Wilson a few times to know the route he took home and eventually pulled him over with the hand-made police sign.

'He said they made him put his hands on the roof and then handcuffed him. Wilson said, "Take my car and take my money but don't hurt me".

'Kevin told me that he had told Flannery that he (Kevin) had killed Debbie. He said that this was to keep Flannery off his back. He said that he was worried about Flannery knocking both of them. This was one of the reasons that we have been more or less on the run for the last four and a half months.'

It all ended when the three were arrested in outback New South Wales near Bourke in July. A passer by noticed a camper with a pistol and told the police. When asked his name, Williams responded with characteristic stupidity: 'Chris Flannery.'

It would be like Lord Lucan trying to pass himself off as Elvis.

Police believe the arrest might have saved Williams' worthless life. They believe Flannery was about to head off to try and find the couple to kill them both. Police in Melbourne acting on the information that 'Flannery' had been arrested interstate rang notorious private detective Tom Ericksen to tell him 'his boy' Flannery was in custody.

Ericksen had been meddling in the case, running a defence for Flannery, including spreading stories that Wilson was still alive. Ericksen immediately rang Flannery and quickly confirmed he was still free – and that whoever had been arrested at Bourke was not him. The pair immediately realised that the man in custody must be Williams and this meant Debra Boundy would be under pressure to talk to the police.

Flannery abandoned plans (at least in the short term) to get at Williams and Boundy and moved onto a macabre Plan B: moving Wilson's body. According to Clarkson's driver and bodyguard, George Marcus, Clarkson said: 'Chris had to go and shift the body. He was as sick as a fucking dog.'

Marcus said Clarkson 'went on to say that now Chris was the only one who knew where the body was.'

The bodyguard said that when he heard Flannery felt he was owed money Clarkson responded, 'Fucking Chris shouldn't be complaining: he got well over $35,000 from me ... over the job on Wilson.'

The witness said Clarkson claimed the body was buried with lime and would disappear in nine months.

The man chose to continue to work for questionable characters and was shot dead in a gangland-related shooting in 1997.

Willgoss told police Flannery gave Williams a book for some on-the-job training. 'Flannery wanted it back as it was his bible. It was a pathology book mainly on gunshot wounds. It had pictures in it showing the type of bullets and shells from shotguns and other firearms and what the effect of each of them was from a particular distance. Flannery gave it to him to read. I had a look at a couple of pages but couldn't stomach it.'

Once, after drinking too many bourbon and cokes, Williams told Willgoss there was another job where Flannery had 'lashed' him. He said he was supposed to get $10,000 for killing a man as part of the Wilson deal but he was paid only $2000. 'Kevin went on and said that he wasn't going to kill the fellow for a lousy grand so he stabbed him in the neck.'

He said Kevin said, 'I watched him for a couple of nights. This night he came home, put his car in the garage and walked down to shut the gates. I jumped him and stabbed him in the neck a few times. He was fighting me off. He was pretty strong and I took off down the road.'

Bank executive Timothy Marcus Clarke was stabbed outside his Toorak home in Melbourne as he went to shut the gates to his property. The date was 28 January 1980 – just days before Wilson went missing.

THE woman at the counter of the Collins Street Bank of New South Wales was one of those demanding types who didn't understand the value of paperwork or the patience for process.

She arrived with a cheque for $12,800 from Falkiner Holdings (the company Clarkson was trying to take over) and wanted it processed quickly. She was breathless and talking quickly. She was, she explained, trying to organise a last minute trip to America.

It was nearly closing time on 29 February – more than four weeks after Wilson had gone missing. She wanted $6000 in US traveller's cheques for the trip and she wanted them immediately. One of the tellers remembered that the pushy woman was in a hurry: 'I went to my desk to get the cheques and I noticed the man and woman kissing at the counter. She was excited and appeared to be in a great hurry.'

So much so that she took the paper work from the teller and tried to complete it herself. She was in a rush because she wanted to go to the nearby Pan Am office to book their tickets.

The cheques were issued – half under the name Kathleen Mary Flannery and the other under Tom Banjanin – Chris's alias.

The couple flew to America via Tahiti on 3 March and returned 21 March. There were other signs of wealth: a few days after Wilson went missing Flannery had bought himself a sports car.

And according to Debra Boundy, just days before Wilson went missing Kath bought some new jewellery – including a gold chain with a gold coin attached for her husband.

Beats thirty pieces of silver.

FOR some time Flannery appeared to be living beyond the means of a nightclub bouncer. Many wondered how he found the money to become a shareholder in Mickey's Disco.

The manager of Falkiner Holdings – the subject of Clarkson's takeover target – was becoming increasingly uncomfortable with the corporate raider's methods.

Business deals went sour, money taken from the business on supposedly legitimate pretences was not returned and Clarkson was beginning to behave more like a CIA operative than a company director.

The manager recalls that Clarkson wanted to place his own industrial spy, a man known as Chris Owen, inside the company's Brisbane factory.

Later, at a local hotel, Owen told the manager he had worked for the mysterious businessman on several jobs and 'that Clarkson had helped him to establish a big nightclub in Melbourne.'

Chris 'Owen' was Chris Flannery.

When it became clear that Clarkson and the Flannerys were being investigated for murder, they attempted to set up a paper trail to make the money paid for the hit on Wilson look as if it had come from legitimate business transactions but fraud squad detectives were able to show the documents were falsified.

In July 1980 Clarkson was arrested and Flannery went to ground. When he was finally arrested in Geelong on 24 August he tried to bluff his way out.

'Christ, we were only out for a Sunday drive. We are not criminals, are we? You are treating us like it,' he blustered to police.

He at first gave his name as Mark Philip Jones. When police asked if his real name was Christopher Dale Flannery he responded, 'Never heard of him.'

Back in the police station he had one more roll of the dice. While being searched he claimed to be ill. 'I'm nervous – I think I'm going to be sick. I'm gonna spew,' he told police.

But while in the police station toilet, something other than carrots came up. A revolver.

Police saw the gun he was hiding down his pants before Flannery could wrap a finger around the trigger and they managed to wrestle it from him.

He was charged with murder later that day. Eventually, four would be charged. Clarkson, the Flannerys and Williams.

Murder cases without a body were always notoriously difficult to solve and the people accused of killing Wilson were desperate to leave an impression the victim was very much alive.

They spread stories that he was having an affair and left Australia for America with $250,000 and his mistress by using a false passport made out under his mother's maiden name of Stewart.

Mischievously, one of the defence lawyers placed a large newspaper ad in a Melbourne paper accompanied by a photo of Wilson that read, 'Roger, no need to hide any more. Contact me. Tony.'

Police had a compelling list of witnesses that could prove Wilson feared for his life, that Clarkson had threatened him and that the Flannerys had been mysteriously paid for something following the disappearance.

But the star witness was clearly Debra Boundy. She made a statement (which she later refused to swear to in court) that she was present during the planning, was told by Flannery they were going to kill a man and saw them leave and return.

While other witnesses could recall damaging details, Boundy was the one who was inside the alleged killers' camp during the act.

If she stood up in court, police believed they were home. So when Boundy walked into the coroner's court and winked and curtsied to Williams, detectives knew they were in trouble.

While still in court she said to Williams, 'Hello Sweetie' and then passionately kissed him.

She said she wanted to marry Williams and have his children, declared she did not make the signed statements over the Wilson murder and that she had no knowledge that could help the inquest.

She complained about police protection, saying it was if she were under 'house arrest.'

'They think I might abscond or that something else might happen to me.'

She asked for the protection to be removed and police reluctantly agreed. During the inquest, Boundy was charged with perjury and given bail.

But even without her evidence the three men were committed for trial on 17 November 1980. The murder charge against Kath was dropped but she was immediately recharged with being an accessory after the fact.

She, like Boundy, was given bail. But the accused three knew that police had 'turned' Williams' girlfriend once. What if she turned again?

On Christmas Day, Boundy had lunch with her parents, reported for bail at the Collingwood police station and then slipped over to a Richmond pub for drinks.

She didn't expect to stay long as she had only $13 and was expected home for dinner with her sister about 6.30pm. She has never been seen since.

Police initially believed she had fled to avoid giving evidence. The theory gained credence after her father received a letter written in her hand and posted 28 December. It read, 'Dad, sorry to leave you this way. Pressure too much. I know what you and mum have done for me. I'll get in touch, ring or write to you. Love Deb'.

The grief-stricken father said 'At least she's safe – for the time being ... It's hard to believe she's done this to me.'

The truth was: she hadn't.

Top: Ray Chuck (a.k.a. Bennett), the Great
Bookie Robber, executed at Melbourne
Magistrates Court in 1979.
Middle: Laurie Prendergast, who helped
Bennett and Vinnie Mikkelsen (police
sketch below) allegedly kill Les Kane
in 1978.

Russell 'Mad Dog' Cox, who was not mad and whose real name was Melville Schnitzerling. A dashing crook who lived to (not) tell the tale. Yet.

Helen Eva Deane, trained nurse and Cox's faithful wife before, during and after years on the run.

Hideaway: the Mt Martha 'safe' house where Cox shot his hench-man Ian Revell Carroll.

Tools of trade (1): cache of weapons found at Cox's house.

Tools of trade (2): The Cox & Carroll do-it-yourself robbery kit, including pistols, holsters, ammunition, bandages, sub-machine guns with handbooks.

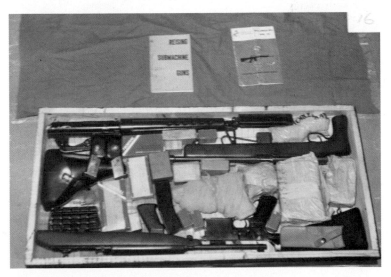

Full bore: the car was shot to bits but Cox walked away unharmed but mighty unhappy.

Run to ground at last: Cox under arrest at Doncaster shopping centre. His singlet must have been bullet proof.

Trophy hunters: Cox humours Victoria's finest with a picture opportunity but no smile.

Touching moment: Cox's getaway car and detective's car almost collided.

Cop that: buckshot in the boot of Cox's Fairmont.

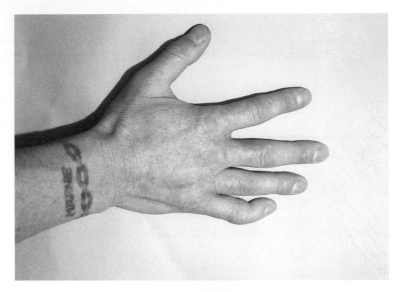

Finger of fate: Santo Mercuri's hand, wounded in fatal Brunswick robbery.

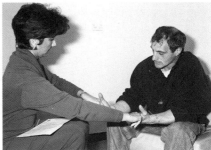

Scientific proof: Mercuri submits to examination of the bullet wound.

Identikit (1): the gunman who shot Ray Chuck, a.k.a. Bennett, at Melbourne Magistrates Court.

Identikit (2): the bogus 'gardener' who set up the gunman's getaway route.

On the wall: a message to Ray Chuck on the court cell wall before he was shot.

Snub noses: short-barrelled revolvers similar to the one used to shoot Ray Chuck, a.k.a. Bennett.

After the event: a detective examines the upstairs court lobby where Ray Chuck was shot.

Tinny: someone had made a hole in the wall of the magistrates' garage ... but who?

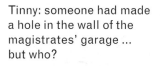

Christopher Dale Flannery: mad, bad, dangerous to know.

Charming, handsome, well-dressed ... and a psychopath. Flannery reputedly killed fourteen people.

Kath Flannery: blood loyal to career killer.

Roger Wilson: clean-living lawyer, businessman, husband and father duped into pulling over for a 'police car' that wasn't. His body was never found, although Flannery had to move it once to make sure.

Debra Boundy: she recanted her evidence against Flannery and his co-accused, but it was too late. She vanished. Some say Alphonse Gangitano was the last to see her alive.

Dab hand with a blowtorch: former Sydney detective Roger Caleb
Rogerson making an honest living.

Lennie 'Mr Big' McPherson: standover man, murderer, rapist and thief with cops and politicians on his pay roll. Below: McPherson kangaroo shooting with visiting American mobster Joe Dan Testa and friend.

'Tough Tom' Domican: dodged Flannery's attempted hit and most charges levelled against him ever since.

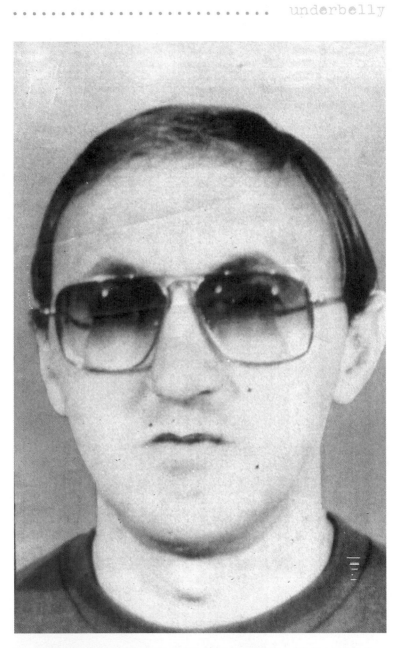

Tony 'Spaghetti' Eustace: a staunch crook who wouldn't reveal who had shot him.

George Freeman: if
he didn't kill Flannery
he knew who did.
Rubbed shoulders with
the cream of Sydney
society.

Although police ended up putting Debra Boundy on the top ten wanted list, she was gone forever.

What really happened was someone she knew well lured her from the Royal Oak Hotel in Richmond then forced or tricked her into writing the letter. And then she was murdered.

But who was the killer?

The chief investigator in the case, Frank Bellesini, says one name was nominated as the gunman. 'Alphonse Gangitano.'

On 22 October 1981, after Victoria's longest murder trial, the three men were acquitted and so in the eyes of the law Mark Alfred Clarkson was an innocent man. The evidence of a policeman's wife who swore she had sold Wilson a raffle ticket in Lakes Entrance the day after he went missing did not help the case.

There were hugs and tears. But Flannery's joy was short-lived. He was immediately re-arrested for the murder of massage parlour boss Raymond 'Lizard' Locksley.

The trial would take him back to New South Wales to play out the final scene in his life, which would prove nasty, brutish and short.

SYDNEY

FOR SALE

12

TRAVELLING NORTH

FLANNERY BEATS ANOTHER ONE

'Anyone who wasn't scared by him
didn't know the man.'

THE hit man was sitting in the homicide squad office, crying.

A jury had just acquitted him of murder but he wasn't crying
with relief. He was crying because the moment he had glimpsed
freedom the cell door had slammed shut again. Police had been
waiting outside court busting to give him the bad news: he was to
be arrested immediately and extradited to Sydney.

One of the detectives who served the papers interrupted the
killer as he was giving his wife an affectionate post-acquittal cud-
dle to tell him it was a case of premature celebration. He wasn't
going anywhere except by prison van.

'He was reasonably accepting,' the policeman would recall.
'He just said, "You've just got to have a win, don't ya"?

'But Kath went berserk.'

And that was how Christopher Dale Flannery – and his loyal
wife, Kathleen – got the news that although he had beaten the
rap for murdering Melbourne barrister and businessman Roger
Wilson, he would be charged with another murder: that of Raymond Francis 'Lizard' Locksley – a Melbourne massage parlour

heavy whose body had turned up with four bullet wounds in the southern Sydney suburb of Menai in May 1979.

Flannery would get a little emotional in the homicide office later. Not out of any finer feelings – apart, possibly, from the possibility that he was frightened of his wife. He was reputed to be frightened of little else, a fatal flaw that would later condemn him to the sort of violent death he had inflicted on several others. Such as Ray Locksley ...

'LIZARD' managed a massage parlour owned by one Ron Feeney but he was a glutton for too many fringe benefits – including free sex. This was considered bad manners and bad for business, which led to his sudden death. That was what the police wanted to talk to Flannery about.

A veteran detective called Brian Murphy knew Flannery so he was asked to try to persuade the contract killer to talk.

According to Murphy, he did talk. Murphy made a statement that Flannery confessed to him as follows: 'Lizard was hustling the girls at the parlour and trying to undermine Feeney.'

Police believe Ron Feeney ordered the hit, but demanded it be done outside Victoria.

Police claimed Flannery persuaded Locksley to drive to Sydney with him. The Lizard had been bragging to the girls in the parlour that he was a hit man and the rumour goes that Flannery 'recruited' Locksley on the pretence they were going interstate for a contract killing.

It was said that as they were waiting together, Locksley asked the identity of their victim and Flannery said, 'You!' and shot him.

In that game you ask a silly question and you can get a deadly answer.

Murphy swore that Flannery told him: 'One thing I am worried about is that Lizard stopped for petrol at a garage on the way up. Ray called the bloke over and introduced me to him. I can only hope he can't identify me. I don't think he can because I covered my face a bit.'

Police say after shooting Locksley in the head, neck and twice in the chest Flannery dumped the body and had the gold Ford he was driving 'detailed' twice on the way back to Melbourne.

Murphy believes Flannery had opened up to him because he feared he would not see his stepson and daughter grow up. After one heavy interview with detectives he saw a *Police Life* magazine on the desk and asked if he could take it 'for the boy'.

For once the hit man's mask had slipped. 'He was saying he had made a mess of his life and just wanted the kids to be able to grow up and be normal,' Murphy would recall.

But at that moment two women walked in. One was Ron Feeney's wife and the other was Kath Flannery.

When Flannery saw them, the tears stopped and he returned to his public persona as 'Rentakill' – the ice-cold killer.

One of the New South Wales homicide detectives who came to fetch him was the personable Billy Duff – a man who would later be dismissed for being corrupt. He was found to have had inappropriate relationships with a number of serious gangsters – including Flannery.

But back then he was seen as a good-humoured detective with a ready laugh, a shallow nature and a deep thirst. And a lot of good suits.

Flannery was extradited to Sydney and sent for trial. It looked an open and shut case until three witnesses turned up to say good old Chris had been in Melbourne at the time of the killing.

In October 1982 a jury failed to return a verdict.

The retrial was set for January 1984 but Flannery was desperate to have the case delayed. It has been said he was told the judge scheduled to hear the case was a touch stern and so he wanted to indulge in a little judge shopping. It is also possible he had heard a witness was sick and if he could drag out the court process then the Crown case would be weakened.

Either way, he knew that a delay on medical grounds would be healthy for him.

Enter the colourful medical entrepreneur and onetime owner of the Sydney Swans football team, Dr Geoffrey Edelsten.

When the professional healer met the professional harmer there was instant chemistry.

Edelsten surgically removed a tattoo for his new best friend. (He had one on his stomach – LUNCHTIME – with an arrow pointing down to his groin). When he realised his patient's line of work, the doctor saw an opportunity.

Edelsten was being harassed by an ex-patient and asked if Flannery could help. The hit man explained the rates – $50,000 for a permanent solution and $10,000 for a severe beating. When the doc queried the price he was told, 'Baseball bats are expensive.'

And you can't bulkbill bashings on Medicare no matter how well deserved.

In a tapped conversation between Edelsten and his then wife, Leanne, she asks, 'Bashing up people, is that all he does?'

'No, he kills people. Nice young fella,' the doctor replies.

While the patient was never bashed, Edelsten was later jailed for conspiracy to pervert the course of justice for issuing Flannery with a medical certificate to delay his trial.

For Flannery the ruse seemed to work perfectly. His second trial was due to start 31 January 1984 but because the accused was deemed unfit it was adjourned until later that year.

In June 1984 a judge directed that Flannery should be acquitted because a witness had died, meaning that the jury didn't get to judge the case on the facts. Flannery was freed on a technicality.

The witness, Dr Denis Maxwell Gomez, gave evidence at the first trial that differed from his committal testimony over the time of Locksley's death. But as Dr Gomez had died in May before the re-trial, the matter could not be clarified. He might have given evidence if the trial had gone ahead on schedule.

Flannery walked out of court a free man – and decided to make a new start in Sydney. He saw it as a city with opportunities for a man in his line of work.

'We were never going back to Melbourne,' Kath said. She was right.

THERE was violence in the Sydney underworld but entrenched corruption worked too efficiently to let it interfere with business. The heavyweight crooks made sure they didn't turn on each other.

For bad people, life was good if they were in on 'the giggle'. The top men were 'green lighted' by senior police and politicians to do what they liked as long as the lawmakers and enforcers skimmed their share.

There was one caveat – don't leave bodies on the street that could embarrass the police and politicians who were taking a cut.

In the beginning, the bribe money came from so-called victimless crimes such as vice, drugs, illegal gambling and sly-grog.

But it spread to a share of payroll robberies, professional burglaries and standover rackets: serious violent crimes.

At its worst, a corrupt cell high in the New South Wales police force was franchising crime. Many of the well-known Sydney gangsters had become celebrities and were invited to A-list functions to be photographed with fawning community leaders who leaned on them for donations to their favourite charities. Big-time crooks were attending the opening of new bars when they should have been behind them.

Flannery began working for a casino operator called Bruce Hardin but eventually moved up the pecking order and became a heavy for underworld supremo George Freeman.

Freeman was a cunning crook who had grown rich on his ability to read the play. For a quarter of a century, everyone seemed to know he was an organised crime figure – everyone, that is, except New South Wales's finest.

By the time he was a teenager, Freeman had started his apprenticeship in crime. His record was long but unimpressive.

It included convictions for evading rail fares, stealing knives, shirts, fountain pens, a tin of biscuits and a car radio. Mr Big he wasn't, but he was learning.

In 1954, he was sentenced to three years hard labour for breaking and entering. In the early days, street police seemed to have no trouble catching him but, as his influence grew, he seemed to vanish from the law-enforcement radar.

He was regularly referred to as a crime boss, yet police arrested him for only a few minor gaming offences. He was able to pay the fines out of petty cash.

Freeman made the leap from street crim to mobster by capitalising on the contacts he needed to survive and thrive. He built bridges with other influential criminals, including Stan 'The Man' Smith and Lennie 'Mr Big' McPherson, and he had influential friends in legitimate society.

Stan the Man once tried to expand his business into Victoria. He got as far as the airport when a remarkably switched-on top Consorting Squad detective 'found' a matchbox filled with cannabis in Smith's coat pocket. Stan got the message and returned to Sydney. 'They run red hot down there,' he said. But he later did jail time in Melbourne, where he teamed up with Flannery.

Freeman was one of the few gangsters who could look as comfortable in the members' reserve at Randwick races with then chief magistrate, Murray Farquhar, as standing around a bar drinking with wharfies. His network included gunmen, gangsters, jockeys, tame reporters, greedy police and upwardly mobile politicians.

The police he corrupted along the way eventually moved into positions of power where they were able to protect Freeman's growing empire.

Freeman always saw the big picture – even before he was a Mr Big. In 1965, he met suspected US Mafia figure, Joe Testa, and three years later he flew to Chicago to stay with his new friend.

They were to set up a construction company together but there was no evidence they were interested in the building trade.

Freeman became friendly with a US gaming figure heavily connected with 'The Mob'. The man had links back to the notorious Meyer Lansky. Letters intercepted by police show that Freeman sent the mobster monthly payments in the US and the pair met regularly.

Before one trip, where they were to meet at the Beverly Wiltshire Hotel, the organised crime figure asked Freeman to bring some contraband with him. Not drugs but something possibly worse: budgie smugglers. And he didn't mean small birds.

The US gangster wrote, 'If at all possible, I would like to have three pairs of Speedo Bathing Shorts, size 34 – one yellow and two in other bright colours. I'll leave it up to you, as you know what I like.'

Sadly, George probably did.

Freeman was shot in the head Anzac Day 1979, but survived. The man who allegedly fired the shot, John Marcus 'Mad Dog' Miller, didn't. He was shot dead outside his Coogee house six weeks later.

Freeman was said to be the killer. He left his home that night, dressed in black – the colour he wore when he suspected someone would die. As usual George only punted when he had the inside mail.

Royal Commissioner and former New South Wales policeman, Justice Donald Stewart, found that Freeman was linked to race fixing, SP bookmaking and illicit protected casinos. Stewart also exposed Sydney's worst-kept secret – that Freeman had improper relationships with senior police, lawyers and members of the judiciary.

Illegal phone taps on Freeman's phone showed he regularly tipped Farquhar which horses to back. No wonder the chief magistrate liked him. The tips were 98 per cent successful. It would take someone with more character than the greedy Farquhar to resist such an exquisite temptation.

In August 1984, Freeman was charged with wounding Frank Hing, a man named in the New South Wales Parliament as having Triad connections. But witnesses were reluctant to give evidence and the case against Freeman failed.

Freeman saw the old pecking order was breaking down and that new splinter groups wanted a larger piece of the pie.

This was the background to Flannery's rise and fall in Sydney.

Flannery started to push himself on Freeman, bragging about the murders he had committed. He saw his criminal record as an underworld CV and he told Freeman that if he needed anyone killed, he was the man for the job.

Freeman later declared that he was polite to the hit man because, 'Flannery scared me. Anyone who wasn't scared by him didn't know the man.'

Freeman always maintained he did not employ Flannery but the reality was he paid him a weekly retainer and liked to show off his new intimidator. Freeman recalled that at one party Flannery was determined to leave an impression.

'He wanted to meet everyone, pushing his own violent image all the time. He wanted people to fear him – and he wanted customers.'

According to Kath Flannery, Freeman was keen to have her Chris on his team. She said he helped raise $22,000 for 'Rentakill's' legal fees between the first and second trial.

She said Flannery would often accompany Freeman when he collected his gambling debts. His job, she said, was to keep Freeman alive. 'He was supposed to be between George and anybody who wanted to kill him.'

But if Freeman thought he could control Flannery he was mistaken. The man from Melbourne was a loose cannon with a concealed .38.

As with his time at Mickey's Disco in St Kilda, when Flannery began by working for Ron Feeney but eventually wanted to be the boss, he was never going to be content with only being hired muscle. He wanted to be a player.

He arrived in Sydney just in time for an underworld war fought over turf and egos. There were several factions, each with its own group of corrupt police backing them.

But the brash outsider was a one-man faction, the wild card in the pack.

13

CODE BREAKER
THE SHOOTING OF MICHAEL DRURY

'I was a giant in the trade;
I thought I was invincible,
and unpinchable.'

IF only there hadn't been a sale at the Melbourne Myer store.

Then a policeman wouldn't have slipped away to buy his wife some sheets and then he wouldn't have been a little bit late for a briefing on a drug sting to be carried out by a visiting New South Wales undercover detective.

Perhaps then he would have heard the exact instructions on when to move in after the heroin was exchanged and before the $110,000 buy-bust money was out of sight.

Because if those instructions had been followed then one of the main targets would have been arrested outside the Old Melbourne Motor Inn in textbook fashion and the case would have ended with criminal convictions and police commendations.

Instead it started a long, painful and fatal chain of events that would lead to at least two killings and the attempted murder of an undercover detective. The chain would also lead to the ultimate exposure of deep and sinister corruption in police ranks.

Mick Drury was the undercover policeman who almost died. He was young, smart and ambitious and, like most detectives, keen to keep control of his investigation.

It was a New South Wales drug operation but eventually it bled over the border into Victoria. This meant it would have to become a joint job involving both state forces.

This was always fraught with danger as there had long been a simmering distrust between the two groups. The Victorians were sometimes dismissed as 'Mexicans' because 'they were only good down south,' while the New South Wales force was often referred to as the 'best police that money could buy.'

In reality, the drug problem had been recognised in New South Wales and more resources were devoted to enforcing drug laws than in Victoria. The drug squad in Sydney considered it was the best and would tell anyone who cared to listen and those who didn't. Most Victorian detectives weren't impressed. They had seen many of their jobs burned as crooks were tipped off when information went over the border.

In one job that went to New South Wales, Melbourne drug squad detectives photographed money to be used in an undercover buy but Sydney surveillance police 'lost' the suspect (and the money) after the exchange. Later it was found that the money had been divided among bent Sydney police.

In another job the drug courier didn't get far from the Sydney airport before he was ambushed and his cash stolen. Detectives in Victoria blamed their Sydney counterparts.

In 1981 Victorian police had solid information that New South Wales Deputy Commissioner Bill Allen (who was being groomed for the top job) was the bagman for some government figures and that each Wednesday he would deliver a share of the bribe money to a senior minister. The information was that police collected $100 a month from each SP bookmaker and $5000 a week from illegal casinos. Further information was that Allen used two corrupt men in the 21 Division, which was police gaming, to run the scam.

Victorian police secretly went to Sydney and photographed Allen getting into a car on a Wednesday and driving in the direction of the minister's office.

When the information was passed to the New South Wales Commissioner his response was both useless and predictable. He sent a senior officer to 'investigate' whose insightful questions included: 'Are you in a position to advise me on whose authority those photographs were taken?'

Translation: 'Keep out of our patch.'

Bill Allen remained Deputy Commissioner – until he was finally exposed as a crook. He was found to have regularly met crime boss Abe Saffron and retired in disgrace after being demoted to sergeant. He was later jailed for bribing the head of the Special Licensing Police on at least five occasions.

But while the Victorians were quick to blame corrupt Sydney detectives they tended to be blind to the crooks in their own ranks.

It was in this climate that they came together to co-operate. The two controlling police were Johnny Weel from Victoria – laconic, tough, brave and straight as a gun barrel – and Mick Drury, who was loud, funny and cocky.

They were different types of men but they were both good at what they did. But above them there were tensions. The New South Wales police arrived and tried to take over while the Victorians tried to protect their patch. If the arrests were made it would be dealt with in Victorian courts and they would get to run the case.

The Sydney police refused to hand over documents and Melbourne officers were slow to come up with the $110,000 for the undercover buy. But eventually a plan was hatched and the deal was set for the Old Melbourne in North Melbourne in March 1982.

The room would be bugged. Armed police would be in adjoining rooms and units stationed outside in the street.

With a little luck, police would get the Sydney connection, Jack Richardson, the distributor, Brian Hansen, and the major supplier, Alan Williams, in the operation.

On the day it began slowly and then went downhill. Drury and his money were there and so was Hansen, but Williams simply refused to turn up with the heroin. And a heroin sting without any heroin is not much of a sting – more just a waste of time.

After nearly nine hours, Williams – stoned, distracted and still suspicious – finally fronted and the deal was done outside the hotel. Drury pressed a squeal button hidden under his armpit to trigger the arrest.

But the police who were meant to move in got it wrong. They rushed in too fast, and the car that was supposed to block the dealer's escape overshot the spot by thirty metres. It was enough to give Williams an out – and he took it – driving off with the heroin.

He dumped the gear and ran through Melbourne University, where he had once worked as a cleaner, and disappeared.

Eventually, he was arrested but the case was no longer simple. Having failed to catch him with the heroin, the prosecution would rely heavily on police evidence and that would prove to be confused and deeply flawed.

But Williams wasn't going to take chances. He had an inside man in Victoria – a well-respected long-term investigator – and through him he first tried to buy back the key evidence: the heroin found dumped at Melbourne University.

Within a week, the word was out that he would pay $30,000 to have the gear – by then at the forensic laboratory – swapped for harmless powder. But John Weel was told of the plan and quickly had the suspect powder tested to ensure that even if there were a quick switch, the evidence already existed to nail the crook. This meant that Williams' first attempt to bribe his way out failed. But no matter. At the committal the magistrate found sufficient evidence to send Richardson and Hansen to trial but ordered that Williams be freed.

However, the Crown eventually decided that Williams should be directly presented on the case.

Having seen the flawed prosecution case, Williams knew that he could only be convicted on Drury's eyewitness testimony and he started to use contacts to see if Drury could be bought.

Considering the reputation of New South Wales police at the time, it was a fair bet. But he was a good player out of luck.

His approach, through an old mate, hit man Christopher Dale Flannery, to rogue detective Roger Rogerson and then to Drury, was rebuffed. But it speaks volumes about the state of play at the time that Rogerson could calmly ask a fellow officer to cop a bribe without fearing it would be reported to higher authorities.

Many New South Wales police were convinced they were above the law and frankly, in effect they were probably right.

When Drury knocked back the approach (but didn't report it) Williams and Flannery decided that if they couldn't buy the undercover detective, they should kill him.

On 6 June 1984 Flannery, possibly in the company of his old mate Laurence Joseph Prendergast, shot Drury at his Chatswood home.

Against all odds, the policeman survived and his testimony would ultimately expose the cancer within New South Wales law enforcement.

There are many versions of what really happened. Some have been told – some haven't.

Roger Rogerson was never convicted of attempting to bribe Drury or involvement in the attempted murder.

He maintains his innocence.

Flannery's version will never be known because he went on the missing list before he could be charged. Prendergast was also murdered and his body never found.

Williams' co-offender Jack Richardson could not assist after his body was found in country Victoria with two bullets in the back of his head. Almost certainly the last person he saw was Flannery – who took the contract to kill likeable Jack on behalf of Williams.

Williams was frightened the former star ruckman, who played more than 100 games with West Adelaide and Sturt, would roll over and talk to police. And he was right. The man they called Melbourne Jack was starting to indicate he wouldn't mind a chat to the right detective.

Richardson was last seen talking to two men in a Fitzroy Street ice-cream parlour in St Kilda on 4 March 1984. It was only a few hundred metres from where Flannery used to work at Mickey's Disco.

Timing is everything. Richardson disappeared the day before he was due in court for a preliminary hearing on Williams' heroin trafficking charges.

Another man close to the crew was Melbourne drug dealer Leslie 'Johnny' Cole, who was shot dead outside his Sydney home on 10 November 1982. His biological son, Mark Moran, would be killed in eerily similar circumstances when he was ambushed outside his home in June 2000.

The only man who survived – at least for a time – to tell his story was Williams himself, who admits he was prepared to pay $100,000 to have Drury killed.

Williams spoke to the authors just weeks after he was released from Goulburn Prison in 1992. He said he wanted to make a fresh start. Sadly, he didn't make it.

He recalled that on the day of the deal in the Old Melbourne his instincts told him there was something wrong but greed and a brain clouded with heroin made him go ahead regardless.

'I knew Brian Hansen – he said he had a drug buyer (Drury) down from Sydney. The deal was supposed to kick off at lunch-time, but for about nine hours I smelled a rat. I didn't want to do the business. Brian, on the other hand, was insistent, he said he had counted the money and that everything was sweet.'

Williams was in another suburb, but after being badgered he agreed to go to the Old Melbourne with the heroin. But he was 'light'. He was supposed to supply a pound but had already sold four ounces to a regular customer.

Still wary of the stranger from Sydney, he wanted the deal done in public. 'I didn't go into the hotel, I waited in the car outside.

'To cut a long story short, Brian went into the hotel, came back with Drury and introduced him. Well, he didn't want to get into the car. (Drury wanted to control the situation and signal waiting police to move when he saw the heroin.)

'I smelled a rat. I showed him the gear but there was some-thing wrong.' Moments later, Williams saw an unmarked police car in his rear view mirror speed around the corner.

'They were so keen to block me in that they skidded past the car. I put it in gear and just took off.'

Williams may have been filled with juice but once he aban-doned his car close by, near Melbourne University, the former star footballer could easily outpace his pursuers on foot. He knew the university layout well and escaped after dumping the drugs. About four months later, he was arrested in Adelaide and charged with heroin trafficking.

The committal was a shambles. Police who declared they could identify Williams were discredited. Only Drury's evidence survived. The case was certainly not helped by New South Wales and Victorian police squabbling with each other. Despite repeated requests, Drury's statement was not delivered until the day of the hearing.

When the Director of Public Prosecutions decided to directly present the case to a higher court, Williams believed only one man stood between him and a long stretch in Pentridge Prison and that man was Michael Drury.

'I knew I needed help because the only bloke who stuck to his guns in the committal was Drury. He was unshakeable. It wasn't his efforts which fell down for the prosecution; it was the Melbourne police around him, trying too hard.

'Mick Drury said it like it was, the others painted a picture which couldn't be finished. They ran out of paint.'

Williams had had enough dealings with corrupt police to believe he could still buy himself out of trouble but he needed an 'in'.

He needed someone to get an offer to Drury that he could make a big dollar if he just massaged his evidence a little. He wouldn't need to tell obvious lies, just forget a few key facts and stumble a few times with his answers. That would surely be enough.

In the underworld there is a loose group of 'mates' who try to look after each other when they get a chance – favours are called in, monies paid and advice given.

Williams had a mate in Sydney he thought could help him – Christopher Dale Flannery – known as Rentakill. Flannery and Williams had first teamed up as juvenile offenders and as young adults had pulled armed robberies together. In jail they sometimes shared a cell.

'I knew Chris, I always found him to be a thorough gentleman.' Alan, it must be said, was never a good judge of character, although he did add as an afterthought about Flannery: 'He was also a murderer and a paid killer.

'I ran into him in Melbourne and mentioned to him that I had been pinched by an undercover copper from Sydney. I asked him if he could do anything in regard to getting him to change his evidence or slow it down.

'He said he would see what he could do, that he had a couple of jacks (police) in Sydney sweet. He said it would cost and I said I wasn't worried about the cost side of it.'

According to evidence given in a series of court cases, Roger 'The Dodger' Rogerson approached Drury with a bribe offer on behalf of Williams, an offer Drury refused.

Williams may have been nasty but he wasn't mean. The offer, for the standards of the early 1980s, was generous. 'I offered $30,000 at one stage, $50,000 at another stage, $100,000 and an open ticket in the end.'

According to court testimony, Williams met with Flannery and Rogerson at a Sydney restaurant where he was told the bad news that the bribe offer had failed.

Williams was devastated. He knew he was looking at a long stretch inside. Then Flannery broke the silence: 'Well, if it was me, I'd put him off (kill him).'

Williams didn't immediately respond then just said: 'That's a big step'. But it didn't take long for him to take it.

'The deal was done in the restaurant,' Williams said.

That deal, done in cold blood over cool beers, was to kill Drury for $100,000. The contract called for a down payment of $50,000 and the rest after the killing.

'I was using the gear (heroin) at the time. If I had my full faculties there is no way I would have been involved in the plan.

'I was a giant in the trade; I thought I was invincible, and unpinchable. But I stepped over the line with the Drury thing. It is something I will regret for the rest of my life.'

It was madness. But the fact they could even suggest that you could kill an undercover policeman in his home in front of his family and resume business as usual shows how out-of control Sydney was in the 1980s.

The corrupt syndicates – some linked to the highest police, legal and political networks – really believed they could fix anything.

The Drury shooting would prove to be the tipping point. The fallout would result in the destruction of many of the established criminal fiefdoms and the cosy police-gangland franchises that had controlled organised crime in Sydney for decades.

It would lead to setting up integrity commissions and external reviews. No longer would police be a law unto themselves.

Williams sent the deposit to Flannery and then waited for the inevitable. He did not know when and where Drury would be killed – he left that to his paid 'experts'.

And Williams, through dumb luck, ended up with the perfect alibi. He had been picked up for speeding and had to produce his licence at the Greensborough police station. It proved he was in Melbourne at the time of the shooting.

Drury was gunned down while he was washing dishes at home. 'When I knew he had been shot it was panic-stations. The heat was on. Basically I didn't realise the repercussions this would cause. It was just a stupid thing to do.'

When Williams stopped being a stick-up merchant and moved into the drug trade he tried to stay clean and to treat it as a business. But soon he was just another junkie – a rich one with an endless supply – but still just a junkie.

'I started smoking, and then it was up the snozzer and then up the Warwick Farm (arm). I was stoned all the time, I wasn't thinking straight.'

Williams said that when he heard that Drury was shot he, 'started getting into the gear (drugs) even heavier than ever.

'I knew I was the number one suspect from day one. But I also knew that the police who had anything to do with me knew that

I was not the sort of gangster who would premeditate this sort of murder.'

If so, the police were wrong.

For all his talk of remorse, at the time Williams was happy that Drury was out of the way and could not give evidence in his heroin trial.

'I was more concerned about the matter at hand than Drury,' he admitted later.

But the Sydney undercover detective, fighting for his life in hospital, made what everyone thought was a dying deposition outlining the attempted bribe by Rogerson.

Everyone, including his colleagues, expected him to die. He had been, after all, shot twice at point blank range. Even Flannery was convinced, assuring Williams: 'He's lost a lot of blood; I don't think he'll make it. He's lost a lot of blood and is very weak.'

But this time Flannery, who had more experience with gunshot wounds than most surgeons, was wrong.

'When he realised he was going to live, Chris said not to worry about sending the other $50,000. The job hadn't been completed,' Williams said.

Flannery may have been a cold-blooded killer but he expected to get paid only on results. But his honour did not extend to refunding the $50,000 he had already been paid. And Williams was not game to raise the subject.

The ultimate irony is that Drury recovered and gave evidence against Williams in his heroin trial but the drug dealer beat the charges on the evidence.

'The whole plan was a waste.'

Drug dealing heavyweight or not, Williams was now the weak link. Once Drury made his statement implicating Rogerson in the attempted cop killing, all roads led to Melbourne.

Williams was the only one who could implicate Rogerson and Flannery in the attempted murder.

Within days stories in the media suggested the shooting related to the 'Melbourne Job.' Clearly this meant people on both sides of the law began to look for him.

Williams was still regularly reporting on bail and would be easy to find. He agreed to have a coffee with two well-known Victorian detectives in a Greek café in Melbourne.

One of them, the legendary thief-catcher Brian Murphy, told Williams that New South Wales police were out to kill him and he should not go home that night.

It was a bluff. 'I just wanted to stir him up so he would talk,' the streetwise Murphy said later.

It worked. 'He went to a public phone and rang his wife, telling her to grab a few things and get out.'

Williams had few friends outside the underworld.

'Squareheads' tend to ask too many questions about unexplained wealth and lazy lifestyles. But Williams' brother-in-law Lindsay Simpson was the exception.

A friendly man who worked in the building trade, Simpson would drink with Alan and not pry into areas where he was not welcome.

But on the day Williams was told he was a marked man, 'good blokes' like Simpson were the last thing on his mind.

'I was told I was to be knocked. I was completely paranoid and I clean forgot that Lindsay was to come to my house that night,' Williams said.

Waiting outside the house to kill Williams was Roy Pollitt, a crim known as the 'Red Rat'. It was a nickname that was defamatory to rats, unfairly maligned ever since the Black Plague.

Pollitt had escaped from jail and was being harboured by 'Mr Death' – Dennis Bruce Allen – a prodigious Melbourne drug dealer and killer later found to have direct links to Rogerson.

It was Allen who commissioned Pollitt to kill Williams. When Pollitt saw a man pull up at Williams' home in Lower Plenty, he drew his gun and made the victim kneel on the ground with his hands behind his head in a hostage pose. The innocent man kept trying to tell the gunman that it was a case of mistaken identity and that his name was Simpson.

It did him no good. He was shot dead in cold blood.

It may have begun as a case of mistaken identity but when Pollitt pulled the trigger he knew his victim was not Williams. He shot him to remove a potential witness.

'Lindsay was a good family man. It took him eight years to have a baby with his wife. Six years of hospital and doctors' appointments. Finally he has a kid and just before its first birthday, Lindsay is dead.' Allen paid Pollitt a $5000 deposit in counterfeit notes for the hit and then refused to pay the rest after it was found he'd killed the wrong man.

Williams used to deal drugs with Allen, who died of chronic heart disease in 1987. 'Dennis was a conniving man and particularly dangerous in his own little world of Richmond. But he lacked a lot of heart and he had to be juiced up to do anything. He was frightened of going to jail – every time he hit the nick he'd get the horrors.'

For Williams, the writing was on the wall. His life as one of the biggest drug dealers and most powerful men in the underworld was coming to an end. The man who could sit in a Sydney restaurant and effectively sign a death warrant for a detective, was now frightened and on the run.

He had already confessed to Murphy that he had tried to bribe Drury but still denied he was involved in the murder attempt.

Williams knew it was only a matter of time before the next set of killers came knocking. His co-offender Jack Richardson was dead. His brother-in-law Lindsay Simpson was also dead. He knew he would be next unless he could cut a deal.

He was placed on the top ten most wanted list and arrested in

Melbourne. He went to Sydney, and in 1986 he quietly pleaded guilty to conspiracy to attempt to bribe Drury.

Ironically, only months earlier, Roger Rogerson pleaded not guilty to similar charges and was acquitted.

Williams was given a 12-month suspended sentence but if he thought that would be the end of the matter, he was wrong.

He moved to the Northern Territory and gave up the drugs – at least temporarily – working for nearly eight months as a plant operator.

Then a New South Wales police task force, code named 'Omega' came knocking. They were the team Commissioner John Avery had selected to find the would-be killers of Drury.

The two targets were Rogerson and Williams. 'When I was arrested in the Territory I was told: "The deal is this, you can either do a life lagging over a crooked copper or you can tell us what happened and jump the box (give evidence) against him".

'I knew I was there to be knocked.'

Williams pleaded guilty to conspiracy to murder Drury and was sentenced to fourteen years jail.

Then he gave evidence in one of the most publicised criminal trials in Australian history.

Rogerson, a highly decorated and brave New South Wales detective, was charged with plotting to kill a brother policeman. Williams, a known criminal, was the key witness alleging that Rogerson was guilty.

In the end, the jury chose to acquit Rogerson, who had always maintained his innocence.

Rogerson was sacked from the force over an unrelated matter.

Williams found himself behind bars after he confessed while the man he claimed was his partner in crime walked free.

'I am not bitter about it. I was part of the conspiracy and I have paid the price,' Williams would say. He served four years, six months before he was released.

'I feel like a new person. It's the first time I don't have to look over my shoulder. I have been offered a new identity but I don't think I need it.

'Roger beat the charges, good luck to him. I am dirty on him, but good luck to him. I'm just happy that it's over for me.'

Rogerson was later jailed for conspiracy to pervert the course of justice. The charge related to the unexplained deposit of $110,000 in false bank accounts. Key evidence given against the former star detective came from a protected witness 'Miss Jones', who had once worked for Dennis Allen.

Williams says he regrets the attempt on Drury's life but doesn't believe he broke any codes by going after a detective.

'The code was broken by some New South Wales police years ago, long before I ever came on the scene. Some of them declared open season on some crooks.' He said some corrupt New South Wales police were prepared to kill to protect their corrupt empires.

'Basically it was down and out murder because they created ripples in the kickback scheme of making a quid.'

Of Drury, he says: 'I can understand if he was bitter to the day he died. But I just hope he is remembered as a bloke who stuck to his guns and was vindicated in what he did.'

Williams' attempts to stay off 'the gear' failed and he returned to becoming a hopeless drug addict.

Riddled with hepatitis and suspected of having Aids, he spent his last weeks trying to kill the shrewd Melbourne policeman who unwittingly saved his life – Brian Murphy.

It was Murphy who fabricated the story that New South Wales police were to kill him at home. If he hadn't, Williams would have headed home on 18 September 1984 and would almost certainly have been murdered by 'Red Rat' Pollitt.

Williams found a gun but died in August 2001 before he could use it. A few days earlier he missed Murphy in a Carlton restaurant by a matter of minutes.

Timing was never his strong suit.

14

FRIENDLY FIRE
THE GREEN LIGHT THAT KILLED DANNY CHUBB

```
He was taken out to sea and set
the challenge of swimming back.
Unfortunately he was attached to
a gas cooker at the time.
```

FOR a prolific drug dealer Danny Chubb was also a kind and thoughtful son. After a morning conference with two of Sydney's most notorious gunmen he popped next door to grab his mother a nice piece of fresh fish for tea.

It was a spur of the moment thing. So much so that when he walked into Bob and Di's Fish and Chip Shop he ordered the fillet and then told the owner he had no money with him and would 'come back shortly to pay.'

The owner knew the man driving the new green Jaguar was good for it and handed over the fish without hesitation.

He would never get paid. Within two minutes Danny Chubb was as dead as the fish he carried – shot by two gunmen. The unwrapped fillet was found still in its paper beside him.

Both a Sydney murder taskforce and a National Crime Authority investigation codenamed Curtains would find that, as is the case with many underworld murders, the victim was set up by so-called friends rather than sworn enemies.

Chubb's marriage had recently collapsed and he had moved out of the house he shared with his wife, child and two step-children. While he could have afforded the rent for a secure penthouse he decided to move back with his mother in the Sydney suburb of Millers Point – near Sydney Harbour.

About 10.30am on 8 November 1984, he received a call. It had to be someone close who would have known of the marriage break-up and the phone number of the family home.

Chubb, 43, told a friend who had dropped in he was heading out for a quick meeting and would be back shortly.

He drove a short distance to the Captain Cook Hotel to meet two of his best customers – Arthur 'Neddy' Smith and Graham 'Abo' Henry.

Big, brash and not particularly bright, Smith should have been no match for trained and dedicated detectives. But the man they called 'Neddy' was born in the golden era of Sydney crime and crooked police gave him the 'green light'. For Neddy, it was better than a royal pardon.

The man himself said of his novel arrangement with the lawmen: 'Thank Christ for corruption.'

One of his closest friends and protectors was the notorious Roger Rogerson, said to be the king of bent police. And in New South Wales that was saying something.

The Woodward Royal Commission on drug trafficking found that Smith's drug syndicate was moving eleven kilograms of heroin a month.

In 1992, the Independent Commission Against Corruption began an investigation into claims that a corrupt cell of New South Wales detectives was organising the armed robberies.

Commissioner Ian Temby found that Smith was a pivotal figure. 'I conclude that over a period in excess of a decade, Smith was helped by various police officers, who provided him with information, looked after him when charges were laid or threatened and generally acted in contravention of their sworn duty. The evidence shows that Smith was friendly with a number of police officers and very close to a few.'

When he was finally jailed he wrote his memoirs, *Neddy – The Life and Crimes of Arthur Stanley Smith*, which exposed the system in New South Wales. It made staggering reading.

'In Victoria, there isn't much corruption. They kill you down there. They certainly don't do too much business.

'But when I was working in New South Wales, just about everyone was corrupt and anything was possible. Late 1980 was the beginning of a decade of crime and corruption within the New South Wales police force that will never be equalled.

'There has always been crime and corruption within the New South Wales police force but nothing like it was then. And I was in the middle of it.

'I had police organising crimes for me to do, then keeping me informed as to how much – if any – progress was being made in the investigations. I had what is commonly known within criminal circles as the "Green Light", which meant I could virtually do as I pleased. Nothing was barred, with one exception – I was never to shoot at any member of the police force. But apart from that, I could write my own ticket.

'I bribed hundreds of police and did as I pleased in Sydney.

'There was no limit to what I got away with. I could never have committed any of the major crimes I did, and got away with them, without the assistance of the New South Wales police force. They were the best police force that money could buy.'

While Neddy and 'Abo' were well-known underworld figures, Chubb was in many ways more powerful. As the axis of influence started to move from gunmen to drug dealers, Chubb was well placed to take advantage of the new demand.

The former able seaman had become a very able drug dealer, moving massive amounts of heroin and hashish.

His official criminal record was modest – a thief and a small-time safe breaker – but through his network on the docks and his connection to Asian heroin suppliers he was able to provide virtually endless supplies of drugs to crooks – including Smith and Henry.

Smith wrote in his autobiography: 'Danny arrived and we had maybe two more beers, discussed our business then stood on the footpath talking for a few minutes.'

Chubb then went next door to the fish shop, grabbed the fillet and drove the 300 metres home pulling up just before 11am.

As he stepped from his car, two men in balaclavas greeted him. One fired a shotgun from point blank range, removing the left side of Danny's face and his throat. He was also shot four times in the chest with medium calibre bullets.

Not surprisingly, he was dead before he hit the ground.

Neddy would later say that he left the Captain Cook with a woman he refused to name and Henry left in a second car. They then met again at a second pub.

Neddy took a call at the pub and was told the news that Chubb was dead. 'I had only just left Danny: I couldn't believe he was dead. He had no enemies I knew of.'

As usual Smith was being economical with the truth.

Kath Flannery would later tell the National Crime Authority that Smith had told her husband, Chris, that he organised the murder. 'He said Chubb owed him money and he was annoyed that Chubb was keeping better quality drugs and selling them rubbish.'

The good drugs, he claimed, were going to Mick Sayers, a major drug dealer and Chubb's good friend.

It was unlikely that Chubb owed Neddy anything and more likely the other way around. Chubb had a reputation for giving a long line of credit to his favoured clients and in the drug business it is more dangerous to be owed money than to be in debt. Debts in the underworld can be cancelled at the end of a gun.

In fact, Chubb had given Sayers $400,000 worth of heroin on the nod, which showed he was certainly not short of cash.

The New South Wales murder taskforce found, 'Within a period of several years he progressed from a middle-class income, with associated assets, to become a very wealthy man.'

He had a double-storey house at Shoalhaven Heads – a beach-side town on New South Wales' south coast. The house was elaborately furnished complete with a huge swimming pool, impressive outdoor entertaining area, a two bedroom flat and a row of professional greyhound kennels. He had bought a block of land at the back with the intention of building a tennis court.

He had also bought two blocks of land at Cunjurong Point. Police believed he had probably bribed officials to make sure he was the successful bidder as both blocks were sold by ballot.

He owned several greyhounds, had bought his Jaguar a month before he was murdered, owned a luxury cruiser and was part owner of a seafood pie business.

The taskforce reported, 'There are unconfirmed reports that Chubb had several million dollars in overseas banks.'

Certainly, one associate had changed five to seven million dollars at the Pitt Street ANZ branch from small notes for bigger denominations in the previous twelve months.

The associate said the money was for Chubb who he described as a 'mammoth punter.' Not that he bet on mammoths but he would have if they weren't extinct.

For a land-based sailor Chubb had done well for himself and as a drug dealer he had learnt to diversify.

He had two major sources: a Chinese gang based in Singapore that supplied heroin and a local cartel that included Sydney doctor Nick Paltos and Graham (Croc) Palmer to supply Lebanese hashish.

Paltos and Palmer were targets of a Federal Police investigation – code named Lavender – into a five-tonne hashish importation by Paltos, Palmer, Chubb and Ross Karp, a solicitor.

The phone taps the police gathered gave a unique insight into the New South Wales crime scene.

In the 1980s only the Feds had the power to tap phones and while Sydney police did it illegally on an ad hoc basis it was the federal force that gathered the bulk on the electronic intelligence.

Investigators found that many high-profile Sydney detectives were working with the major gangsters so their operations would be sabotaged.

Certainly the investigators from the Stewart Royal Commission and the National Crime Authority knew they were being white-anted by New South Wales police. At least twice witnesses who were pivotal to organised crime probes disappeared days before they were to meet investigators.

Corrupt law clerk Brian Alexander was in hiding. He knew where all the bodies were buried and knew he could join them. In 1981 an investigator contacted Alexander's mother, who arranged for her son to come in to talk. That night he disappeared – his body was never found. It was said he was taken far out to sea and set the challenge of swimming back. Unfortunately he was attached to a gas cooker at the time.

A beautiful call-girl named Sallie-Anne Huckstepp always maintained police had murdered her boyfriend, Warren Lanfranchi.

She remained an outspoken critic and in February 1986 had an appointment to see senior crime authority investigators. She never made it: her body was found in a shallow pond in a Sydney park.

Paltos was a doctor whose roll call of patients included Bob Trimbole, Lennie McPherson and George Freeman. After Trimbole fled Australia, Paltos stepped up to fill the gap in the drug market.

The syndicate bought a dilapidated freighter, the *Gulf Freo*, and transported 240 large hessian bags of hashish to Australia. Near Melville Island the ship ran out of fuel and Chubb used his wharf contacts to organise a trawler to meet the vessel.

They transferred the load and scuttled the freighter. The drugs were smuggled into Darwin and Chubb helped drive some of the load to Sydney in a furniture removal van.

Later the Federal Police would recover two tonnes and arrest Karp, Paltos and Palmer.

Much later police raided a safe cracker who was a member of Neddy Smith's gang.

When they checked his flat they found cannabis from the Paltos importation. They also found Fiocchi shotgun shells – the same type of ammunition used to kill Chubb.

Kath Flannery said Smith had mentioned that the safebreaker and another man were Chubb's killers.

There were several suspects for planning the murder but Neddy Smith was considered the hottest prospect by far. It seemed highly likely he organised the meeting with Chubb to allow his hit team to be in place for the killing when he returned. Neddy and Henry headed straight out of the area and placed themselves at another pub so they would have the perfect alibi.

But why would Neddy want to kill his heroin supplier?

Smith knew that Chubb was under investigation. He had told associates that a kilo of 'heroin' he had bought from Danny was in fact pure chalk – indicating that Customs or Federal Police had exchanged it and were closing in.

The taskforce found: 'In addition to supplying heroin to Sayers, Chubb was also supplying Smith. It has been suggested that he was giving preference to Sayers but the validity of this assertion cannot be established. It has also been suggested that Smith and Sayers worked in concert to have Chubb killed, thereby cancelling out all the monies owed to him; but this would have cut off their source of supply.'

A prisoner told detectives that Neddy had discovered an alternative source. 'With the removal of Chubb it would have enabled him (Smith) to gain a monopoly of the local market.'

Certainly Sayers lied to police, saying he was with his lawyer at the time of the shooting. But Sayers told another crook that he had been on his way to Chubb's when he accidentally witnessed the shooting.

Sayers told an associate that the death of Chubb really hurt his business. With growing debts and his main supplier dead, Sayers was in deep trouble.

But before Sayers could be re-interviewed by detectives he was shot dead.

Sydney was about to have its own underworld war and no amount of corrupt cops could stop it.

It was game on.

15

TOMMY GUN

SYDNEY HARD MAN V. MELBOURNE MADMAN

'I don't think he intended to
kill Domican that day because
he didn't take gloves or a mask
with him, as he would usually do
in these circumstances.'

CHRIS Flannery had seen the look many times. The look of terror on the face of a victim just before the bullets hit.

But on 27 January 1985, he was to feel for the first time what it would be like to be on the wrong end of the gun muzzle.

He and Kath had been to the Arncliffe Scots Club for the afternoon and after seeing some visitors off began walking up the driveway to their house in Turrella Street, Turrella.

It was 5.45pm when a green car pulled up and war was declared.

The gunman in the car opened up, firing around 30 shots at Flannery. The couple hid behind their Ford LTD and Flannery was shot in the hand and ear as he pushed his wife's head beneath the car for protection.

The Flannerys' eleven-year-old daughter began to come out the front door and (Kath said later) two bullets missed the child's head 'by inches.'

The killers had the Flannerys hopelessly exposed. There was nowhere for Chris to run – a case of shooting fish in a barrel. But at the critical moment the gunman changed magazines or suffered a momentary jam so Chris ran and vaulted the fence, hoping to draw the fire away from his family.

Kath ran inside and grabbed a Ruger rifle and gave it to her husband but the car sped off before Flannery could launch a counter attack.

Incredibly, he survived with just a nick to his ear and hand, a bruised ego and a burning desire to seek revenge.

When police arrived, a shaken Kath was prepared to make a statement until Flannery told her to say nothing. He also refused to let the children speak to the police. It was clear Flannery decided that he, and not the police, would be in charge of the investigation.

He was taken to the St George Hospital but discharged himself as soon as he was treated. From that moment on he was on the move – first heading to Queensland, then returning but moving from motel to motel, and changing hire cars every two days.

Initially he thought the killer was from Melbourne – the last surviving Kane brother, Ray 'Muscles' Kane.

So why did he think he was in danger from Kane? Flannery was a close mate of Laurie Prendergast, who had been one of the three gunmen charged with killing Les Kane. Perhaps Flannery was suspected of some involvement in the murder of Brian Kane in the Quarry Hotel in November 1982. He had been bailed just weeks earlier, after the first Locksley jury failed to reach a verdict and was certainly available for selection at the time.

Or perhaps it was because he had killed Les 'Johnny' Cole (a Kane ally), who'd been shot dead in Sydney just over two weeks before Brian Kane was killed. But for once, 'Muscles' was innocent. Within hours, Flannery decided the gunman was Marrickville garbo turned underworld heavyweight, Tommy Domican.

Born in Ireland in 1943, Domican was a London nightclub bouncer who migrated to Australia in 1968. A fearsome-looking fitness fanatic with deep and disturbing links to inner-Sydney ALP branches through local politics; he was a dangerous enemy with serious ambitions.

He was the man suspected of having organised the horrendous bashing of local politician (later Senator) Peter Baldwin in his own home. No one was ever charged. It would be the story of Domican's life. Accused of many crimes, he was rarely convicted.

So what caused Domican to be blamed for launching the attack on Flannery?

Just twelve days earlier there had been a bust-up over lucrative video poker machines running in an ethnic club in Enmore. Underworld heavyweight Lennie McPherson had his machines there but it was alleged Domican had them removed and replaced with another set. The new ones were later thrown out and damaged.

A murder taskforce reported that, on 15 January, 'Domican is reported to have had a heated exchange with McPherson over the phone, during the course of which they each threatened to kill each other.'

Police speculate that as McPherson and Freeman were business associates George may have lent Lennie his hit man to go to war.

There was a suggestion that Flannery broke into the home of the front man for the McPherson machines and threatened to kill his children. Whether this is true doesn't really matter. What is important is whether Domican believed Flannery was after him.

Enter the New South Wales police. Despite Domican's reputation, he felt perfectly comfortable calling a policeman to ask him to rat the confidential intelligence files for information on the Melbourne gunman.

On 19 January Domican rang the policeman and asked him to find out about Flannery.

'I've heard rumours he could be looking for me. He's done about fourteen murders. I don't even know what he looks like,' Domican said.

Tom told the policeman Flannery had shot Mick Drury and was known as 'Rentakill'. The policeman did make a call but did not report the approach even though he must have known Domican may have planned a pre-emptive strike.

'He (Domican) once told me that if anything ever threatened his life or family he would do something about it first. He is a man totally capable of it,' the policeman later told the taskforce, far too late. Certainly McPherson was concerned for his own welfare as he described Domican as 'quite mad.'

Around the time Domican was known to be trying to find out about Flannery, the latter's young stepson noticed a green two-door car parked near the house.

It was on 25 January, when Chris was in a paddock at the end of the street. His stepson Peter saw a Mazda two- door hatchback parked opposite their house. 'This car was parked so that the occupant could see the front of the Flannery home,' the National Crime Authority found.

At different times an orange Ford Falcon was seen in the street with the occupant apparently conducting surveillance of the Flannery house – but more of that car later.

Peter later identified the driver of the green car as Tom Domican – even though the gunman was believed to be wearing a wig and a false moustache.

National Crime Authority investigators, including Glenn Woolfe and Bob Ryan, went back to the street and did what apparently the New South Wales police failed to do – a simple door knock of the area.

One neighbour remembered that on the day of the shooting he heard what he believed was a car backfiring but when his father said it was a machine gun they dived into the garage. When he looked again he saw a green Mazda 121 driving off with one man in the front seat and one in the rear. His brother also saw a green car but could not identify the make.

At least two other neighbours made statements that they had seen a green car drive off in the street immediately after the shooting. It would be pivotal evidence.

In 1981 Domican had bought a silver two door 1978 Mazda 121. But later he had it spray painted – green. In an amazing coincidence, Domican reported the car stolen the day after the attempt on Flannery's life. It was never recovered.

The National Crime Authority concluded: 'The natural and logical inference to be drawn here is that Domican reported his car stolen because he suspected that some people may have witnessed it leaving the scene.'

Domican had called Newtown police at 3.30 pm to report his car was missing but when told he would have to report it in person he said he could not come in immediately.

The National Crime Authority noted that the car was allegedly stolen just 300 metres from the station and yet Domican could not walk up to the station to make the report.

Why?

Perhaps he feared the police could tip off Flannery, who might then have set up an ambush. Or, as the National Crime

Authority found: 'The inference here is that Domican was hiding in fear some considerable distance away after his unsuccessful attempt on Flannery's life the previous day.'

It was probably a wise move. Flannery was soon back after a week in Noosa and immediately began planning a counter attack.

'Chris went to Domican's house and watched him take the rubbish out. Chris recognised him as the man who shot at him,' Kath later said. Flannery told his wife he planned to kill the man they called 'Tough Tom' – even discussing how long his jail term would be if he were caught.

Certainly, Domican knew there would be a backlash and he wouldn't have to wait long to feel it.

While Flannery had a sense of theatre and a sense of timing, he was not known for his sense of humour. But in the days leading up to his attempt to kill Domican, Rentakill showed just a glimpse of his lighter side.

His hastily formed hit team needed a 'clean' car and Chris always preferred to use Valiants on a killing mission (closely followed by Fords; he was never a Holden hit man).

Two men went to a Sydney car yard and bought a Valiant for $650 cash. When asked the name of the purchaser they gave it as 'Thomas Domican'. The scallywags even provided Tough Tom's previous address.

On the morning of 3 April, Victor John Camilleri and Kevin Victor Theobold drove to Domican's house in Kingsgrove. The two were regular visitors and used the gym in Tom's house almost daily.

Both men were considered tough but in an underworld war, medium-size fish are always in danger from the sharks and Flannery was a maneater close to the top of the foodchain.

Theobold told police they drove there to tell Domican they would not be training with him that day (clearly petrol was much more reasonably priced in those days and cheaper than a simple phone call).

The trip was a waste of time as, according to Theobold, Domican was out for a (convenient) training run. After a quick cup of coffee with Mrs T the two men drove away in an orange Ford Falcon. Exactly the same type of car spotted doing surveillance on Flannery.

As the two men were driving along, the Valiant drove past and Flannery opened fire, hitting Camilleri in the neck with the bullet passing through his lung and into his stomach.

Camilleri spent ten days in hospital but refused to co-operate with the police investigation. Later, when the Valiant was found abandoned, it was clear that Flannery's team had not escaped unscathed. The back windshield had been shot out and there was damage to the nearside rear fender – probably from a .44 calibre bullet.

The murder taskforce was told that Domican was actually in the Ford and returned fire during the attack. When interviewed, Flannery denied involvement but said he was convinced Domican was trying to kill him.

So what really happened?

The most likely version of events is that Flannery went to the area near Domican's house on 3 April with two men, the same two believed to have killed Danny Chubb on behalf of Neddy Smith.

It is likely it was a dry run or a simple surveillance operation. Flannery preferred to do his killings at night and prided himself on his preparation. But this time it went wrong from the beginning.

Later, Domican was alleged to have told an underworld heavy he saw Flannery's team parked at Bexley North Railway Station near his home and dispatched Theobold and Camilleri to try and ambush them.

Domican then went by foot and hid in some long grass. He was able to fire first, but he missed. Flannery returned fire, shooting out the back window, and began firing at the orange Ford, hitting Camilleri. When Flannery's Valiant was recovered there were bloodstains in the back seat that were never identified.

Of all those involved most won't talk because they are not so inclined or can't talk because they are dead. Except for Kath Flannery, that is. Her recollections were clear.

'He (Chris) was looking for Domican to kill him. I think Domican was also searching for Chris to kill him ... I don't think he intended to kill Domican that day because he didn't take gloves or a mask with him, as he would usually do in those circumstances, so that he wouldn't be recognised or leave fingerprints. All of a sudden, he came face to face with Domican and his group, which forced the situation on for which he hadn't planned.

'Domican fired one shot at the car, then Chris opened fire on the orange car and that was it.

'He was forced to act in self-defence. He thought the shots were coming from another car. The last thing he would be involved in would be shooting people in broad daylight unless forced to.'

After the shooting Flannery came home, she said.

'Chris told me to go to the airport and hire a car because after Camilleri was shot he had to get rid of the car, the Valiant I am talking about.

'What happened was Chris came running home and he was bleeding from the hand and he said that he had been shot and that he had shot at another car.'

After they had dumped the car, the gun and the clothes they drove back to the crime scene for a look. 'I think the police had been there and gone by then although there were still people about.'

Flannery was determined. Little more than a week later, he had another go.

On 12 April Domican went to the Kingsgrove police station to be questioned but yet again someone let the cat out of the bag, or in this case the crook out of the boob. On his way home, a motorbike went past with two people on it. Domican recognised Flannery as the passenger. According to Neddy Smith, the other rider was Flannery's Melbourne mate, Laurie Prendergast.

In his book *Neddy*, Smith wrote, 'They had the bike running and Chris had a .357 magnum revolver ready in his hand. They spotted Domican and moved off. They made a pass to make sure it was him. Silly move, as Tom saw them straight away. They turned around for another run and Chris started shooting, missing with every shot. Tom grabbed a gun and started shooting back at the two escaping on the motorbike. He, too, missed.

'Chris fucked up badly with his cowboy tactics and the fact that he had missed was the beginning of his demise. He lost any respect that he had had.'

Certainly Coroner Glass was sure there had been a second attempt to kill Domican. 'I concluded from the evidence that this was an attempt on the life of Domican and the probabilities are that the person responsible was Flannery and an unknown companion.'

So both sides had thrown what they had hoped would be the knockout blow and missed.

Now it was time for round two.

16

END OF THE LINE
MICK SAYERS' SHORT CUT TO THE MORGUE

But in New South Wales
some police just weren't
that curious.

TO the second hand car dealer he looked like another tyre kicker. He tried to hide his boredom when the rough-looking punter asked the price of the Mercedes coupe sitting in the busy Parramatta Road lot. Then he tried to hide his look of surprise when the customer produced the required $36,500 – in cash – from a paper bag.

But the customer wasn't finished. He wanted the car to be fitted with the personalised number plate MARIAN because he was buying the Merc for his girlfriend, Marian Ware.

It was 20 December 1983 and Michael Sayers was buying the car as a last-minute Christmas present.

That was the sort of guy he was. But then again, prodigious drug dealers can afford to be impulsive and generous when the mood strikes.

It had been a good year and better was to come. Just over twelve months later he bought himself his own present – a new Mercedes. A snip at $77,000.

Business was good and Mick was flying – for the moment.

Sayers was an old-school Melbourne armed robber who saw drugs as the short cut to wealth and Sydney as the land of opportunity.

But, unfortunately for Mick, he was also seen as a friend of Chris Flannery and that was a short cut to the morgue.

His first major conviction had been in 1969 for an armed robbery in Melbourne where he was sentenced to a minimum of six years.

When he was released Sayers moved to Sydney, where he became a burglar before graduating to drug trafficking – selling cocaine, cannabis and heroin. He wasn't fussy, or maybe he was just multi-skilled.

Even though he was 38 and had been charged 25 times in Victoria and New South Wales he had no plans to reform any time soon.

And why would he? In just two years the Melbourne battler had turned himself into a millionaire.

He owned two adjacent houses in Kean Street, Caulfield. He bought the second one for $95,000 in 1984 just weeks before he was finally busted for drug trafficking.

His Sydney house in Bronte was worth $250,000 when he bought it in September 1983 and he had no hesitation pouring in another $100,000 for renovations. He also had an assortment of investment properties scattered around Sydney.

In July 1984 he was charged with drug trafficking, but after four months was finally granted bail. As it turned out he would have been better off if he had stayed inside.

The man who put-up the $20,000 bail was a registered bookmaker who wouldn't have tipped that his mate was soon to be shot.

Saturday 16 February 1985 had been a typical day for the drug dealer, horse owner, SP bookmaker, mad punter and man about town.

Sayers had been to the Canterbury races during the day with Marian Ware and his bookie mate. Following the races they picked up the bookie's wife and went out to a Pitt Street restaurant.

After dropping off the couple, Sayers and Ware returned to their Hewlett Street home (just a few hundred metres from the iconic Bondi Beach) around 9.55pm. He pulled into the driveway, left the motor running and hopped out to open the garage door.

According to Ware, there were several pops similar to a car backfiring. Sayers continued walking, then stopped and looked as if he were trying to determine the direction of the noise.

As shots started to hit the garage door, Sayers realised he was under attack. He moved from the garage and crouched behind the front mudguard of his Mercedes. He then moved to the back of the car and bolted towards Bondi Beach.

Ware watched him run before seeing him stumble to the ground at precisely the wrong moment. Then, as if in slow motion, a masked gunman walked over and fired into the helpless victim.

Sayers was shot twice in the back, with one bullet passing through both lungs and nicking the aorta.

Ware would swear the man she saw fire the shot was armed with a rifle. The New South Wales murder taskforce, set up to investigate the gangland killings, believed she had to be mistaken.

Investigating police would establish the hit team had planned to shoot him from a distance but missed. They then had to chase him to finish the job.

Police found fragments from three .22 bullets in the garage and believed from the angle of the entry points they had been fired from two locations.

As no spent cartridges were recovered, police wrongly concluded the guns were revolvers that would not spit out the spent cartridges.

'The bullet taken from the body of Sayers is probably of .38 or .357 Magnum calibre ... the fact that no fired cartridge cases were found at the scene is indicative that the firearms were revolvers.' This would be in conflict with Marian Ware's description of a rifle but there does not appear to be any other explanation given the number of shots fired.

Unless of course the hit men picked up the spent shells or police simply didn't look hard enough.

So who was Mick Sayers?

He was rumoured to be one of the biggest SP bookmakers in Sydney until he moved into the drug business.

He owned five racehorses valued at $45,000, including the prophetically named Final Episode. While under surveillance he was seen to lose up to $10,000 a night playing Russian poker without apparent concern. He was also a regular at a Double-Bay card-school run by Federal Police target, Graham 'Croc' Palmer.

As a prolific SP bookmaker he was posthumously, and perhaps conveniently, blamed for one of Australia's most notorious racing scams – the Fine Cotton Affair.

In August 1984 city racehorse Bold Personality was swapped for the bush plodder Fine Cotton in a race at Eagle Farm in Brisbane. More than $1 million were wagered, pushing the odds from 33/1 to 7/2.

Many people were implicated and some of those said Sayers was the driving force behind the rort. But, of course, by that time he was dead and could not defend himself. In New South Wales the only thing better than a live ring-in is a dead scapegoat.

Two months before the Fine Cotton ring-in, police raided his Bronte home and arrested Sayers' father over an SP operation. Police claimed the cash turnover for the day was $81,000.

Certainly while the drug business was good Sayers was a big spender who owed money around town. He was paying back

$400,000 to his good mate Danny Chubb at $20,000 a week but that debt had died when Danny did just a few weeks earlier.

Sayers owed an SP bookmaker $120,000 and it was eventually agreed he would settle at a meeting at a Double Bay hotel in May 1984.

The bookmaker saw Sayers approach carrying a brief case when Mick was intercepted by two men in suits and taken away.

Later a shaken Sayers returned with the briefcase, which was now empty. Mick told the bookmaker that Federal detectives had grabbed him but agreed not to lay drug trafficking charges in return for the $120,000.

It would later be established that the 'detectives' were Flannery and a mate and the 'arrest' was just another Sayers scam.

But Sayers and Flannery were not always play-acting. They were the prime suspects for the murder of Melbourne crook turned Sydney drug dealer, Les Cole.

Leslie John Cole was shot in the garage of his Sydney home 10 November 1982. He had survived an attempt two months earlier but this time he was shot twice in the chest and once behind the right ear.

Eighteen years later his son, Mark Moran, would be shot dead outside his Melbourne home in similar circumstances.

Police said Cole was aligned with the Melbourne Kane Clan, the standover family involved in its own underworld war. Intriguingly Cole had been in Melbourne the day before he was killed, and just over two weeks later Brian Kane was shot dead in Brunswick.

Were the deaths connected or was it coincidental? The trouble was that each murder was investigated by a different police force that often concealed information from each other. So the truth is no-one will ever know the truth.

DESPITE his debts, his occupation and his recent drug charges Sayers appeared to be relaxed, that is, until the attempted murder of Flannery.

His good friend Danny Chubb had been shot dead and then Flannery miraculously survived an attack where 30 shots were fired at him. Sayers was quickly on the phone to assure Chris he had nothing to do with the attack.

Sayers knew that as crooks were being asked to take sides he would be seen as a potential ally of Rentakill and as such a threat to be neutralised.

But Flannery and Sayers were no longer close and Mick was as concerned about his so-called mate as his known enemies.

According to Kath Flannery, 'Chris had a terrible fallout with Michael Sayers.' As usual, it was over money. Flannery had loaned Sayers $15,000 at 100 percent interest and expected $30,000 back. And you reckon the Reserve Bank is tough.

Kath said Mick was slow to return the money and this broke up the friendship.

But she also claimed George Freeman wanted Sayers killed and planned to use Flannery as the hit man. According to her, Freeman told her husband that Sayers planned to kill Flannery and he should get in first.

Kath said Freeman gave him a Valiant, a gun and a false beard to do the job. Tellingly, Rentakill took them – at least initially.

Eventually Flannery met Sayers to discuss the bad blood between them. 'They worked it out and everything was fine. Chris went and gave George the gun back and the car. George wasn't happy about it all and that was the start and the end for Chris.'

If the meeting were designed to reassure Sayers, it didn't work. He came back and told his girlfriend, 'If I die, Chris Flannery is responsible.'

But on the day of the killing, Flannery had an alibi. He was dining in an upmarket Surfers Paradise restaurant with his old mentor Ron Feeney, from Melbourne's Mickey's Disco. Flannery even paid with his American Express card.

So if it weren't Chris, then who did it?

It was not so much a suspect but a suspect car that gave police their best lead.

A week before the murder a panel van pulled up in the street and the driver asked if Mick Sayers lived here. The man then said something that stuck with the witness, 'I'm a heavy, don't mess with me.'

On the night of the killing a neighbour saw a panel van parked near Sayers' house – hardly unusual considering how close they were to Bondi Beach.

But what made the car stick in the mind of the resident was that he noticed the two men in the panel van were not 'surfie-types' but fit men aged between 30 and 40.

Just after the shooting a man and a woman saw a Holden HQ panel van driving from the area with its lights off – only to relight them as it moved away.

Police eventually concluded the two gunmen killed Sayers and then ran through a vacant block to Bronte Marine Drive, jumped into a dark coloured panel van and drove away.

Coincidently Tom Domican owned a Holden HQ panel van just like the one seen opposite Sayers' home. But while Tom was lucky with court appearances, (he was charged with one murder, one attempted murder and five counts of conspiracy to murder – and beat the lot), he was unlucky with cars.

On 28 January – the day after the attack on Flannery – Tom reported his car stolen. It was a Mazda – the same type alleged to have been used by the hit team in their failed attempt to kill the Melbourne gangster.

Now someone of Domican's status could not be expected to rely on public transport so on 29 January – the day after Tom's car went missing – someone bought a 1973 HQ Holden Panel

Van (GQD-603) from a motor auctions company for $2,850 cash, under the name of Kevin Ryan.

The murder taskforce was able to establish that Domican sold the same panel van to a policeman, just a day after the Sayers murder for the under-the-odds price of $400 (this was the value of a rifle Domican had received from the policeman).

The car was parked just a couple of streets from the murder scene in Jackman Street, Bondi and the helpful Tommy Domican produced the keys and drove the car to the policeman's house.

It was the same policeman who had attempted to provide information on Flannery to Domican just before the murder attempt on Rentakill.

The policeman was apparently unable or unwilling to see the obvious links. He was happy to do business with Tough Tom, even giving the notorious Sydney identity his address so he could drive the car to his house.

The experienced investigator didn't seem to wonder why someone like Domican would sell him the car for such a bargain basement price – at a massive discount of nearly 80 percent.

But in New South Wales some police just weren't that curious.

Later when the policeman realised the car may have been used in a murder, he helped conceal it. Despite this, and his questionable relationship with Domican, the taskforce remained sympathetic saying while the actions were 'rather silly, they do not disclose any criminal offences.'

Others might disagree.

The taskforce effectively discounted the theory Sayers was killed over his many debts. The dealer may have owed money but he had shown time and again the capacity to make bucketloads of it. He was paying back Chubb and had previously paid gambling debts.

But once he was dead no-one was going to get paid.

The New South Wales police murder taskforce concluded, 'Although heavily indebted to a number of persons, to have Sayers murdered would have been of little value, other than to exhibit to others the folly of not settling promptly ... It is more feasible that Domican, being unable to locate Flannery, has identified Sayers as his ally and at the same time settled an old score. The evidence would tend to suggest that the Holden van recovered during the course of the investigation is the vehicle used in the murder. Should that be correct then there is evidence which places Domican and an associate in possession of that vehicle 12 hours after the killing.'

Certainly there was logic to support the police view that to kill Sayers over a debt would be self-defeating, as the debt would die with him. But whoever said drug dealers were logical?

In Sydney at the time the established underworld pecking order had collapsed. In January 1985 one of Sydney's most influential gangsters, Frederick Charles (Paddles) Anderson, had died of natural causes leaving a void many wanted to fill.

The new breed of drug dealers was challenging the men who had controlled illegal gambling for decades under the umbrella of police corruption.

Plus, Sayers had been charged with drug trafficking and if convicted he wouldn't be able to pay his debt. Maybe he would be better as a dead-set example of why it could be fatal to fall behind, than to leave him to a long prison term.

The New South Wales murder taskforce produced some impressive work. Its investigators concluded the killers were Tom Domican and his good mate, Roy Thurgar. But they lacked the evidence to lay charges.

It was one of the cases that could have gone no-where. The homicide squad couldn't create the breakthrough and then a second investigation by the murder taskforce couldn't press charges.

But there was another group of investigators who had moved into offices in Sydney. The National Crime Authority was a new agency, one with some of the powers of a Royal Commission. This was hardly surprising as it was born out of political necessity following the findings from two judicial inquiries. One was headed up by Melbourne QC Frank Costigan who looked into the crime-riddled Painters and Dockers Union. The second, by Justice Don Stewart into drug trafficking and the Nugan Hand merchant bank.

Both men were very different and ran their inquiries very differently. But they concluded that corruption, infighting and lack of powers left law enforcement with little chance of effectively investigating organised crime.

The National Crime Authority was an attempt to deal with the problems on a national basis using state and federal resources. Don Stewart was its first head and the National Crime Authority's initial chief investigator was the former head of the Melbourne homicide squad, Carl Mengler.

Mengler, whose warm personality and ready laugh concealed a determination to expose corruption, was tasked with reinvestigating the Sydney murders in an operation code named Curtains.

Senior Sydney police did not welcome the National Crime Authority investigation for several reasons. Firstly, no police force would want the new boys on the block to succeed where they had failed. And secondly, they knew if the full story were told the chronic corruption of New South Wales dirtiest could no longer be hidden in dark places.

Within the National Crime Authority was a carefully positioned New South Wales mole, who reported back on a daily basis to senior Sydney police on the progress of the supposedly secret operation.

In February 1986 Mengler told his team they had to go back to the beginning. He didn't want them just to read existing statements and pick holes in the grammar. He wanted them to get out of their air- conditioned offices and back on the streets. He told them they must treat the old crime scenes as active sites and imagine the murders had just been committed.

Some of the team assigned to look at the Sayers murder were not convinced, but Mengler made them an offer they couldn't refuse – get on with it or get out.

The National Crime Authority was seen as the law enforcement body of the future. It had coercive powers, bugging equipment and hand-picked investigators but it was old-fashioned policing and a ballpoint pen that would create the first breakthrough.

In August one National Crime Authority detective placed his pen in the bullet holes in the garage door of Sayers' house and then followed the invisible line back to the vacant block across the road.

Using simple garden tools, the police dug up two spent .223 WW Special cartridge cases. New South Wales police, using metal detectors, had previously searched the area but had drawn a blank.

Tests found the bullets were fired from a 5.56mm Colt self-loading assault rifle. The second breakthrough came when rifling marks on the cartridges were found to match a weapon seized a year earlier from the Hunter Valley property of major drug dealer, Barry McCann. The bullets also proved a match to the shots fired at Flannery in the failed murder attempt in January 1985.

McCann hated Flannery and was also a great mate of Domican.

Snap.

So why would McCann be involved?

McCann and Flannery fell out after a violent confrontation in the Lansdowne Hotel. There are several versions of what happened. Kath Flannery claims that during an argument, McCann's wife threatened to glass Flannery who responded with a short right to her jaw that left it swollen and badly bruised.

Another man produced a shotgun and the Flannerys decided to take their custom elsewhere.

They were banned from that day on from returning to the pub. This was hardly surprising, as it was owned by McCann.

Later Chris sent flowers as a form of apology. Who says chivalry is dead?

And, according to Kath, McCann had also crossed Sayers off his Christmas card list.

'Michael Sayers was killed because he ripped off McCann for $250,000 worth of hash outside the Lansdowne Hotel in the boot of the car.'

Many colourful characters enjoyed the hotel. Bob Trimbole's son, Craig, provided the amusement machines in the bar and Aussie Bob was an occasional patron.

McCann was big and getting bigger. He was able to buy a 1000-hectare horse stud in the Hunter Valley for $450,000 cash.

One of McCann's team was to brag that he threw away his carpet underlay and replaced it with $100 notes – to conceal $3 million.

The boss was said to have kept up to $4 million in cash on his property.

So who ordered Sayers death? The National Crime Authority alleged that McCann and four others decided he had to die – ostensibly because he owed Barry $400,000.

But Sayers still had plenty and could have at least made a part payment, so it wasn't purely the money. McCann had plenty of that. It was a statement – a show of strength directed to old school gangster and rival drug dealer Neddy Smith – that he was a force to be reckoned with.

One of the men eventually charged over the Sayers murder was former boxer turned gunman Ray Thurgar, although the case was thrown out by a magistrate due to lack of evidence.

By 1990 Thurgar had lost his strong silent image and had became chatty with the Independent Commission Against Corruption, whose investigators visited him inside Long Bay Jail at least four times.

In December 1990 he was released from prison declaring he would make a clean start by buying a small laundromat in Randwick. But in May 1991 he was gunned down outside his business in Alison Road.

In August 1991 Tom Domican, Victor John Camilleri, 31, and Kevin Victor Theobald, 32, were found not guilty of conspiring to murder Sayers.

One of the major sticking points was the use of a police informer and notorious liar as a key witness.

The evidence about the discovery of the bullets at the scene was also contested, with the defence asking why it took so long to find the key evidence.

The jury heard that National Crime Authority officers found the spent cartridge shells 18 months after Sayers was shot.

National Crime Authority Inspector Geoffery Schuberg, admitted he wasn't going to search, but his supervisor ordered it 'in no uncertain terms' on 15 August 1986.

They then found the bullets within an hour.

When asked why he had not previously searched the area, Schuberg said, 'I'd accepted the search had been carried out at the start of the murder investigation. I honestly didn't believe anything would be found 18 months after the murder.'

The main target of Operation Curtains was Tom Domican and in October 1986 he was charged with the attempted murder of Flannery.

But the charges kept coming, including conspiring to murder Flannery and conspiring to murder his wife, Kath.

He was charged with the murder of Sayers, and three further murder conspiracy charges.

Many thought that he would be buried under the weight of charges but Domican, the former London bouncer, fought and fought.

Even when he was convicted of the attempted murder of Flannery and sentenced to 14 years he vowed to clear his name. One by one he was acquitted of the charges and after a battle that went all the way to the High Court, the Flannery conviction was quashed.

Understandably bitter, he told accomplished Sydney journalist Neil Mercer in 2003: 'It was all political to stop me saying anything about the Labor Party, to destroy my credibility. The National Crime Authority was part of all that gang war shit, then with the help of the media they built me up into this underworld figure.'

So what does McCann say about the claims?

Not much.

He was shot around 30 times in a Marrickville park on 27 December 1987.

McCann had a reputation as a Sydney kneecapper, yet the autopsy showed that while McCann had been riddled with bullets, his knees remained intact.

Irony in a full metal jacket.

17

IN THE BACK
THE DRUG DEALER WHO WOULDN'T GIVE UP HIS KILLERS

What better way to test
Flannery's loyalty than
to get him to kill one
of his best mates?

TONY Eustace was a man of few words and he wasn't going to waste any while taking his dying breaths in the emergency unit of the St George Hospital.

When a policeman asked him who had shot him six times in a Sydney street an hour earlier, his response was as brief as his life expectancy. 'Fuck off,' he responded.

These were his last words on that subject – or any other – as he died shortly afterwards on the operating table.

Eustace was born in Liverpool on 26 November 1942 and migrated to Australia just after turning 21. He was a low-level crook charged as a young man with possession of stolen property and SP bookmaking. Like many of his ilk he didn't hit the big money until the first drug wave hit.

Eustace became a heroin-dealing middleweight. He could move enough gear to live well but, at least for a while, he could avoid close police attention.

He was on the move but those in front of him were not prepared to get out of his way. He eventually attracted the attention
of the Australian Federal Police and was charged with serious
drug offences.

Like fellow Sydney underworld murder victims, Eustace had
strong Melbourne connections. In 1985 he was on bail in Victoria
after federal police charged him with conspiring to import cannabis valued at more than $8 million. The cannabis charges were
not his biggest problem. The taxman had already destroyed him
financially.

He had been forced to sell his house in Coogee and put his
Mercedes in the name of his girlfriend's mother. But while his
girlfriend was obliging, the relationship had come at a cost as he
had to pay his wife about $40,000 in a messy divorce settlement.

Eustace, known as Liverpool Tony, Spaghetti Eustace and the
less complimentary Useless Eustace, was a good heroin dealer but
a lousy legitimate businessman. He was a not-so-silent partner in
'Tony's Bar' in Double Bay and dabbled in the export business
with spectacular lack of success. He owed $50,000 to a wholesale
seafood business after he couldn't pay for lobsters he exported to
Greece in 1980. Clearly he ignored the old proverb: Beware of
Greeks making bisque.

He also laundered $30,000 in drug money through a business
selling factory-seconds towels. When the Sydney underworld
war heated up, Eustace was one of the few who remained loyal
to Flannery. After the first attempt on Flannery's life in January
1985 it was Eustace who helped hide him. They were known to
be so close that Tony was on a short list of suspects thought to
have helped Flannery go hunting for Tom Domican for a payback shooting.

Certainly, Domican later told police he suspected Flannery,
Eustace and a Melbourne painter and docker as the hit team that
tried to kill him near his home.

If it were Eustace helping that day, he was about as good an assassin as he was a seafood exporter. They got the wrong bloke. On 3 April, Domican's mate, Victor John Camilleri, was shot and wounded while Domican did not have a hair on his balding head harmed.

From November 1984, friends say, Eustace was apprehensive and began to fear that mid-range drug dealers with big-time ambitions could be an endangered species.

And his fears grew as he found himself offside with both sides of the warring bodies.

As a friend of Flannery's and a suspect in the Camilleri shooting he was a target for the so-called Domican camp (although Tom has always maintained he was not a gangster but a misunderstood political number cruncher).

When asked why he was concerned, Eustace told a friend: 'Some madman from the western suburbs wants to run Sydney.'

As radio commentator Steve Price lives in the east, he probably meant Domican. In fact, as Price didn't move to Sydney until years later, he almost certainly meant Domican.

He began to move from house to house regularly and told friends he could be 'off' because he had been protecting Chris Flannery. He started to carry a gun and his fears increased when he spotted two men using walkie-talkies watching him while he was eating in an upmarket restaurant in Double Bay.

Later, he thought two men were following him in a green Commodore. Police would allege that Domican and one Roy Thurgar had access to an identical Commodore registered in the name of a close family associate.

But while Eustace was dodging the Domican faction he had reasons to fear the George Freeman forces for several reasons.

According to Kath Flannery, when Freeman wanted Chris to kill Mick Sayers the hit man sought Eustace's advice.

They met at the Royal Oak Hotel in Double Bay where Eustace told Flannery he shouldn't carry out the hit because Sayers was a 'good bloke.' Intriguingly, he also said Sayers wouldn't be a problem because he was soon to be arrested by the Federal Police on drug charges.

Tony was on the money. In July 1984 Sayers was arrested as part of a joint federal-state police operation and spent four months inside before he made bail.

But if Freeman knew that Eustace had persuaded his favourite hit man to refuse a contract he would have been unimpressed.

Worse was to follow. The man with few words opened his mouth too much. He asked a hypothetical question to another crook: 'What happens if George goes?'

The crook reported it to Freeman, who was already on war footing. Those five words were effectively Eustace's death sentence. And what better way to test Flannery's loyalty than to get him to kill one of his best mates?

On 23 April 1985, the weather in Sydney matched Tony Eustace's mood – both were filthy. He had taken the risk of protecting and hiding Flannery – and now the Melbourne hit man was asking him for $25,000, saying he was set to disappear overseas.

Eustace got a call while sitting at his favourite restaurant that afternoon from Flannery wanting yet another favour.

Enough was enough. He agreed to meet Flannery but his patience was running out. 'Fuck these Melbourne people,' he said after hanging up.

He was running late and parked his car near the meeting place at the Koala Inn. The Mercedes was booked for being at an expired metre at 2.35pm. Nearby a brown Valiant was booked for being at an expired metre around the same time.

Someone had bought the car less than two weeks earlier for $1945 cash under a false name. It was, of course, Flannery's favourite make of car to use when carrying out a hit.

But according to Kath, Flannery was worried for his mate and even warned him he should stop driving his readily identifiable gold Mercedes as it made him an easy target.

As they left the meeting Eustace promised to get some money and meet later at the Airport Hilton. It is reasonable to assume the meeting place was picked because Eustace believed that once he gave him the money Flannery would head overseas and become someone else's problem.

Tony went back to Tony's Bar and had a drink with a mate – who bought him a second and was keen to settle in for the evening. But Eustace was in a hurry and said he had to go to the airport. It was pouring rain and his mate told him he was crazy to head out but Tony said he had no choice.

Before he left he went over to one of the staff who was owed wages and peeled off $500 from a large stack of cash he had inside a paper bag tucked in his shirt. Police believe this was the money he was to give to Flannery.

Eustace headed towards the airport in the rain. He didn't make it. He parked in Gertrude Street, just 200 metres from the hotel, about 6.30pm. Several witnesses said they saw a gold Mercedes parked nose to nose with a brown Valiant.

They saw the internal and external lights illuminating the empty Mercedes and three people in the Valiant.

Witnesses heard several shots before watching a man holding a gun run back to the Valiant, do a three-point turn and drive away. Some said they saw another person in the front seat of the Valiant. We will never know the identity of the second man – or woman. One intriguing theory is that the second person in the car was George Freeman himself, who used Flannery to lure the victim to the dark street for the ambush.

Certainly Freeman was not home that night and he went out wearing his 'lucky' black outfit – the clothes he wore when he was about to commit a major crime.

In phone taps recorded during the Federal Police's Operation Lavender, Freeman's bent doctor Nick Paltos was caught talking about the case with Graham 'Croc' Palmer.

Paltos: *I'll tell you who shot Useless, I've got to be honest with you.*

Palmer: *Freeman?*

Paltos: *Yeah, he did. George Freeman, he shot him, all right ... He owned up to it today.*

Police believe Eustace hopped into the Valiant and gave Chris his $25,000 farewell present. After his last goodbye and as he walked back to his car Flannery (or possibly Freeman) hopped out and emptied six shots from a .45 pistol into the back of his good friend.

About fifteen minutes later a local young man saw the man on the ground and called out, 'Are you OK?'

'I've been shot,' the dying man responded.

He was asked how many times and muttered, 'About four or five times.' He was the master of understatement.

The young man asked who did it and Eustace answered: 'I just stopped to help them – they looked as though they needed help and they shot me.'

To the end Eustace showed Flannery loyalty he didn't deserve.

The Valiant was later recovered in the airport carpark. It had travelled only about 170 kilometres since its new owner had bought it on 12 April.

At 5pm on 23 April, Flannery hired a Falcon from Budget Rentals at Mascot Airport. He returned it the following day and paid $73.40.

In what must have been seen as an amazing coincidence, just three weeks earlier when Flannery was dumping a Valiant he used at the time Camilleri was shot, Kath hired another car – also from the airport.

The murder taskforce concluded: 'The evidence points to Flannery as the murderer.' The National Crime Authority went further. 'It is the opinion of the investigators that Christopher Dale Flannery, quite probably through his association with George Freeman, played a major role in the murder.'

Flannery may have got away with the murder but his cards were marked.

By killing (or setting up) his best ally he showed all the warring elements – and more importantly the police power brokers – he was prepared to turn on anyone, which meant no-one was safe.

The underworld war was bad for business. If it kept going it could prompt a royal commission that would expose the fact that corrupt police 'green lighted' favoured gangsters to let them commit crimes with impunity.

Flannery was out of control. Freeman, Neddy Smith, Mc-Cann, Lennie McPherson and key detectives knew he had passed his use-by date.

The 'green light' racket meant selected crooks could do anything short of killing a policeman. But Flannery had already tried to kill undercover detective Mick Drury.

And then he made the mistake of threatening the wrong man. According to Neddy Smith, during a vicious argument Flannery once yelled at a powerful police figure: 'You're not a protected species, you know – you're not a fucking koala bear.'

But neither was he. And he was the one who would soon be extinct.

18

RENTAKILLED

VALE CHRISTOPHER DALE, ROGUE MALE

> 'My first reaction was
> one of relief. I hoped he'd
> been killed.'

BY early 1985 Chris Flannery was running out of friends. This was hardly surprising, as he'd killed most of them.

Flannery had built a fearsome reputation for killing on command but when an attack dog begins to snarl at its master it's time for the big sleep.

Flannery had made too many enemies in the underworld. Police alleged that Sydney hard man Tom Domican was out to kill him, although no charges would ever stick. A heavy drug dealer called Barry McCann was no fan of the mad dog from Melbourne, either. This may have related to the fact that Flannery had once punched McCann's wife in the face. He later sent her flowers as an apology but a left hook followed by a few orchids was never going to work.

Flannery's boss George Freeman had lost patience with him and was a little frightened of the unpredictable gunman. Flannery was said to have refused Freeman's contract to kill Mick Sayers – so he was no longer obedient.

He had also killed his good friend Tony Eustace – proof that he was no longer loyal. He had shown he would kill anyone for anybody if the price were right or even if he just felt like it. He was on every team and therefore he was on no-one's. It was a dangerous place to be.

But more importantly, perhaps fatally, Flannery had lost his pull with the corrupt detectives who were the main stabilising element in the Sydney underworld.

Flannery had threatened police and had shot one – undercover detective Mick Drury. Even when the notorious Neddy Smith had been given the 'green light' to pull virtually any crime he wanted, he was warned he would be protected only if he did not harm police.

In the end, Flannery had managed to alienate all the players that influenced the Sydney underworld. It was not a recipe for longevity. But the truth was, even when he was just a cocky youngster, he'd lived by the rule 'live fast, die young'. Which is exactly what he did.

FLANNERY might have been half crazy but he was no fool. There had already been one attempt on his life and he knew it would not be the last. His sister-in-law described him as being jumpy – 'a caged animal that could not relax'. In the end his cat-like reflexes would not be enough. He was about to run out of his nine lives.

He abandoned his family house and kept moving between hostels, hotels and private homes. He would also wear disguises and change cars every few days and always carried a loaded gun. As the pressure grew, he took to leaving the safety catch off and the gun cocked. It was risky but better than giving an enemy any advantage in a shoot out. He knew half a second could make all the difference in a showdown.

But eventually he became sick of packing his bags, and in April 1985 rented an apartment under an assumed name in the prestigious 30-storey Connaught Building, conveniently across the road from the Criminal Investigation Branch. Perhaps he thought being nestled next to the police would give him extra protection.

If so, he was horribly wrong.

He leased the apartment at $350 a week for three months under Kath's brother-in-law's name of Mougalis.

It is almost certain that key members of the underworld and corrupt police had a council of war and decided that Flannery had run out of time. But the hit man would be hard to trap. He was cunning, dangerous and frightened. He kept his address secret and stopped being seen in public. He was short of money because he could no longer act as Freeman's bodyguard.

At one stage Freeman even suggested he should disappear. 'Go away for a while and things will be taken care of.' He chose to ignore the advice.

As is usual in the underworld, it would be left to a 'mate' to set up the target and this time the friend was Freeman himself.

On 8 May Flannery agreed to meet members of the murder taskforce informally to talk about the Eustace murder. He denied any knowledge of the case and said his mate had not turned up for the second meeting that was supposed to go ahead at the Airport Hilton.

But what if Flannery had been seen meeting the detectives? Flannery was frightened, so perhaps some were concerned he was trying to broker a deal with the police that would involve implicating Freeman.

On the very same day he met the murder taskforce detectives, his pager went off with a message – 'Ring Mercedes' – Freeman's code name. Flannery did what he was told and Freeman organised a meeting for next morning.

Dangling a bait, Freeman told him he wanted him to come around to inspect a modified sub-machine gun fitted with a silencer. It was from the batch modified by Linus Patrick Driscoll and used in the Bookie Robbery and to kill Leslie Herbert Kane in Melbourne.

Flannery, a gun nut, couldn't resist.

The trap was set.

But, according to Kath, Rentakill was nervous. 'Poor Chris was a wreck,' she said. That night he began to worry if he were being set up. He speculated to Kath that if Freeman wanted to kill him he would lure him into the house and then use the gun with a silencer to finish the job. For her part, Kath had also feared for her children's safety after an earlier attempt to kill Chris in a drive-by shooting.

On the morning of 9 May Flannery dressed for his meeting with Freeman. He was wearing the uniform of the day – pants, a tracksuit top, and the mandatory gangster jewellery in the days before it was called bling. He had with him a passport in the name of Christopher James, a light brown wig and a loaded .38 handgun – cocked with the safety catch off.

When asked by the National Crime Authority if her husband had been armed that day, Kath responded as if it were a stupid question. Would you ask a surgeon if he had washed his hands before he entered the operating theatre?

'Oh, he had a gun and it was loaded and ready to go ... Yes, it was a silver .38, a little silver one,' she explained.

But when asked to identify the weapon she became a little vague.

'There were so many coming into Chris from others and going from Chris to others that I can't be sure what type it was but I do know that at the time he had a handgun and from memory it was a pistol.'

He planned to ring Freeman from a public phone at the Miranda shopping centre near George's house to tell him to lock up the dogs and open the front gates so his favourite hit man could slip in without delay.

Flannery took the lift down to the underground carpark and walked over to the Valiant he had bought a few days earlier while his brand new car was being repaired after someone ran into the back of it, causing $5500 worth of damage.

But the engine on his old Valiant wouldn't turn over so he returned to the apartment, telling Kath he would take a taxi and be back in a couple of hours. She would later recall that he said to her, 'Ring Marshall Batteries and get a new one. I'll be back at 11.30 and we'll go to the movies.'

He was seen leaving by the building's security officer at 8.15am. He was never seen again.

Kath did as she was told and rang the battery supplier. But when the serviceman arrived and turned the key the motor jumped into life. It is almost certain one of the hit team had disconnected the battery to force Flannery out of the front door of the building so he could be picked up, and had then reconnected it later to cover the trail. They wanted it to look as if Flannery had decided to do a runner rather than having just run out of time.

There were a hundred theories about what happened to Flannery, but one thing is certain. He died that day and it was his friends who set him up. The irony is obvious. The man who made so many disappear suffered the same fate. In other words, the karma bus flattened him.

But who was driving?

In his autobiography, *Neddy*, Smith claims, 'Rumour has it that Chris was picked up by a policeman he knew well and trusted, who offered him a lift. The car went only a short way before it stopped at a set of traffic lights, where two ex-police climbed in. The car took off and Chris was then shot several times in the head and chest as the car drove along.'

New South Wales Coroner Greg Glass heard from 132 witnesses during his three-year investigation into the death and was able to debunk several of the more colourful theories such as the one that Flannery was garrotted in a boatshed and dumped in the harbour, shot by police while driving on the Newcastle Highway, murdered and buried in a Sydney building site and hit from behind with a meat cleaver and fed into a tree-shredder.

But he did confirm underworld folklore that it was friends and not known enemies who had done the job.

'I am therefore comfortably satisfied that Flannery was betrayed, deceived, possibly lured into a motor vehicle, by someone, or by some persons, whom he trusted and was then killed, with the remains being disposed of in a manner unknown,' Glass said.

He said the evidence raised a 'strong suspicion that Roger Rogerson was involved in Flannery's disappearance and his death, or at least knew what happened to him. Rogerson had the motive and opportunity to cause harm to Flannery.'

He found Freeman may have been 'connected with Flannery's fate'.

Rogerson has always maintained he was not involved. Much later 'Roger the Dodger' told Channel Nine's *Sunday* program, 'Flannery was a complete pest. The guys up here in Sydney tried to settle him down. They tried to look after him as best they could, but he was, I believe, out of control. Maybe it was the Melbourne instinct coming out of him. He didn't want to do as he was told, he was out of control, and having overstepped that line, well, I suppose they said he had to go but I can assure you I had nothing to do with it.'

Kath Flannery told the National Crime Authority that she quite liked the charismatic cop they all called 'Roger'.

'I got to know him in '72 when he was one of those who ver-balled Chris and they hated each other and then when I got to know him I didn't mind the guy.

'He's always been good to me. He's always been good to the children. I don't think for a moment he probably doesn't take a bit here and a bit there but I don't think he is as bad as some of them going around.'

But she claimed that about two weeks after her husband disappeared, Rogerson turned up with an offer of $50,000 from Freeman to shut up about the case. She refused: 'I told him to stick it up his jumper.'

Freeman also maintained he was not involved. In his book he wrote that when he first heard of the earlier failed attempt to kill Rentakill outside the Flannery home, 'My first reaction was one of relief. I hoped he'd been killed. No such luck.

'Kath Flannery has tried every means possible to fit me for her husband's disappearance and alleged murder – but I'll stack my credibility against hers any time.'

Kath Flannery may have been many things but no one could doubt that she was blood loyal to her Chris.

Flannery, on the other hand, believed monogamy was a board game. He regularly visited brothels and had a two-year torrid love affair with a part-time model known as Ms P that ended the previous year.

Flannery rang Kath three times a day when he was on the road to tell her he was still alive and kicking. When he didn't ring from Freeman's house Kath knew the worst. He was gone.

She rang Freeman and immediately suggested not only was her husband dead, but Freeman was involved in the murder.

At 3pm she rang and Freeman responded, 'Why don't you go

and see your mate Rogerson, or Billy Duff (another corrupt New South Wales detective)? He's probably locked up somewhere.'

She rang her solicitor who checked with the police. Flannery was not in custody.

Kath went to the murder taskforce at the CIB building at 4.30pm to report that her husband had been murdered but she refused to give detectives her address across the road.

There was good reason for this. In the apartment were Chris's tools of trade – guns and disguises – and she did not want police to be able to seize them. If Freeman were behind the death of her husband she might have had some use for that equipment at a date to be fixed.

Kath again rang Freeman and this time the conversation was more pointed. 'I'll see you later. We'll see about you,' she said.

'Good, do your fucking best, lady,' he responded.

Hardly the way to speak to a grieving widow.

Kath's prompt visit to the taskforce gave police their first real opportunity. If they could get a break they would be able to find the crime scene and perhaps a body. But if they didn't locate the area where Flannery was murdered they would always be hard pressed to identify the professional killers.

The head of the taskforce, John Anderson, rang the suspended Rogerson and told him Flannery was missing. This was quite reasonable because Rogerson, having a known link to the hit man, might have been able to shed some light on the case. But if Rogerson had in fact been directly involved in the murder he was unwittingly given an early warning that the taskforce was on the case.

Later Coroner Glass would say the strong links between Flannery and Rogerson should have been aggressively investigated. He said the connection, 'strangely was not the subject of inquiry after 9 May.'

From the outset, Kath made it clear to the police she believed Freeman was involved. So what did they do?

You would expect they would have grabbed a warrant and raided the last known location Flannery was supposed to visit: Freeman's house.

But they didn't. For some reason the police called Freeman first to tell him they wanted to pop over for a chat and a bit of a sticky-beak. George said that without a warrant they were not welcome. Police made an appointment to see him the next day.

If Freeman were involved it would be lunacy to warn him that a search was going to take place. Or was it?

Kath had told them she believed Chris had been shot in the house, hidden in a secret compartment in the billiard room, then transferred in the boot of an old car to a boat and dumped at sea.

On 10 May two detectives went to the house. Freeman, through his lawyer, refused to comment but offered them an invitation to search the house.

The detectives, without calling any forensic back up, conducted the search and found nothing.

On 20 May – eleven days after Flannery was killed – police returned with forensic experts for a thorough search. They found the secret compartment that Kath had told them existed in the house. It was in the den and not the games room. Twisting shelves that swivelled open revealed the compartment hidden between two wall cavities. As would be expected, it was clean.

'Nothing was turned up,' Freeman later gloated.

Meanwhile Kath had to make herself busy. She knew the police would come to their apartment so she grabbed the guns – a .45 pistol and a sub-machine gun – and put them in the Valiant.

The car started first time, adding weight to the theory the car had been disabled by someone to force Flannery onto the footpath where he could be grabbed. She drove the car to a friend's house where she hid the guns to be used later.

So what really happened?

It is the authors' opinion that in late April 1985 there was a secret meeting in Sydney attended by corrupt police and several major crime figures including Barry McCann, Lennie McPherson and George Freeman.

At the meeting it was agreed that the war had to end as it was bad for business and the growing media pressure could result in a royal commission. It was unanimously decided that Flannery had to go if the murders were to stop. McCann said he was prepared to pay for the hit and Freeman agreed to control the planning. As Flannery was still on the move, difficult to find and always armed, a drive-by street shooting was considered unlikely to succeed, remembering that an earlier attempt had failed spectacularly.

Freeman decided on the high-risk strategy of killing Flannery in his own home. For Freeman the advantages outweighed the risk. While there was a risk of leaving some forensic evidence he knew that if it were done within the walls of his house, there would be no witnesses and the body would never be found as it could be disposed of discreetly.

Many would just think Flannery had run away because of fears for his life. Without a corpse and with no witnesses, who could know for sure?

In addition, Freeman knew that if he shot him from behind he could finish the job. It would ensure the hit would not be bungled a second time. The motive not to fail was strong, because no one would be safe from Flannery's revenge.

This is a theory like many others but what can be established is that in the days before the murder Freeman sought advice from the underworld doctor of choice, Nick Paltos, on removing bloodstains after a murder.

Just two days before Flannery was killed, Paltos was recorded talking to Croc Palmer on Federal Police phone taps.

Paltos: *He said mate, "I need your help ..." Freeman said to me ... "I'm gonna knock someone off ... I wanna know about blood, how long blood lasts ..." He's said gonna do it at home, he's gonna brick a bloke at home.*

(Freeman said) "What I think's gonna happen they're gonna come to my house they'll never think ... It's so fucking dicey".

Palmer: *Surely not that fucking stupid.*

Paltos: *I said, "I'll give you some good fucking advice, you want to be very fucking careful ..." "Anyway, I know what's going on," he says... "Everything's right for five years, there'll be peace for five years, after this week".*

Palmer: *Are they just going to make this cunt disappear?*

Paltos: *I think so ... He says it's gonna be blood on the carpet, he says, "You know I'm worried if they see the carpet," and I said, "You're a fucking mug, a miserable fucking ..." I said, "Cut the fucking bit out, cut the fucking bit out and throw it away" ... He said, "You're fucking right".*

Palmer: *It's not safe fucking bringing someone to your home and fucking killing them.*

Paltos: *It's the only way maybe ... But they'd want to do it in a way that everyone would know they've done it too, without proof.*

Palmer: *Oh they can't be smart fucking people.*

Paltos: *No, none of them are smart.*

But then again they weren't stupid enough to blab on phones tapped by the feds.

Flannery knew what was coming, he just wasn't sure when. By May the pressure was getting to him. He was fidgety, nervous and sleeping badly. He told his mother-in-law that Freeman had once told him, 'The one that gets you will be a friend you think you've got but you haven't.'

He told one of his few remaining friends he feared that police would try and kill him to stop the gang war.

He told his sister-in-law, 'I think I'm going to die ... They're going to get me ... I just can't keep running like this.'

But there was one policeman (or at least a suspended one) that he (almost) trusted – Roger 'The Dodger' Rogerson. While on the run he kept in contact with Rogerson – although he was wise enough to never let him know where he was hiding.

But then on 8 May – the day before Flannery disappeared – the rogue detective cast a giant shadow over the case. It was Rogerson who contacted the taskforce and said he could organise a meeting with Flannery.

The officer in charge, John Anderson, was not ready to put allegations to Flannery but thought a meeting could break the ice.

Anderson later told the inquest, 'I was sort of taken back a bit but, nevertheless, I took the view that I had nothing to lose by meeting Flannery so I said yes ... I would speak to him. Rogerson later got back to me and said he would not come to the CIB he had this contact with Flannery ... so the venue was set to meet him at a club in the city and I went there about 1.30 on 8 May and I took Detective-Sergeant Coughlin with me.

'I wasn't really ready for the meeting but I thought something positive was going to come from it ... I was hoping Flannery would tell us about the background to the confrontation but it wasn't to be. I came away a little bit disappointed actually.

'At the club I didn't have any great conversation with Rogerson because they were both there when we arrived ... Rogerson did the introduction ... Flannery was seated at a table and having done that introduction Rogerson moved away from the company. I don't know why. He wasn't asked to move away. We tried to be as sociable as possible.'

As the pair sat and talked at the New South Wales Cricketers' Club, Anderson could see that Flannery was there under sufferance. 'I don't think he liked our presence there. I think he was keen to get away from us as soon as possible. He gave the appearance he was anxious to leave.'

So it would appear that it was Rogerson who pushed for the meeting.

Flannery told Anderson he didn't know who shot at him in January, but it was obvious that he was blaming Domican. Anderson said that Flannery appeared very nervous, with Flannery implying that the feud between him and Domican had 'come too far to be resolved'.

It was clear that the war would end only when either Domican or Flannery was dead.

'It was obvious to me that he (Flannery) was not going to sit back and allow people to shoot at him without taking some sort of action himself. I came away with the apprehension that he would do something further himself,' Anderson said.

But Anderson noticed that when Flannery left, Rogerson hung back and walked out a few moments later.

'I expected them both to leave together ... it caught me by surprise when one went prior to the other,' Anderson said.

The question remains, did Rogerson set up the meeting so that he or his team could follow Flannery to his secret address just two kilometres away?

Rogerson was suspended from the force and was soon to stand trial over attempting to bribe Mick Drury.

The erratic and dangerous Flannery could have been a star witness against Rogerson if he could be turned, and the hit man was running out of options. A new identity and a new start could have been his only way out.

Six weeks after Flannery disappeared, Rogerson was acquitted of the charge. It is certainly reasonable to conclude that as a result of that meeting Flannery's hideout was exposed. But the exact apartment number may still have been a secret, giving him at least some protection. Even then, if the flat number were known there was no way a hired killer would risk bursting in on Flannery, who was always armed. Freeman and his associates didn't want a shoot-out; they wanted an ambush.

And Freeman – the professional punter – always wanted the odds on his side. Just hours after Freeman left the detectives and Rogerson at the club, Freeman paged him to organise a meeting for the next day.

If Flannery were allowed to drive to Freeman's in his Valiant he may have been seen entering the secure property and the car would have to be dumped. By disabling the sedan it put Flannery on the street outside the building. This part of the theory tallies with Neddy Smith's version of what happened.

But it is believed that after accepting a lift from police who just happened to be passing, they drove him to Freeman's.

Present with Freeman was his crony, underworld heavyweight, Lennie McPherson. Although on his guard, Flannery was lured into the den where Freeman used the silenced sub-machine gun to kill Flannery. The light calibre of the bullets was such that they did not pass through the body. Linus Patrick Driscoll modified the gun and one from the same batch was used to kill Les Kane in his Melbourne bathroom years earlier. Then, as in the Flannery case, no bullet holes were found in the walls and the body was never recovered.

With Flannery dead, Freeman thought he would have some time to dispose of the body and clean the house but Kath was on the phone within hours.

It is known that on that afternoon Freeman had left the house for unexplained reasons. Certainly when Kath rang a second time he was not home and his wife, Georgina, took the call.

If police had gone to the house straight away, perhaps they would have found some evidence to back up the theory. But having unintentionally warned him he was a suspect with a call on 9 May they did not complete a comprehensive search until 20 May, giving George plenty of time to get his house in order.

The taskforce concluded: 'Two days before his disappearance Freeman had a conversation with Dr Paltos indicating he intended to kill somebody at his home. There can be little doubt that the intended victim was Flannery. Should Flannery have been murdered on 9 May, it would appear that he had been intercepted prior to his arrival. It does not seem feasible that Freeman would carry out the execution in his own home where his wife and five children could become involved. There is no scientific evidence to support such an occurrence and it is more likely that Flannery has been intercepted by persons he trusted prior to his arrival there.'

It found: 'What is believed to have occurred is that there has been reconciliation between McCann/Domican and Freeman/McPherson whereby Flannery became isolated. With his removal there would be reason to believe that the previous conflict would be put to rest. In order to achieve this and appease McCann/Domican the scene was set where Flannery was betrayed by alleged friends.'

As Kath Flannery was to tell the National Crime Authority: 'When Chris was killed we were virtually trying to sell the house to move to Queensland. He knew he couldn't survive in Sydney. They were too strong. You see they'd been doing what they had been doing for a hundred years.

'These people were not going to stop until they got him. They were so blatant about it. George sold Chris out because they've said, "Look, we know that Chris sold out Drury now you've got to get rid of him because he's told a certain police officer that if I start he'll kill him".'

But while police would never find sufficient evidence to

charge Freeman, Kath was convinced he was behind her man's death and she was determined to get her revenge.

One of Flannery's friends was the son of a respected New South Wales public official. The friend had dabbled in cocaine trafficking and when one of his partners refused to pay, Chris paid a visit and the partner paid up.

Flannery would part finance two trips to Bolivia for the friend to buy cocaine. One of the importations netted each of them $170,000.

Just days after Flannery went missing the cocaine smuggler met Kath at the Melbourne Airport Travelodge. 'She looked terrible – she appeared very tired and weepy eyed,' he would later tell the National Crime Authority.

She told him that Chris was dead. At a later meeting at a Melbourne restaurant she said that Freeman organised the hit but McCann paid for it.

Eventually, the drug importer agreed to back up another Melbourne criminal in an attempt on Freeman's life.

But, quite unwittingly, Federal police from Operation Lavender would save Freeman's life – not once, but twice.

The perfect place, the Melbourne team decided, was when George Freeman went for his regular Thursday medical checks with Dr Paltos. Some say he needed his asthma monitored. Others said he was addicted to morphine that was supplied by the obliging Dr Nick.

On two Thursdays Flannery's mate sat off the surgery (each time with a different Melbourne gunman) ready for the hit but on the first occasion he noticed a suspicious van and on the second he saw men near the surgery he believed were Freeman's bodyguards. In fact, they were Federal police from Operation Lavender who were trying to conduct discreet surveillance on the good doctor. The would-be hit man said he believed Freeman had been tipped off. He said when Freeman arrived, 'He had a nasty scowling look on his face. He started pointing at us while he sat in his car.'

Freeman later wrote, 'The underworld grapevine ran hot that night. It was no secret who had taken the contract out on me.'

But Kath was too loyal to let it rest. Heartbroken and isolated, she turned to Melbourne for support. The painters and dockers raised $10,000 for her. Perhaps believing that the Sydney gangsters who arranged her husband's murder would come after her, she decided to fight back. According to a secret National Crime Authority witness, she got ten sticks of gelignite from Alan Williams and was set to blow Tom Domican and another Sydney identity into the next world. The plan was to plant the gelignite in the exhaust pipes of two cars so that they would explode as the engines heated.

But the New South Wales police were tipped off about the gelignite plot by an 'extremely reliable but confidential source in Victoria,' which probably saved a couple of worthless lives.

On 3 June Freeman opened his mailbox to find a letter with a photo of a small child coloured blue. He took it to be a threat against his children.

The Sydney gangsters weren't going to let Kath pick them off and threaten them, so it was inevitable she would get a warning she could end up with her husband.

Two weeks after Flannery's death, Kath's car was torched. Police believed her enemies did it as a warning but some wondered if she had done it herself to raise public sympathy. The car was insured.

In July, members of the Sydney underworld who had once been at war were seen sitting and talking amicably. A few days later a crew of heavies were seen cruising around near the Flannery family home.

On 19 August, Kath called the police after finding a suspicious device under her Ford LTD. It was a bomb rigged to go and designed to be set off by remote control.

Some police believed that she set the bomb herself, claiming the gelignite was from the same lot she sourced from Williams. It seemed unlikely, given that her plan had been to use hot exhaust pipes to explode the gelignite rather than a complex remote control.

The taskforce found it 'had been constructed by a person with expertise in the area of electronics.' It was doubtful that Kath had done it herself.

Soon after, she sold her house and moved to the Gold Coast with her children. Since then, apart from the occasional minor legal problem, it appears Kiss of Death Kath has left the underworld behind.

BIBLIOGRAPHY

Apart from extensive original research and interviews with sources on both sides of the law, the authors have drawn on published sources listed below. We wish particularly to acknowledge the work of the late Richard Hall and of Keith Moor, Bob Bottom, Tom Noble and gun-for-hire John Kerr.

Booth, Pat: *The Mr Asia File.*
Bottom, Bob: *Connections.*
Bottom, Bob: *Connections 2.*
Bottom, Bob: *Shadow of Shame.*
Bottom, Bob: *Without Fear or Favour.*
Freeman, George: *An Autobiography.*
Goodsir, Darren: *In the Line of Fire.*
Hall, Richard: *Greed.*
Hickie, David: *The Prince and the Premier.*
McCoy, Alfred: *Drug Traffic.*
Moor, Keith: *Crims in Grass Castles.*
Noble, Tom and Smith, Arthur: *Neddy.*
Reeves, Tony: *Mr Big.*
Reeves, Tony: *Mr Sin.*
Silvester, John and Rule, Andrew: *Tough: 101 Gangsters.*

Silvester, John and Rule, Andrew: *Underbelly* series, 1-11.
Whitton, Evan: *Can Of Worms*.
Wilson, David and Murdoch, Lindsay: *Big Shots*.
Wilson, David and Robinson, Paul: *Big Shots 2*.

Government Reports

Victorian Coronial reports into the deaths of Ray Bennett, Les
Kane, Brian Kane, Norman McLeod, Laurie Prendergast and
Roger Wilson.
NSW Coronial report into the presumed murder of Christopher
Dale Flannery.
Final report of the NSW Drug/Murder Taskforce.
Nagle, John: Special Commission of Inquiry into police investi-
gations into the Donald Mackay murder.

Royal Commission reports from:
Costigan, Frank.
Stewart, Donald.
Williams, Edward.
Woodward, Philip.
Supreme Court transcripts (various).

BIOGRAPHIES

Leslie Herbert Kane. Born Carlton 1 December 1945. One of three gangster brothers and heavily connected in the notorious Painters and Dockers Union. In the 1970s considered Australia's most violent man. Shot dead in the bathroom of his Wantirna unit 19 October 1978. Body never found. Three men charged – and acquitted – of the murder.

Raymond Patrick Bennett. The mastermind behind the 21 April 1976 Great Bookie Robbery. Charged and acquitted of the murder of Les Kane. Shot dead inside the Melbourne Magistrates Court 11 November 1979 allegedly by Les's brother, Brian.

Brian Raymond Kane. Melbourne standover man and suspect for the murder of Ray Bennett. Shot dead in the Quarry Hotel 26 November 1982.

Alan David Williams. Footballer, armed robber and drug dealer. A Melbourne-based gangster connected with failed attempts to bribe and then murder New South Wales undercover detective Mick Drury. Died of natural causes mid 2001.

Christopher Dale Flannery. School drop-out who became an underworld drop-kick. Born Melbourne 15 March 1949, the

317

youngest of three children. Became Australia's most notorious hit man – reputedly killed 14 people. Charged and acquitted of two contract killings, moved to Sydney and became a key figure in a major underworld war. Known as Rentakill, went missing 9 May 1985 – body never found.

Kathleen Flannery. Blood loyal wife of Chris. She stuck with him when others wouldn't and was dragged into an underworld war as a consequence. After his death she reclaimed her life and raised her children away from the underworld.

Tom Ericksen. Former insurance salesman who became an influential figure with connections to police and gangsters. A one-legged private detective known as 'Hopalong Tom.' In the 1970s, Ericksen employed another shadowy character, Gianfranco Tizzoni, in his repossession business. Tizzoni was the man who later helped organise the murder of anti-drugs campaigner Donald Mackay. Strongly linked to Chris Flannery and almost certainly helped set up the hit man's murder contracts. In 1988, National Crime Authority officers charged him with 195 counts of giving secret commissions (bribery) and 11 counts of making threats to kill. On 10 August that year, he was due in court to answer the charges. He died earlier that morning, a 52-year-old blind one-legged diabetic.

George David Freeman. Colourful Sydney racing identity who protected himself by bribing police. Royal Commissioner and former New South Wales policeman Justice Donald Stewart found Freeman was linked to race fixing, SP bookmaking and illicitly protected casinos. He employed hit man Chris Flannery until the underworld and corrupt police decided to make the hit man redundant. Flannery went missing on the way to Freeman's house and has never been seen again. It wasn't crooked police but a crook chest that got George in the end. Freeman had chronic asthma. The man who survived being shot in the head died from complications from an asthma attack in March 1990.

(Dr) **Nicholas George Paltos**. Born Kastellorizon, a small Greek island, in 1941 the youngest of ten children. Migrated to Australia with his family aged six. Completed an electroplating diploma. Won a Commonwealth Scholarship and studied medicine at the University of New South Wales while working nights as a taxi driver. Became a fashionable GP whose patients included Kerry Packer and many of Sydney's major crime figures such as George Freeman, Danny Chubb and Robert 'Aussie Bob' Trimbole. Alleged to have provided morphine for Freeman's raging habit. Organised the importation of 5.5 tonnes of hashish resin with a street value of $40 million. Arrested as part of the Australian Federal Police Operation 'Lavender' – sentenced to a minimum of 13 years. Struck off the medical register. Found guilty of conspiring with former detective Roger Rogerson, of perverting the course of justice for using false names to hide money in bank accounts. Released 1994. Died of natural causes 2003.

Roger Caleb Rogerson. Born January 1941. Rose to the rank of Detective-Sergeant of the New South Wales Police Force. Received bravery awards and the Peter Mitchell Trophy for outstanding police work. Had suspicious links to underworld figures including Arthur 'Neddy' Smith, Graham 'Abo' Henry and Christopher Dale Flannery. Smith claimed Rogerson protected him while he committed major crimes. Rogerson was responsible for the shooting death of Warren Lanfranchi. During the inquest the coroner found he was acting in the line of duty, but a jury declined to find he had acted in self-defence. Rogerson was later commended by the police force for his bravery. However, it was alleged by Lanfranchi's partner, Sallie-Anne Huckstepp, and later by Neddy Smith, that Rogerson murdered Lanfranchi for robbing a police protected heroin dealer and for firing a gun at a policeman. Served three years for conspiring to pervert the course of justice and became a colourful after dinner speaker.

Robert 'Aussie Bob' Trimbole. Born 19 March 1931. Struggling businessman who discovered he could make a fortune as the front man for the Griffith mafia. Key figure in organising the murder of anti-drugs campaigner Donald Mackay. Connected to the Mr Asia heroin gang. Fled Australia in 1981 when tipped off he was under investigation by the Stewart Royal Commission. Escaped extradition when arrested in Ireland in 1984 and died a free man in Spain in 1987.

Donald Bruce Mackay. Born 13 September 1933. Ran a Griffith retail store called Mackay's Furniture. Studied law and learnt Italian. Became known locally for his tough stance on drugs and his desire to expose local members of the crime group known as The Honored Society. Disappeared 17 July 1977 after having a drink at a local hotel. His body was never found.

Paul Delianis. Former head of the Victorian armed robbery and homicide squads. Involved in the investigations into the Great Bookie Robbery, the murders of Leslie Herbert Kane, Roger Wilson, Isabel and Douglas Wilson, Bob Trimbole and the Mr Asia Gang. The first policeman to grasp the significance of the Terry Clark drug syndicate and to realise it had infiltrated key law enforcement agencies in Australia. Retired in 1987 as Deputy Commissioner.

John Carl Mengler. Former head of the Victorian Homicide Squad. Chief Investigator Stewart Royal Commission and later National Crime Authority. Helped crack the Donald Mackay case after New South Wales police failed to do so. Involved in the investigations into Trimbole, the Mr Asia Gang and the murders of Isabel and Douglas Wilson. Described by the *Sydney Morning*

Herald as 'possibly the greatest detective of his generation.' Retired as Deputy Commissioner Victoria 1990.

Peter Lamb. Spent three years with a wool-classing firm before joining the Commonwealth Police in 1961. Heavily connected to Operation Lavender and many of his investigations uncovered the corrupt links between New South Wales police and Sydney gangsters. Had three postings overseas as an Australian Federal Police liaison officer where he learnt the latest international organised crime investigation tactics. Promoted to Assistant Commissioner Federal Police, Director of Operations with Independent Commission Against Corruption in New South Wales and General Manager of the National Crime Authority.

Frederick Joseph Parrington. Honest New South Wales policeman who doggedly investigated the murder of Donald Mackay. Unfortunately he was barking up the wrong tree. Concealed evidence from Victorian police in the hope of convicting the killers in New South Wales.

Brian Francis Murphy. Colourful Victorian detective with contacts on both sides of the fence. Deeply religious, a gregarious teetotaller with Irish charm and a persuasive manner. Charged and acquitted of manslaughter after a prisoner in his custody, Neil Stanley Collingburn, received fatal injuries in an interview room. Joined the Victoria Police 1954. Retired 1987.

Albert Jaime Grassby. Born Albert Grass Brisbane 12 July 1926. Immigration Minister in the Whitlam Government and colourful front man for multi-culturalism. But it was the political connection for the Griffith Honored Society that helped fund his election campaigns. Charged in 1980 with criminal defamation over asking state politician, Michael Maher, to read in the New South Wales Legislative Assembly a letter claiming Mackay's widow Barbara and her family solicitor were responsible for the murder.

Cleared of the charges in 1992. Died April 2005, his reputation deservedly in tatters.

Terrence John Clark. Born 1944. Small time New Zealand crook who became a big time international drug dealer. Made millions importing heroin into New Zealand, Australia and Britain. Ordered the murders of drug couriers Isabel and Douglas Wilson after he was told they were informing to police. Convicted of killing long-time drug associate Marty Johnstone, whose handless body was found in Eccleston Delph, a flooded quarry in the north of England. Died in prison 1983. Death listed as non-suspicious but there were suspicions he was killed by IRA inmates who suspected he was an informer.

Karen Soich. New Zealand lawyer who embarked on an affair with Terry Clark. Later regained control of her life and is now a successful entertainment lawyer in New Zealand.

Isabel and Douglas Wilson. Key couriers for the Mr Asia drug syndicate. Their bodies were found buried on the back beach at Rye, May 1979. The Wilsons were killed on the orders of the Mr Asia drug syndicate boss, Terrence John Clark, after corrupt police told him the couple were talking to Queensland detectives.

Gianfranco Tizzoni. Migrated to Australia 1955 and later naturalised. Became a private investigator and worked with notorious underworld figure Tom Ericksen as a debt collector. From 1971 became the Melbourne distributor of cannabis for the Griffith cell of the Mafia and distributed about 200 kilograms a week. Helped set up the murders of Donald Mackay and drug couriers Isabel and Douglas Wilson. Became a police informer code named 'Songbird' and died Italy July 1988 aged 53.

James Frederick Bazley. Known as Mr Cool. Career gunman and key member of the Painters and Dockers Union. Police allege he completed the contract killings of Donald Mackay and drug couriers Isabel and Douglas Wilson. Expected to die in jail but was released from prison in 2000 aged 75.

Russell Cox. Born Melville Schnitzerling Brisbane 15 September 1949. Became known as Cox the Fox because of his cool head and ability to plan armed robberies. Escaped from the maximum security Kattingal section of Long Bay Jail 3 November 1977 and spent 11 years on the run. Released from prison 2004 and returned to Queensland a reformed character. Remains a suspect for the murder of Brian Kane.

Thomas Christopher Domican. Born Ireland 1943. A London nightclub bouncer who migrated to Australia in 1968. A fearsome fitness fanatic with links to the New South Wales division of the Australian Labor Party. Has always rejected claims he was connected to the underworld. Charged with a series of offences, including murder and attempted murder in Sydney. Beat the lot.

THE CAST

ROLE	ARTIST
Robert Trimbole	Roy Billing
Terry Clark	Matthew Newton
Allison Dine	Anna Hutchison
Chris Flannery	Dustin Clare
Dave Priest	Jonny Pavolsky
George Freeman	Peter O'Brien
Jim Bazley	Scott Burgess
Frank Tizzoni	Tony Poli
Joe Messina	Peter Phelps
Liz Cruickshank	Asher Keddie
Brian Alexander	Damian de Montemas
Laurie Prendergast	Teo Gebert
Dr. Nick Paltos	Wadih Dona
Andy Maher	Damon Gameau
Brian Kane	Tim McCunn
Les Kane	Martin Dingle Wall
Maria Muhary	Jenna Lind
Merv Wood	Anthony Phelan
Bill Allen	Jeff Truman
Warwick Mobbs	Matt Passmore
Ray 'Chuck' Bennett	Nathan Page
Young Alphonse Gangitano	Elan Zavelsky
Lennie McPherson	John McNeill
Vinnie Mikkelsen	Wayne Bradley
Doug Wilson	Gareth Reeves
Isabel Wilson	Ashley Fairfield
George Joseph	Harold Hopkins
Donald Mackay	Andrew McFarlane
Greg Ollard	Chris Sadrinna
Karen Soich	Katie Wall